BACKYARD WILDLIFE

BACKYARD WILDLIFE

HOW TO ATTRACT BEES, BUTTERFLIES, INSECTS, BIRDS, FROGS AND ANIMALS INTO YOUR GARDEN

CHRISTINE AND MICHAEL LAVELLE

Photography by Peter Anderson
Special wildlife photography by Robert Pickett

This edition is published by Southwater,
an imprint of Anness Publishing Ltd
Hermes House
88–89 Blackfriars Road
London SE1 8HA
tel. 020 7401 2077
fax 020 7633 9499

www.southwaterbooks.com
www.annesspublishing.com

If you like the images in this book and would like to investigate using them for publishing, promotions or advertising, please visit our website www.practicalpictures.com for more information.

UK agent: The Manning Partnership Ltd
tel. 01225 478444; fax 01225 478440
sales@manning-partnership.co.uk

UK distributor: Book Trade Services
tel. 0116 2759086; fax 0116 2759090
uksales@booktradeservices.com
exportsales@booktradeservices.com

North American agent/distributor:
National Book Network
tel. 301 459 3366; fax 301 429 5746
www.nbnbooks.com

Australian agent/distributor:
Pan Macmillan Australia
tel. 1300 135 113; fax 1300 135 103
customer.service@macmillan.com.au

New Zealand agent/distributor: David Bateman Ltd
tel. (09) 415 7664; fax (09) 415 8892

Publisher: Joanna Lorenz
Senior Editor: Felicity Forster
Photography: Peter Anderson
Special Wildlife Photography: Robert Pickett
Illustrator: Liz Pepperell
Copy Editor: Richard Rosenfeld
Jacket Design: Nigel Partridge
Designer: Lisa Tai
Production Controller: Christine Ni

ETHICAL TRADING POLICY

At Anness Publishing we believe that business should be conducted in an ethical and ecologically sustainable way, with respect for the environment and a proper regard to the replacement of the natural resources we employ.

As a publisher, we use a lot of wood pulp to make high-quality paper for printing, and that wood commonly comes from spruce trees. We are therefore currently growing more than 750,000 trees in three Scottish forest plantations: Berrymoss (130 hectares/320 acres), West Touxhill (125 hectares/305 acres) and Deveron Forest (75 hectares/185 acres). The forests we manage contain more than 3.5 times the number of trees employed each year in making paper for the books we manufacture.

Because of this ongoing ecological investment programme, you, as our customer, can have the pleasure and reassurance of knowing that a tree is being cultivated on your behalf to naturally replace the materials used to make the book you are holding.

Our forestry programme is run in accordance with the UK Woodland Assurance Scheme (UKWAS) and will be certified by the internationally recognized Forest Stewardship Council (FSC). The FSC is a non-government organization dedicated to promoting responsible management of the world's forests. Certification ensures forests are managed in an environmentally sustainable and socially responsible way. For further information about this scheme, go to www.annesspublishing.com/trees.

Previously published as part of a larger volume,
How to Create a Wildlife Garden

PUBLISHER'S NOTES

Great care should be taken if you decide to include pools, ponds or water features as part of your garden landscape. Young children should never be left unsupervised near water of any depth, and if children are able to access the garden all pools and ponds should be fenced and gated to the recommended specifications.

Although the advice and information in this book are believed to be accurate and true at the time of going to press, neither the authors nor the publisher can accept any legal responsibility or liability for any errors or omissions that may be made nor for any inaccuracies nor for any harm or injury that comes about from following instructions or advice in this book.

CONTENTS

Introduction 6

WILDLIFE IN YOUR GARDEN 8

What is wildlife gardening? 10

Working with natural cycles 12

Predators and prey 14

PLANNING AND DESIGNING A WILDLIFE GARDEN 16

The role of gardens for wildlife 18

The weather in your garden 20

Garden soils 22

Design principles 24

Surveying your garden 26

Drawing up a plan 28

A large country wildlife garden 30

An urban wildlife garden 32

A courtyard wildlife garden 34

A wild garden 36

A bee border 38

A butterfly border 40

A bird border 42

GARDEN HABITATS 44

Grasslands 46

Wetlands, ponds and bogs 48

Hedgerows 50

Woodland 52

Soil habitat 54

Minor habitats 56

Habitat loss 58

CREATING WILDLIFE HABITATS 60

Establishing a wildflower meadow 62

Making a wildlife pond 64

Planting ponds and water features 66

Planting a wildlife hedge 68

Planting trees and shrubs 70

Creating woodland edges 72

Establishing climbing plants 74

Creating flower borders 76

Naturalistic planting 78

Establishing a herb garden 80

Planting vegetable gardens 82

Planting roof gardens and patios 84

WORKING IN YOUR WILDLIFE GARDEN 86

Watering and feeding 88

Composting 90

Weeding and weed control 92

Pests, diseases and disorders 94

Pruning 96

Raising native plants from seed 98

Division, cuttings and layers 100

Getting a close-up view 102

Recording wildlife in your garden 104

CARING FOR WILDLIFE 106

Plants as food 108

Providing extra food 110

Bird feeders 112

Feeding beneficial creatures 114

Providing natural shelter 116

Constructing extra shelters 118

Bird boxes 120

Hibernation sites 122

Calendar of tasks 124

Index 126

INTRODUCTION

The aim of this book is to show how you can encourage and care for backyard birds, insects and animals by designing and planting wildlife-friendly gardens, and by supplying additional food, shelter and hibernation sites. As well as helping your local wildlife and attracting a colourful array of visitors that are a joy to watch, you will also find that welcoming beneficial creatures improves the health of your plants. Gardeners and wildlife can share the same space without conflict and to mutual benefit.

Above: *Birds are probably the most popular and engaging visitors to gardens, where they find food, shelter and nesting sites.*

WHY HELP WILDLIFE?

This book is concerned, as are many gardeners, with the state of the environment and the effect we have on the natural world. Increasingly, people are realizing that plants and animals that were once common are now threatened as modern living and developments ruin their homes and habitats. Gardeners are particularly aware that we must share our outdoor living space with other creatures, and this book is a guide for both beginners and the more experienced who want to encourage nature back into the garden.

The book is structured in a simple, down-to-earth way, with easy-to-follow explanations that demystify this exciting aspect of gardening. The language is largely non-technical, although many of the techniques described are based on sound scientific principles. An explanation of the underlying principles of the natural sciences is followed by clear advice on how best to design, plant out and maintain areas that are suitable for wildlife.

Gardens can be visited by a wide range of creatures, and consequently the descriptions and explanations cover a wide range of topics and do not simply focus on the narrower requirements of one single geographic region. Despite different climates and surroundings, many of the techniques remain the same across the continents and are easily adapted.

THE WILDLIFE AGENDA

Wherever possible, design ideas are included in the book to illustrate how you can create all kinds of habitats within a garden. Planting plans are included for specific projects, and to inspire your own ideas for making wildlife-friendly features. The text is lavishly supported with illustrations and photographs that bring the ideas to life.

The approach is packed with common sense, and is centred on the creation of outdoor living spaces that are attractive, functional and fun, while simultaneously being great for wildlife. Clear step-by-step guides show how different tasks can be realized, and practical hints and tips are

Left: *Wildlife gardens need not look unkempt – they can be just as neatly designed and ornamental as any other type of garden.*

Below: *Many different insect species, such as this bee, depend upon bright and colourful flowers for their food.*

included throughout. The aim is to make the functionality of your garden space, the needs of wildlife and a beautiful design completely gel, and dispel the myth that a wildlife-friendly garden must resemble a neglected, unsightly and overgrown patch of wilderness.

IN THIS BOOK

Starting with an explanation of what wildlife gardening is, the text clearly outlines the main principles and natural cycles that work both on a global scale and, most importantly, in your own garden. It shows how a wildlife garden works in harmony with nature's rhythms and cycles, and spells out how all the wildlife in your garden has a part to play.

Once the basics are understood, the section dealing with planning and designing explains how to take stock of what you already have, while giving detailed advice on how to assess your own needs, as well as those of the wildlife, and produce the best possible design for your garden. Sample plans show how the basic design ideas can be applied to a range of garden sizes and settings.

The major habitat types are also clearly described, focusing on their relevance to the garden, and the section on creating wildlife habitats gives clear advice and instructions on how to recreate these features in a garden. Considerable emphasis is placed on the importance of getting out there and enjoying the garden. Maintenance should never be a chore, and the wildlife garden ought to be a unique place for you and your family to relax and experience a closeness to nature.

Ideas for helping some of your favourite species, including birds and butterflies, are also covered, with practical advice on feeding and helping all kinds of garden creatures. The aim is to create a super, all-inclusive habitat. You'll find advice on making hibernation sites and providing shelter and cover, and on helping some creatures that, in turn, will actually improve the health of your plants. Practical, effective horticultural practices and advice on watching, recording and enjoying the wildlife in the garden make sure that nothing is left to chance.

Whether your garden is large or small, in the city or the countryside, the design principles and projects in this book will help you to welcome a wonderful range of birds, insects and animals into your backyard, and create a rewarding wildlife sanctuary that you will enjoy for years to come.

Above: *Carnivorous mammals such as this stoat are rare visitors to gardens because they need large hunting territories.*

Above: *Adult ladybirds are small and highly visible beetles that eat aphids and help to control these pests.*

Far left: *Caterpillars are eaten by many garden animals, and these cinnabar moth caterpillars advertise to predators that they are poisonous with their striking black and yellow colours.*

Left: *Vegetarian mammals such as this mouse are common in gardens and are an important food source for larger carnivores that may occasionally visit the garden.*

WILDLIFE IN YOUR GARDEN

There can be few gardeners who have not experienced the thrill of a close encounter with some form of wildlife in their garden. Birds and butterflies are an obvious joy to watch flying among the trees and flowers, but there are many creatures that scurry and slide underneath the plants and into dark crevices that are less well understood and sometimes less welcome. Yet these crawling mini-beasts are actually the unsung heroes of the garden, and knowing why they are important and what they do is a vital first step in becoming a wildlife gardener.

Left: *Birds feeding at a bird table are a familiar sight in many gardens, adding movement as well as colour.*

Above: *Bees are commonly found in the garden and perform a valuable role in pollinating ornamental flowers.*

Above: *Butterflies are among the most colourful and best loved of all garden insects that visit to feed on nectar.*

Above: *Hedgehogs are frequent visitors to European gardens, where they eat a large range of garden pests, including slugs.*

WHAT IS WILDLIFE GARDENING?

The idea of gardening for wildlife has become popular, even fashionable, in recent years with many high-profile gardeners and organizations hailing it as a new approach. The simple truth, though, is that there has always been a huge variety of wildlife living in, or visiting, our gardens although conventional gardening techniques and materials have led to a decline in their numbers.

Above: *Gardens and wildlife have always enjoyed a strong association for many of us, as this garden sculpture shows.*

A NATURAL PARTNERSHIP

Gardens and wildlife have always shared the same space. The ants that forage, the worms that mix the soil and the bees that pollinate flowers are the most obvious examples. But some gardeners with an overly fastidious view of nature don't want to know about anything else, purging homes and gardens of anything verging on the "unclean" or "unhealthy".

While the idea of cleanliness is fine indoors, outdoors it causes a problem. The outside world is a living, functioning system, rich in many types of organism that depend on diversity and balance. In the quest for a sanitized environment, many gardeners have targeted some wildlife species on the grounds of plant health or simply because they don't want to share their space with them. A war began against creepy crawlies involving an array of noxious chemical agents whose effects were – and indeed still are – felt well beyond the confines of the garden. In addition, the combined forces of urbanization and industrial-scale agriculture have diminished the numbers of many other once common creatures.

It is only when the likes of birds and butterflies cease to visit the garden that the damage is noticed by the many, though surprisingly few regard their diminishing numbers as a problem. Fortunately, some gardeners realize that not only are we in danger of losing considerable natural diversity from our gardens, towns and cities, but that gardens are actually an ideal place for solving the problem. Domestic gardeners have a huge role to play in the future of many species of wildlife, especially now, as the traditional countryside in so many continents is under threat from the pressures of modern living.

Below: *Even a relatively small space can accommodate a variety of ornamental plants that, if chosen carefully, will provide a food supply, shelter or even a permanent home for a large range of garden wildlife.*

THE LOOK OF A WILDLIFE GARDEN

To some, the idea of being wildlife-friendly might mean forsaking the perfect lawn, trimmed borders and rose beds. Others might even assume that a wildlife garden means a disordered, untidy eyesore. Nothing could be further from the truth. True, some of the early wildlife gardeners did look to the countryside for ideas, attempting to make tiny, overgrown pockets of "wilderness" in their backyards. Increasingly, though, wildlife gardeners have taken a more fundamental approach, applying the model of nature – a dynamic, self-balancing and regulating system – when designing their own gardens. So, with a bit of know-how, every garden, however small, can act as a private nature reserve with its hedges, trees, flower beds and even sheds, walls and paths providing wildlife habitats. In fact, many gardens need only a little adjustment to vastly improve their wildlife credentials. Whether your passion is for herbs, flowers or vegetables, your garden has the potential to provide a habitat for many different wildlife species.

The most important requirements in a wildlife garden include providing creatures with shelter from the elements and a measure of protection from predators, while also providing food, water and nesting materials and, ideally, an environment in which to conduct their day-to-day lives, including mating and raising their young. Even those without a garden can help. Pots, window boxes and hanging baskets can all provide excellent feeding sites.

Above: *Where space is limited, even a window box can provide a place for wildlife to visit and feed on the nectar-rich flowers.*

Above: *Knowing which particular flowers provide food for which creatures is an important aspect of wildlife gardening.*

In most cases the types of plant used are an extremely important part of making your garden wildlife-friendly. Animals feed in a variety of ways and so ensuring that you have a range of plants, chosen to suit these varying needs, will help to maintain a healthy, thriving population of different animals. These in turn will attract carnivorous species, many of which may take up residence in your garden.

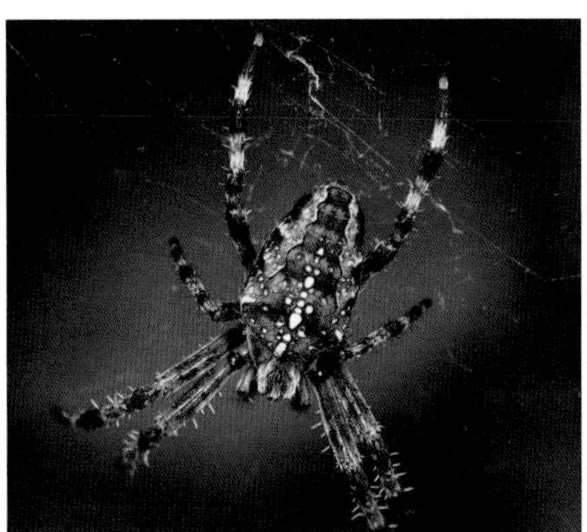

Left: *Spiders cause fear and revulsion for some people, but the majority are harmless to humans, and their tireless feeding activities help to balance the number of flying insect species in the garden.*

Below: *Dragonflies will visit a garden to feed, and if a suitable pond is present, they will readily lay eggs in it. They are superbly agile fliers with excellent eyesight, and are able to capture insects on the wing – a truly spectacular sight.*

Below: *Many species, such as this robin, require not only food but also nesting sites where they can raise their young in safety.*

Above: *The changing seasons often bring cold periods and garden plants must be chosen to withstand these times.*

WORKING WITH NATURAL CYCLES

Many gardeners have an appreciation of the need to work within the constraints of the seasons. Understanding exactly how these natural cycles affect the plants and animals in our gardens is a key factor in successful wildlife gardening. Some cycles can be modified or adapted, whereas others are as inexorable as the passage of time itself, and our actions must fit in with them.

DAILY AND SEASONAL CYCLES

The simplest and most obvious cycle is that of a 24-hour period, marked by dark and light, which affects all life in the garden. Increasing warmth and day length, among other factors, speed up the growing process while lengthening nights signal the need for some animals to hibernate. It is the easiest natural cycle for us to measure, observe and understand.

The gradual passage of the seasons is something that humans have long sought to measure, and it's thought that some of the most ancient artefacts left by our ancestors were designed to help them do this. When it comes to deciding the best time for sowing seed, hedge cutting and pruning, for example, always be guided by the seasons but pay particular attention to the climate in your area. Spring can arrive early or late, and you need to be responsive. Always keep a record of what you did and when, and what the conditions were like, using this as a guide in future years.

WHEN TO PLANT

Much has been written about the best time to sow or plant in the garden. The accuracy of this depends upon where you live and the prevailing conditions. There's no point in sowing seed outdoors until the soil has warmed up and you're sure there will be no more frosts. Autumn, in temperate regions, is generally considered the best time for moving some plants and planting bare-root trees, since it causes them less of a shock when they're not in active growth. Again, though, the exact timing depends on local conditions. Warmth and moisture are vital.

NEW LIFE FROM OLD

Life, death and decay are all part of the wider environmental cycle. The gardener must keep in tune with this by composting, for example, and attempting to keep the garden habitat healthy.

Composting waste matter ensures that valuable nutrients are not lost and can be returned to the soil in a useful form. Organic matter is the food that many nutrient-cycling organisms depend upon, and this (with air and water) provides them with an

Left: *Autumn brings the end of the growing season and is often marked by spectacular displays of changing leaf colour.*

Below: *Spring brings warmth and an increase in light levels, and is when most plant growth commences.*

Left: *Warmer weather and an increasing abundance of food makes spring the start of the nesting season for birds, which must work hard to gather enough insects for their newly hatched chicks.*

Above: *Old leaves and stems naturally decay and release nutrients back into the soil. Mulching has the same effect.*

ideal environment. The more you return organic waste to the soil, the more self-supporting it will be, the healthier the plants, and the greater the range of wildlife.

HARNESSING NUTRIENT CYCLES

Cultivation is an ancient technique that helps to cycle nutrients. Freshly dug ground receives oxygen that encourages soil organisms, and helps them to break down organic matter. It also benefits many micro-organisms that process inorganic elements into a useful form for plants because they too need oxygen to breathe.

Keeping a healthy habitat, free of pesticides and the imbalances that can be caused by the excessive use of artificial fertilizers, is the best way to manage these cycles and benefit your own garden and the wider environment.

WORKING WITH NATURE

One thing that all gardeners have in common is that it is almost impossible to see exactly what the coming growing season will bring. Drought, heatwaves, floods or cold spells can all be features of an average summer and in some cases, the growing season may contain elements of them all at different times. A golden rule for any wildlife gardener should be to work with nature and never against it.

You will of course be able to anticipate some of these problems and if you are in a drier area, you will naturally need to plant drought-tolerant plants. Gardeners in wetter climes or on naturally wet ground will need species adapted to boggier conditions. The biggest problem, however, will always be predicting what the prevailing weather conditions will be, and it is not uncommon for a long hot summer of drought to be followed by a cool summer with heavy rainfall. Reacting immediately to the summer conditions and changing your garden design accordingly may be rather short-sighted and may not always pay dividends in the long run.

NATURAL UNCERTAINTIES

The weather is naturally variable, but in the wake of predicted changes to the global climate – mostly referred to as "global warming" – it may yet become ever more complex and unpredictable. For us as gardeners, we cannot be certain whether global warming will mean drought or flood and so for now the best description would be "climatic uncertainty". Make sure that you don't ever act too rashly and try to remember that we never could accurately predict what the coming season holds – that is all part of the fun of gardening.

When things don't turn out as expected, remember that mistakes are simply part of gardening and that careful and patient observation of these can ultimately teach you as much about your garden as all the successes do. If particular plants have done well, you'll be on safe ground if you decide to make more of a feature of them or closely related species, and if a particular feature is flourishing like never before, you might do well to expand it. Always look on your garden as separate areas that might be affected in different ways by the changes in weather patterns. While the majority of your garden remains unaffected, there might be some areas that become drier or wetter. If this trend is borne out over several seasons you might wish to redesign it in accordance with your ever "uncertain" weather.

Right: *Some birds, such as these barn swallows, travel vast distances to take advantage of the glut of summer insects in different latitudes.*

PREDATORS AND PREY

While some creatures eat only plants, many others rely on hunting and eating other creatures. These animals are called predators. A garden rich in plants will attract many plant eaters, and it doesn't take long before these attract the attention of other, mostly larger animals that want to make a meal of them. These in turn attract yet larger creatures that will eat them, and a complex cycle of "kill or be killed" gradually unfolds that is every bit as exciting as any big game safari.

Above: *Birds, such as this song thrush, are often some of the most important predators of garden pests, including snails.*

ENERGY AND FOOD SOURCES

When ancient peoples worshipped the sun, they were recognizing one inalienable truth. In order for life to continue, it needs a source of energy to power it. Sunlight cannot be eaten as food but certain organisms, principally plants, have evolved ways of capturing it and turning it into energy-rich molecules of sugar through photosynthesis. This food provides the basis of almost all life on Earth and, as a result, plants are described in an ecological sense as "producers".

The vast remainder of living species (or consumers) on the planet are not able to produce their own food and rely, instead, on eating other organisms. Some consumers (the herbivores) eat the plants directly, while others (carnivores) gain their energy by eating another consumer. Creatures such as humans, which eat a combination of producers and consumers, are omnivores. Those that eat material from organisms that have died are "decomposers". These strategies provide organisms with the energy they need to live.

ENERGY USE AND LOSS

The First Law of Thermodynamics states that "energy cannot be created or destroyed, it merely changes form." To put this into context, remember that the energy of the sun is used to power life and, in doing so, the energy changes form. The energy contained in the sunlight is changed into food and used to assemble living tissue. The process is rather inefficient, with around 90 per cent of sunlight energy being lost. The remaining 10 per cent of the energy that is stored in the food suffers a similar fate each time it is used, so when the food is used to power growth and development around 90 per cent of it may be lost. This then means that there must always be more food than consumers because the conversion of food is so inefficient.

Scientists use a diagram – the Pyramid of Biomass – to explain this. Biomass is the term used to describe the amount of living tissue minus the water content, and each layer in the pyramid can only have 10 per cent of the biomass of the layer below it. If the 10 per cent ratio is exceeded, the consumer quickly begins to run short of food and may starve.

PYRAMID OF BIOMASS

For every layer of the pyramid, there is progressively less and less biomass (living material) as each layer must be able to support the consumers above it. At each level, energy is lost.

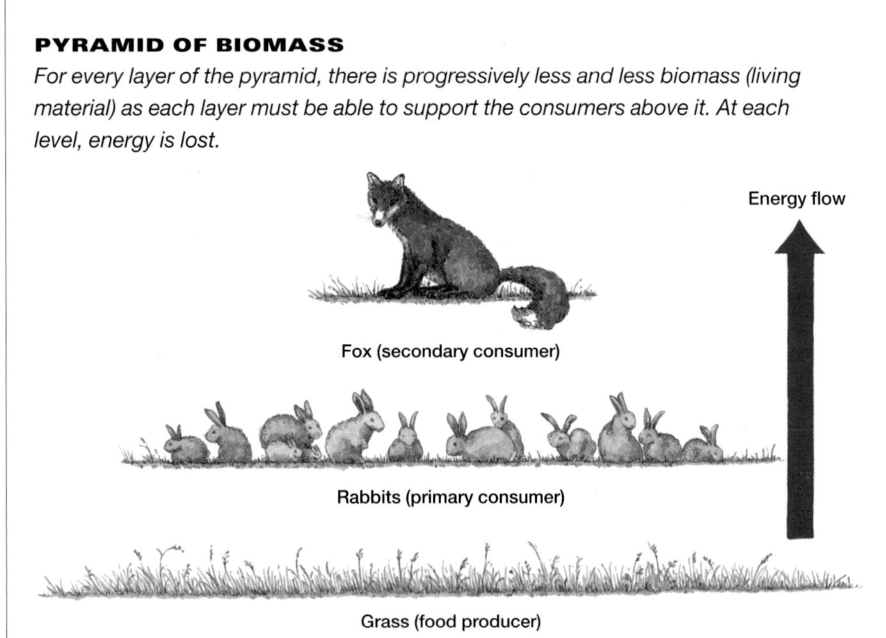

FOOD CHAINS

A food chain is a simplistic but useful way of illustrating the relationship between predators and prey. The chain starts with the producer – a plant – and moves on to a primary consumer that eats the plant. In the example shown, the producer is grass and the primary consumer is a rabbit. The chain then moves on to show how a fox might eat the rabbit, and because few things found in a garden prey upon foxes, the fox is said to be at the "top of the food chain". While this is a good way of illustrating the basic principles of predation, the story is rarely as simple as this. Foxes, of course, feed on a wide variety of prey, and it is not only foxes that eat rabbits. In order to consider the complexity of natural systems, then, we would normally construct a food web.

FOOD WEBS

These help us to understand complex relationships between predators and prey. Their main drawback is that to be fully accurate, they would have to be extremely complex and almost impossible to follow. Nonetheless, they do draw attention to complex interdependences that form the basis of natural habitats. It is not always necessary to be able to construct one of these to understand that the more complex a system is, the more stable it tends to become.

FOOD WEB

The complexity of nature can be shown in a food web. The direction of the arrows shows the flow of energy from one living organism to another, revealing a range of interdependencies typical in natural habitats.

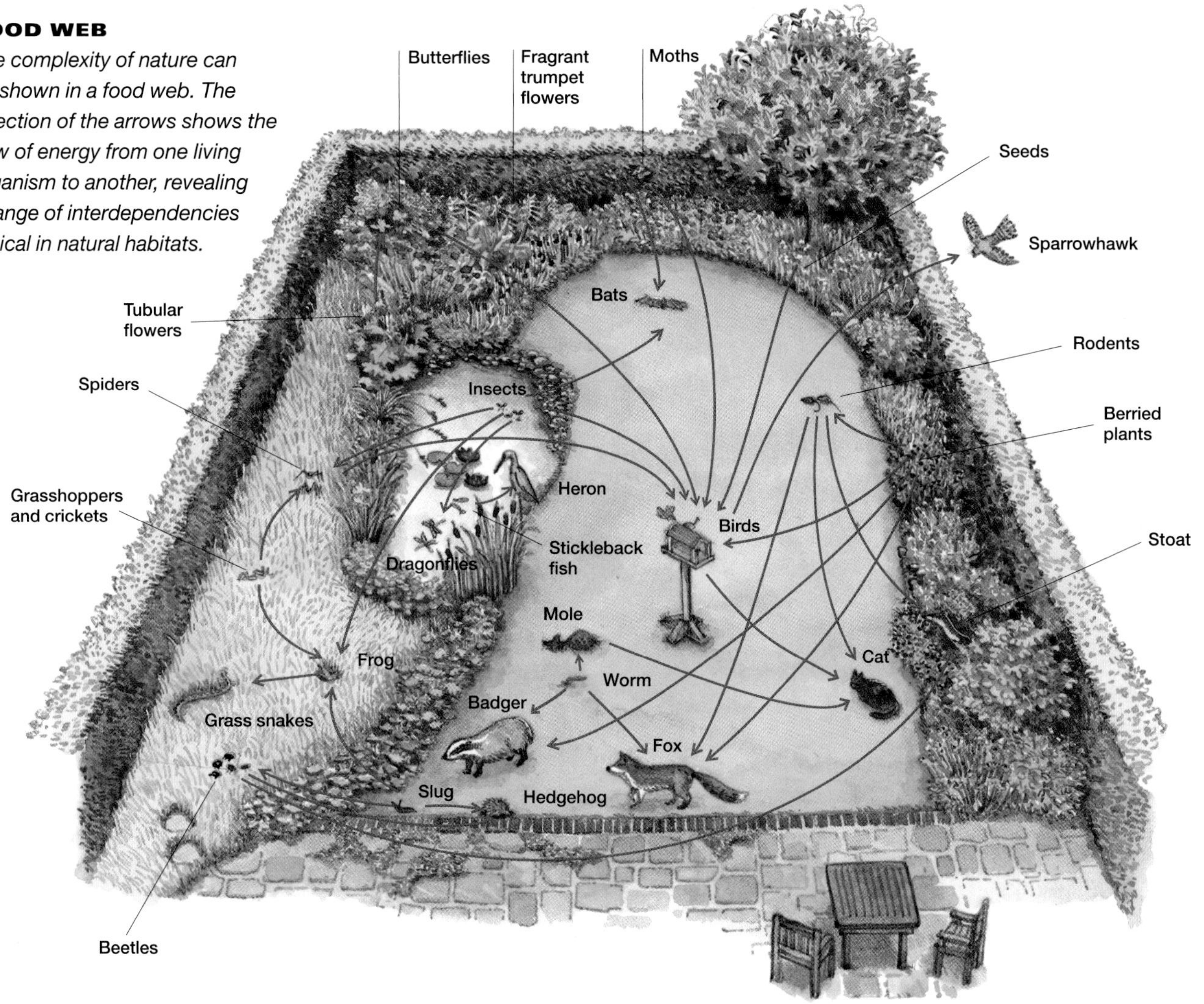

Butterflies
Fragrant trumpet flowers
Moths
Seeds
Sparrowhawk
Tubular flowers
Bats
Rodents
Spiders
Insects
Berried plants
Heron
Grasshoppers and crickets
Birds
Stickleback fish
Stoat
Dragonflies
Mole
Frog
Cat
Worm
Badger
Grass snakes
Fox
Slug
Hedgehog
Beetles

BENEFICIAL PREDATORS IN THE GARDEN

The average garden can play host to a whole range of common species, and some of them are voracious predators. Many offer a useful service in seeking out and eating a range of garden pests that would otherwise damage garden plants.

PREDATOR	WHAT IT EATS
Bat	Bats are mostly night-flying insectivores that locate their prey in darkness using a complex echolocation system consisting of high-pitched squeaks and clicks.
Blue tit	One of many birds that capture and eat garden pests, they are known for their agility, often picking aphids and caterpillars off in flight to feed their young.
Dragonfly	Larvae live an aquatic existence feeding upon various creatures. The adults are extremely agile fliers, capturing and consuming a wide range of mostly flying insects.
Frog and toad	The adults of both frogs and toads are carnivorous and capture a range of mostly invertebrate prey, such as slugs, using their long and sticky tongue.
Hedgehog	Mainly insectivorous, although the hedgehog will eat quite a wide range of animal pests, such as slugs, depending on their availability. Long known as a friend to the gardener.
Hoverfly	Eats aphids.The hoverfly adults feed mainly upon pollen and are attracted to daisy-like flowers. Their larvae are voracious predators of many aphid species.
Ladybird	Eats aphids. Both adults and young of the common garden beetle are voracious predators of these troublesome garden pests.
Shrew	One of the smallest mammals, the shrew must capture and eat around two-thirds of its own body weight in food each day to survive. Captures mainly invertebrate prey.

Bat

Blue tit

Frog

Hedgehog

Hoverfly

Ladybird

PLANNING AND DESIGNING A WILDLIFE GARDEN

The real secret of success with any type of garden lies in how well it is planned. Good design leads to a garden that is both functional and pleasing to look at. Clearly this is less of a problem when starting from scratch, but redesigning your whole garden can be daunting, and it may be best to tackle the job in stages. Measuring the garden and assessing the soil and growing conditions is the first stage. Once you have done this you can think about the design elements that will help shape the perfect garden for wildlife.

Left: *A properly executed design will enable you to build the successful garden you always dreamed of.*

Above: *Garden plans should be drawn carefully and to scale to enable you to build the features and borders accurately.*

Above: *A well-drawn plan can form the basis of a wonderful garden, and is well worth the time and effort it takes to produce.*

Above: *For the more artistically minded, a sketch projection of a garden plan helps you to visualize the finished effect.*

THE ROLE OF GARDENS FOR WILDLIFE

Domestic gardens increasingly represent a direct link with the countryside. Many species, once seen as purely rural in their distribution, have started to move into towns and cities, where they find refuge in parks and gardens. This is often due to the loss of their traditional haunts through changes in land use or agricultural practices. The more suitable we make our gardens for wildlife, the more species are likely to follow.

Above: *Spiders' webs are a common sight in many gardens, and their presence is a sign of a healthy environment.*

HABITAT VARIETY

In nature, habitats, even when they are extensive, are rarely particularly uniform. Even slight variations in the soil and topography, for example, affect the microclimate and suitability for plant and animal species. In such cases a habitat is called a "mosaic", meaning that the total area is generally uniform even though it is variable when viewed in more detail. Suburban gardens may superficially resemble each other but, together, they create a mosaic because of their many differences. In this way they represent the maximum opportunities for species that are either present or are waiting to move in when conditions become more favourable.

Each garden's microhabitat is capable of supporting a particular combination of species (plants, animals, fungi and other organisms) that interact with one another and form a community. Across many gardens, then, the total diversity of species is greater than in any one part, although there is always the chance that an occupant of another part may visit your garden once in a while. Of course, the more opportunities there are for species, the more of them will visit and take up residence and, in time, your garden habitat may become a hotspot for species diversity.

Below: *To many creatures the underground layer is the most important place as they spend part or the whole of their life there.*

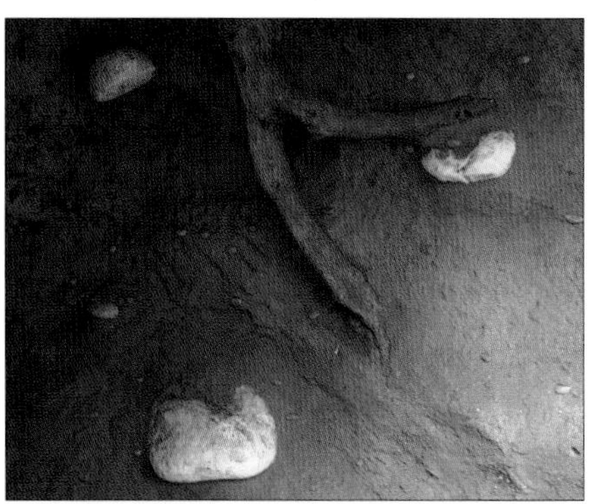

BIODIVERSITY

In recent years, the term biodiversity has increasingly cropped up but few gardeners are aware of what it actually means, or why it is important. Put simply, biodiversity is an all-encompassing word that scientists have coined to describe the variety of life on Earth, and that includes plants, animals, fungi and micro-organisms. But biodiversity doesn't just refer to diversity at the species level, but to the genetic variation that contributes to the differences between individuals, and, at the other end of the scale, to the combinations of organisms, climate and soils that make up various habitats, including your garden.

SHELTER AND FOOD

In order to attract wild creatures, your garden must meet their basic needs, i.e. food, water, shelter and breeding sites. The first three are the easiest to supply in the form of supplementary food and artificial shelters, or preferably by planting the appropriate plant species that they need. If the first three are present, then some creatures may choose to breed, but this is not always the case because they may have very specific needs. This does not mean

Left: *For the insects that fly into our gardens to visit flowers, there is a constant danger. Spiders are important predators of flying insects and help regulate their number, thereby achieving a state of natural balance.*

that they won't visit your garden, though, and many species may appear merely to feed and drink before returning to a home elsewhere in the mosaic. But your garden still has an important part to play.

WILDLIFE CORRIDORS

Birds often fly long distances in search of a winter refuge or summer breeding site, and a garden may provide an ideal spot in which to rest, refuel and have a much-needed drink. Indeed, many modern cities are like deserts to migrating species, offering little comfort were it not for parks and domestic gardens. They often act as oases for both passers-by and residents, and if enough suitable sites are made, creating a continuous "super-habitat", they'll double as wildlife corridors for "through traffic", while also enabling less mobile species to enter from the surrounding countryside. Hedges, street trees and roadside verges are all part of this effect and offer shelter and respite for a large range of species. The more diverse all of these are in respect of the plant species they contain and the less intensively tended they are, the better for wildlife they naturally become.

Gardens are an essential part in this story, and the species that they contain today are increasingly refugees from the countryside, fleeing intensive farming practices and the loss of traditional habitats. It is within the grasp of the gardener to help such species and make our cities both greener and more diverse.

Above: *Many birds, such as this house martin, happily live alongside humans throughout much of their lives.*

Right: *Rodents are just one example of a mammal that quickly adapts to the changes wrought by human settlement.*

Below left: *Many species of birds were once exclusively rural, but as their habitats have been changed by human activities, they often find refuge in urban gardens.*

Below: *Ants mostly go unnoticed until they invade our houses or picnics. They have intricate and complex lives, even farming and protecting aphids to obtain their sweet honeydew secretions.*

THE WEATHER IN YOUR GARDEN

Each garden has its own microclimate, or even several within it. This will be mainly created by the prevailing weather, but will also be affected by factors such as altitude and the amount of available shelter from the wind and shade from the sun. To grow plants successfully, you need to know what kind of weather they will be subjected to, and make sure you choose species that can tolerate these conditions.

Above: *Sunny walls and fences help to capture heat and so make ideal settings to help ripen fruit such as these pears.*

PREVAILING CLIMATE

The prevailing climate for your area could best be described as the average of the weather on a yearly basis. Most places see a degree of seasonal variation and this, combined with a number of climatic influences – principally temperature, precipitation, humidity, light and wind – characterizes the prevailing climate for a particular area. Any and all of these influences can have a dramatic effect on plant growth and development, especially when taken to extremes.

RAINFALL

Water is vital for food production and growth in plants, and for the optimum growth of most plants a steady supply of water is essential. In reality rainfall is very variable in both its regularity and quantity, and the best plants for your garden are those that thrive in such conditions.

HUMIDITY

The level of humidity is the quantity of water vapour in the atmosphere at any one time. It is normally referred to as the relative humidity, and is measured as a percentage of the saturation point (100 per cent humidity). In places that receive heavy rainfall, relative humidity also tends to be high. Plants such as ferns thrive in damp conditions, although high relative humidity can have undesirable effects on plants, facilitating diseases such as grey mould (*Botrytis cinerea*) and exacerbating heat stresses because water cannot evaporate from the leaves to cool them.

LIGHT

The light from the sun is a vital constituent of plant food production – or photosynthesis – and sustains existing plants and generates new growth.

The duration of light in a day, determined by latitude and season, is known as day length, and is characterized by the number of hours. Changes in day length often trigger reactions in plants: chrysanthemums, for example, produce flowers in response to shortening days in autumn. The most important factor, though, is the overall amount of light available to plants. Some will only thrive in bright light, while others, such as ferns and rhododendrons, have evolved to live under trees and do well in shade. Also note that strong sunlight can damage the foliage of

Left: *Cool shady areas such as this enable you to grow a range of "woodland" plant species that in turn provide a habitat for shade-loving creatures.*

Above: *Dry, sunny areas can allow you to plant a range of sun-loving and drought-tolerant species, such as this Mediterranean-style border.*

Right: *This drystone wall provides excellent cover as well as a range of habitats for both plants and animals, and is an excellent feature to include in a wildlife garden.*

some plants, with the leaves being scorched, especially if wet, the light being magnified by water droplets on the leaf surface.

WIND

This can easily damage plants, especially woody trees and shrubs. The stronger the wind, the more damage is likely to occur and, in windy gardens, the plants must be chosen in accordance with their ability to resist such conditions. Even quite moderate winds may cause desiccation of leaves when combined with cold or dry conditions, although a light wind often has beneficial effects by cooling the plant's foliage and alleviating a possible stagnant atmosphere that might promote disease.

TEMPERATURE

The plant's growth and life processes are affected by temperature, with all plant species having their own maximum and minimum temperatures at which they can survive. As a general rule, the maximum temperature for most plants is around 35°C (95°F) while the minimum is highly variable. Plants may enter dormancy beyond these thresholds or, in more extreme cases, may actually die. In some gardens, though, a sheltered site that benefits from the warming effects of the sun may be used for growing plants that are usually suited to warmer climates.

Soil temperature may also vary, with sandy soil warming up more quickly after a cold season than clay, mainly because sand is relatively free-draining and does not hold as much water. Sites facing, or with a slight incline towards, the direction of the sun, will also warm up more quickly than a shady one, enabling you to grow a range of sun-loving plants. Such local variations are termed microclimates.

MICROCLIMATE

Gardeners often exploit their microclimate by growing a wider range of plants than would be possible elsewhere in their region. This doesn't just benefit you, but the wildlife too, creating a greater range of habitats than would otherwise have been possible.

A south-facing garden in the northern hemisphere provides most sun, whereas in the southern hemisphere it is a north-facing site. Away from the tropics, the sun is also higher in summer than it is in winter, resulting in less shade in summer. Lastly, exposure to wind, frost, or shelter will greatly affect the type of plants you can grow.

GARDEN ASPECT

The aspect of a garden mainly relates to the movement of the sun through the day and how this alters the pattern of sunny areas in relation to shade, as this will affect the type of plants you can grow in any particular area. In the northern hemisphere a south-facing garden is the sunniest, whereas in the southern hemisphere they will be sunniest if facing north. In higher latitudes, the summer sun sits higher in the sky, reducing the amount of shade, whilst winter sunlight arrives from a low angle, casting long shadows. Aspect also concerns whether the garden is exposed to wind or frost or is sheltered, as these conditions also affect the plants you can grow.

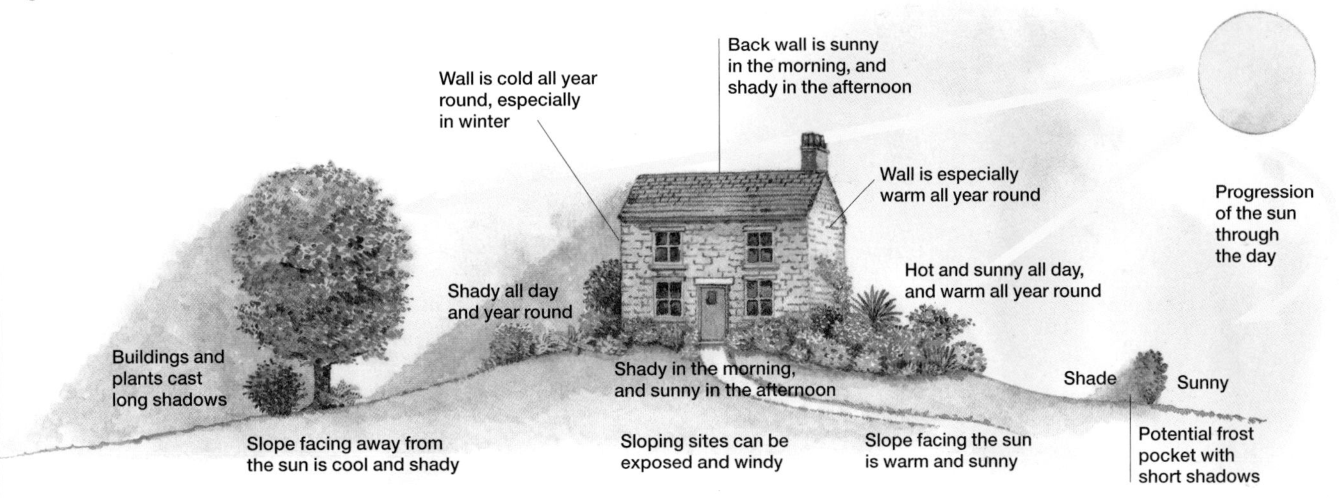

GARDEN SOILS

Understanding your garden soil and which plants it will support is a key aspect of successfully planning a wildlife garden. Soils vary according to the area in which they are found and also, in part, to how they have been treated in the past. Soil can be a complex subject but, by following a few simple rules, you can easily find out what type you have in your garden. Once you know this, you will be better able to choose plants that will rapidly establish, grow and ultimately thrive there.

Above: *Applying well-rotted mulch to a border helps add organic matter to an area and can result in a more open soil structure.*

DIFFERENT KINDS OF SOIL

Soil is made up of many ingredients but, in the main, the majority consist of small mineral fragments produced by the action of the weather on rocks. The fragments are classed according to their size and physical properties.

Clay is the smallest type of mineral particle found in soil, being less than 0.002mm (0.00008in) across. The particles bind tightly together, making the substance very sticky and water-retentive. Clay soils are heavy and can be hard to cultivate. On the plus side, though, they are very fertile.

Silt is larger than clay, being up to 0.02mm (0.0008in) across and, as such, shares some characteristics with both clay and sand. It is sticky when wet but does not form the same close bonds as clay, and may dry to a quite dusty soil in a drought. It makes fertile soil that, if well managed, can be an excellent growing medium for a wide variety of plants.

Sand is the largest particle, being up to 2mm (0.08in) across. While this is still quite a fine particle to our eyes, it is very large in respect of soils and, unlike the smaller clay and silt, is very poor at retaining nutrients. This is because the amount of air that is naturally present tends to rapidly break down any organic matter, and because the particles themselves are unable to hold on to nutrients. As a result, sandy soils tend to be free-draining and hungry, needing to be bulked up with organic matter.

SOIL PROFILE

Made up of a number of layers, each soil section is distinct from the others and plays different roles.

Leaf litter layer This layer is composed of partly decayed plant remains and is home to a diverse range of insects.

Topsoil This can be 5–60cm (2–24in) deep. It is dark in colour and rich in organic matter. It contains the greatest number of soil life species.

Subsoil The topsoil finishes and there is a distinct colour change to the subsoil. Little organic matter is found.

Parent material On shallow soils you may see this layer. It may be found as rocky gravel, such as limestone, or other material.

ORGANIC MATTER

A normal part of topsoil, organic matter is derived from the dead parts of plants and, to a lesser degree, animals that live in or on the soil. Decaying plant matter is broken down by many soil organisms, especially fungi and bacteria, and consequently is not a constant quantity in the soil. If conditions are right, however, it can form a substance called humus that is relatively stable and is excellent at holding on to nutrients, especially when present in sand or silt. Organic matter is ultimately broken down and recycled by decomposers and plants, and needs to be replenished on a regular basis.

SOIL STRUCTURE

The constituents above are the building blocks of soil, but the properties of any garden soil also depend on how they are arranged. Imagine your home: it will have been specially constructed using a range of materials. This is its architecture or structure. Soil is much the same. In order to function, it must have areas of open space, called pores, that provide routes for water and air to move through. A well-structured soil has the right balance of air space to facilitate the drainage of excess water and air movement.

A good soil structure will ultimately help plant roots penetrate the soil and also

TESTING SOIL TEXTURE

1 *This simple method is easy to do in a garden. Start with a ball of soil about the size of a golf ball and moisten it until it can be flattened into a ribbon shape.*

2 *Continue flattening out the ribbon, making it as long and thin as possible. The longer and thinner you can make it without it cracking or breaking, the more clay your soil contains.*

pH TESTING WITH AN ELECTRONIC METER

1 *After loosening an area of soil, moisten it using rainwater, and allow this to soak through the ground for a few minutes.*

2 *Using a trowel, take a sample of the wet soil and place it into a clean jar, adding a little more water if needed.*

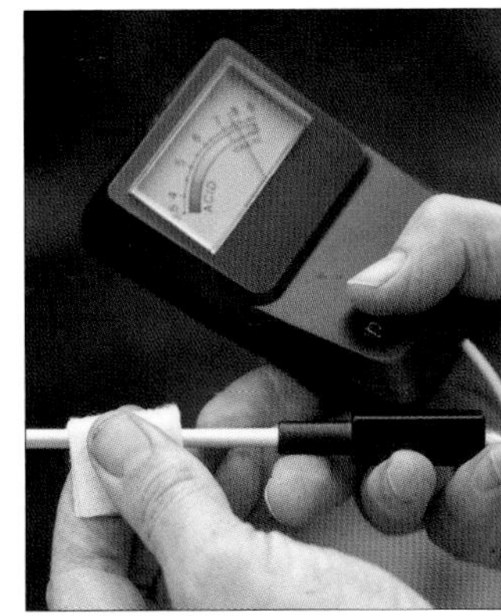

3 *Always clean the probe on your pH meter using a sterilized cleaning solution to eliminate any risk of an incorrect reading.*

4 *Insert the probe into the soil solution and after a few moments the reading on the front panel will appear.*

encourage a myriad of tiny soil organisms, whose activities help to liberate nutrients for the growing plants.

WHY CULTIVATE SOIL?

The simple answer is to give nature a boost. Cultivation enhances the formation of pore spaces while often providing an ideal opportunity to add organic matter. This free flow of air both in and out of the soil allows oxygen to be replenished and toxic gases, that might otherwise build up, to escape. Adding organic matter also provides food for micro-organisms that, in turn, provide nutrients for the plant roots.

SOIL pH

A measure of the acidity of a soil, its pH is an important factor in deciding which plants will grow and thrive in your garden. It is expressed on a scale of 1–14 with 1 being highly acidic, 14 being extremely alkaline, and 7 being classed as neutral. Most commonly grown garden plants prefer, or tolerate, a specific pH range, i.e. acid, alkaline, or near neutral.

A low pH may cause nitrogen or phosphate deficiency for instance, may promote trace element toxicity or deficiency, and may cause a more general deterioration of the soil structure. Soils that maintain a pH of around 6.5, however, generally have the most nutrients available and are suitable for the widest range of plants.

ASSESSING SOIL TEXTURE BY HAND

The amount of mineral constituents present in the soil dictates, to a degree, what the soil will be like. They are often judged as a relative proportion of the total and, although measuring them can be a complex matter, there is an easy test.

Begin with a small amount of soil about the size of a golf ball. Moisten it and knead until it is like putty, and remove any hard lumps or large stones. Then mould the soil into a ball. If it does not readily form a ball, it is sand. If the ball is firm, try forming it into a ribbon between thumb and crooked forefinger. If the ribbon breaks easily while being formed it is loamy sand. If it hangs freely, then the longer and thinner you can make it before it breaks, the more clay it has. The higher the clay content, the more it glistens when smoothed between thumb and forefinger.

Left: *Digging is a good way of improving the structure of the soil by allowing air and water penetration. It also allows you to add organic matter at the same time.*

SOIL pH AND PLANT SELECTION

All plants have their preferred pH at which they will grow best. Generally speaking, good results may be obtained from soils at the following pH levels.

Mineral soils (majority of plants)	pH 6.5
Mineral soils (turf)	pH 5.5-6.5
Container composts	pH 5.5-5.8
Peat/moss soils	pH 5.5 (or lower for specialist uses such as heather or bog gardens)

pH preferences of some common garden plants

Carnations	6.0–7.5
Chrysanthemums	5.7–7.0
Roses	5.5–7.0
Rhododendrons	4.5-5.5
Heathers	4.1–6.0
Hydrangeas (blue)	4.1–5.9
Hydrangeas (pink)	5.9–7.5
Coarse lawn grasses	5.5–7.0
Fine lawn grasses	4.5–7.0

Above: *Ideally, a wildlife garden combines an outdoor living space with a home and a visting place for a variety of creatures.*

DESIGN PRINCIPLES

Careful planning is the key to a successful garden, and this is often best done as a team effort involving the whole family. Planning the garden provides a real chance for everyone who uses it to have a say in what it should look like, making sure it caters for all their needs. The design should reflect the types of activity that you enjoy and should consider not just your current needs but also your longer-term aspirations and the time you can realistically devote to maintaining it.

FIRST STEPS

The first thing to remember about your garden is that it is fundamentally the same as any other living space. It needs to be organized around your activities. If the garden is predominantly for outdoor living and entertaining, then the design should reflect that. If you have children or pets, they must be considered, though of course their needs will change over the years. In addition to this list – which might well include play areas and a vegetable garden – you need a second one containing aesthetic features.

When you have made the list, consider how much space each ingredient requires and position them on a rough sketch. If you are limited for space, start making compromises, and be realistic. You might want to be self-sufficient in vegetables, but will you have the time to take care of them properly? When you have fine-tuned your design, check that each feature works in relation to adjacent areas and the garden as a whole. Remember that ponds, thorny and poisonous plants are best avoided if you have young children, and can be added later.

FORMULATING A CONCEPT

Finally, once everyone has had their say, you can think about a wildlife theme. A small courtyard in a city centre may be best geared towards birds, with feeders, a birdbath and hanging baskets and pots. If space permits, introduce more elements, but always be realistic about what you can achieve and whether particular species are likely to be in your neighbourhood. And remember to separate the areas being most heavily used from those where you want wildlife to shelter. While some species, such as sparrows and the European robin, might not mind close contact, other species are shyer and tend to shun busy areas.

Below: *With a little thought, even a relatively small garden space can provide variety and interest for both people and wildlife.*

CHOOSING PLANTS FOR THE DESIGN

Good garden design can be reinforced by good-looking plants but, for maximum usefulness in a wildlife garden, they must also provide food and shelter.

Form A plant offers a particular shape in three dimensions that is called its form. Use a variety of forms to complement both the surrounding plants and features.

Growth habit A term used to describe the overall branching pattern of a plant. Unlike form it only refers to the skeleton of growth. Note that a dense, twiggy habit offers good cover while an open habit offers perches for birds.

Colour An obvious reason for choosing plants is if they have attractive coloured leaves, stems, fruit or flowers. How you choose to use colour is subjective, but certain flower colours may attract particular insects.

Theme Within a wildlife garden, for instance devoted to butterflies or birds, choose certain plants because they favour particular species, either for food or breeding sites.

Seasonality Establish what time of year certain plants look at their best and are most useful for wildlife.

Food value Some plant species are better than others in providing food for wildlife, and choosing them can make your garden into a super habitat.

Above: *Strong, flowing lines are an important part of larger designs and look especially good near water.*

Above: *Strong, hot colours provide a very warm feeling when they are used in a garden, and are ideal for sunny borders.*

Below: *Blues and purples tend to give a garden a cooler feel, but they can also have a calming effect too.*

You might even want to make a few specialist areas where you can see particular species, planting a range of plants that will best favour their needs. Colour can also be an important element and by choosing carefully you can create subtle moods throughout your garden.

BASIC DESIGN PRINCIPLES

The key to any successful design is to apply a few basic principles. All of these are simple, and if applied consistently, will help you to produce a design that will meet the needs of both you and the wildlife in your garden, and it will look great when finished.

Unity This ties a design together. Avoid clashes and anything that appears out of place by using similar materials, patterns, shapes and colours throughout the design, and make them echo the house and even the wider surroundings.

Rhythm and line This applies to the flow of the design. Remember that strong lines are important, with flowing shapes looking good in larger, naturalistic gardens, and geometric shapes often working well in smaller or more formal courtyard settings.

Scale Simply refers to the relative size of each element, or part of the garden, in relation to the space in which it is placed. Features included should be neither too small and insignificant nor too large and overpowering for the whole scheme.

Balance Refers to the use of space in relation to other features in the garden. It is a matter of taste, of course, but too many features in too small a space can feel cluttered whereas too much open space can leave the occupants feeling exposed.

Variety and contrast They should not conflict with the need for unity. A certain amount of variety is, of course, vital for wildlife and relatively easy to achieve in large gardens, but it needs to be artfully juxtaposed in order to achieve a balance.

Functionality Even in a garden managed expressly for wildlife you still need space. Make sure that such areas don't conflict, for example with barbecues near flammable long grass, and items such as bins or storage areas are best hidden from view.

SURVEYING YOUR GARDEN

Once you have decided what you want from your garden in terms of its function, features and the types of wildlife you wish to attract, you can start planning. A thorough appraisal by surveying the site is the best way to start, and can be done quite easily using a few simple techniques. A survey involves nothing more than measuring the dimensions of the site, and making notes on what is already there.

Above: *If you have recently moved, talking to the neighbours will help you find out about your garden and its microclimate.*

WHY DO A SURVEY?

Before you attempt your design, surveying the existing garden site will help immeasurably, despite the fact that it isn't the most creative job. It'll certainly stop you from rushing blindly in, and can actually save you time in the long run. The survey also determines what plants you can grow because it will not only provide the measurements of the garden and details of existing features and views, but information about the microclimate and soil type.

Left: *Unless you intend sitting out in your garden while you design it, photographs will be useful memory joggers when you draw up your survey at a later date.*

WHAT INFORMATION IS NEEDED?

Find out as much as you can about what is already there. The more you understand your garden, the better the design will be. As you move around the garden taking measurements, make some notes about the following points.

The climate – that will greatly influence your new design. Check the direction of the prevailing wind, the annual and monthly rainfall, annual and monthly temperatures, and if and when frosts occur. All this information can be gathered from your local meteorological station.

The microclimate – measuring this can be more difficult, mostly because the slight differences might not be apparent at first glance. Often it is more a case of looking for the most likely variations caused by the permanent features or the lie of the land.

Sun and shade – extremely important factors when selecting plants. Assess how much sun and shade your garden receives, and where it falls at different times of the day. Always note that even the sunniest garden may have shady pockets created by adjacent houses, fences, hedges or trees.

Site aspect – whether your garden faces the sun is important but a sloping site that faces either sun or shade will accentuate the importance of that factor. A sunny slope is often warmer and may also be more exposed or free-draining than an equivalent flat site. In addition to slope, walls and fences are also affected by their orientation. A wall facing the sun will retain heat, making it even warmer than a sunny fence, and it may be perfect for growing a more tender climber or shrubs that might benefit from this milder setting.

Exposure – an exposed site is often thought to be difficult due to high winds, but some species and seaside plants for instance might appreciate this more than others. Of course not all species of wildlife or plants will tolerate exposure and the type of features you include must either

TIPS FOR MEASURING YOUR GARDEN

Unless you are a trained surveyor, the prospect of measuring your garden might seem a little daunting. This need not be the case, though, as the techniques are relatively simple – it is just a case of being careful and methodical at all times.

Two's company Always work with a friend. It makes life easier, especially when trying to keep a tape straight to take measurements. One person should normally be in charge of measuring, the other recording the information.

Divide the site into triangles Since the time of the ancient Greeks, the value of the triangle as a shape for surveying land has been recognized. The most obvious way to apply it to a rectangular garden is to measure and plot the boundaries, and then measure from corner to corner.

Use two tapes to mark the position of a fixed point You will need to plot the positions of features such as trees and flower beds, which are best measured at right angles from a nearby straight edge such as a boundary line. Stretch a tape along this edge. Place the start of a second tape nearest the object you are measuring towards, and move the other end in an arc across the tape along the edge. The shortest distance you measure across this arc is the distance at a right angle from the first tape line. Note this measurement and how far along the first tape it occurs.

Take photographs They are invaluable when drawing up the initial ground plan, and particularly when you start to draw up the final design. Enlarge a few photographs and cover them with tracing paper, and then sketch on your ideas to get an idea what the finished garden will look like.

Photographs can be stuck around the edge of your drawing to act as a constant visual reminder of what the site looks like and help you envisage the space while you are not actually in the garden.

cater for those that will or be sheltered by a windbreak or hedge.

Soil type – check what you've got so that you know which plants will thrive there, and which ones won't. Also check what's growing well in your neighbours' gardens, and talk to them about their experiences.

Drainage – note any problems.

Existing features – both on, and near, the site including trees, garden beds, driveways and garden sheds. Decide which ones you want to retain. Also note the position of water and gas mains, sewers, meters, taps and power lines (underground and overhead).

Good views – from within the garden, and into it from without. Check which ones you want to retain, and the extent to which the garden should be private.

Once you have collected all this information, you can draw up a plan (see below) that will provide a detailed picture of the site, its features and other information relating to its suitability for growing plants. From this point on, you can begin to plan your wildlife garden.

Left: *Take a soil sample to test later if you don't have time or the equipment to hand when you are measuring the site.*

RECORDING THE SITE DIMENSIONS

1 *The easy first stage is to make a rough sketch plan of what is already there. This forms the basis of your survey so that when you take measurements of the site, you can record them on the sketch plan. In many cases a freehand sketch is all that is needed, as long as you are not planning to undertake any detailed engineering or building work that needs precise dimensions.*

2 *Using two measuring tapes – one long and one shorter – start by establishing a base line along the house or boundary from which to build the survey. Establish the boundary dimensions, taking additional measurements between the corners as cross checks. Note the position and dimensions of other features, including the house and outbuildings.*

3 *Make notes about the microclimate, sunny areas, damp areas, soil, existing plants and the condition of any features. Put this series of observations on the survey drawing. Neatly draw your plan using the information contained in the sketch, the measurements and the notes, keeping it to a scale. Use graph paper, using one large square, for example, to represent 1m (1yd).*

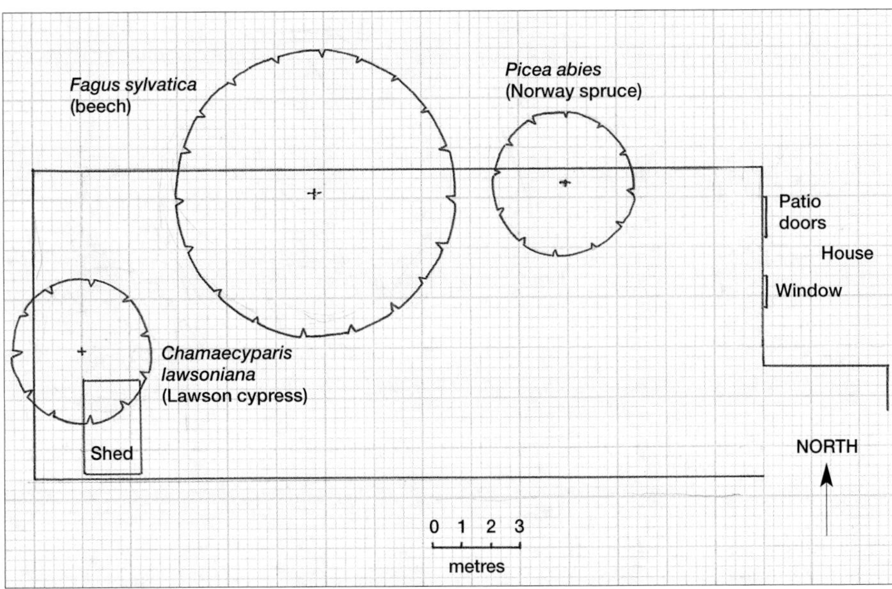

4 *Once you have marked down the dimensions, add the location of doors and windows on buildings, and the position of drains, pipes, power lines and existing landscape features, such as the driveway, paths and trees, that are to remain. Where possible, add the name of each tree and plot the dimensions of the canopy. This information will help at the next stage of planning the garden. Also show the direction of the prevailing wind, the areas in shade or sun, and any other site particulars, including views which you would like to keep or to open up. Finally, it is extremely important to find where north is and chart this on the survey, as this will help determine the plants chosen to cope with sun or shade at the planning stage.*

DRAWING UP A PLAN

Garden plans range from complex designs to sketches, with most domestic settings requiring relatively simple drawings. Even if you find it difficult to come up with a design you really like, sketches and ideas are always useful. Alternatively, if you are prepared to pay for it, you can hire a professional garden designer. Whichever you opt for, it is important that you are absolutely clear as to what you want to get out of your garden for both you and the wildlife you intend to help.

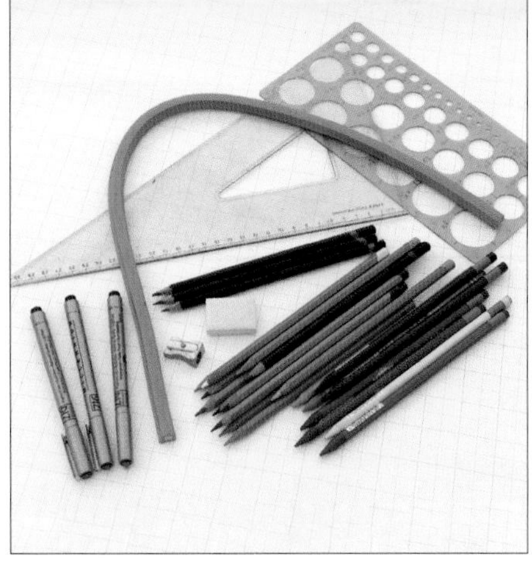

Above: *Drawing up a garden plan does not need anything more complex than simple drawing equipment and graph paper.*

INTERPRETING YOUR WISH LIST

Once you have drawn up the survey sketch plan, use it to create the design for your new garden. The first stage involves using tracing paper to draw the base plan. You need to trace over the garden boundary, and any features on the site (trees, shed, existing paths, etc.) that you intend to keep. This is preferably done using an ink or fine fibre-tip pen. Then place this over a piece of plain white paper. The result is your garden, minus all the features that you will be removing. In essence it is your blank canvas. Place another sheet of tracing paper over this and start to sketch your ideas.

SITING FEATURES

It is very important that you clarify the priorities at this early stage. Start with the basics, e.g. positioning the washing line, dustbins and storage areas. Remember that they will need to be accessible, perhaps even in the dark, while being screened from view. Then add a shed or compost area, and car parking space if required.

Once you have the basic needs, consider the rest of your wish list. Start with the most important items and work down the list. Remember to think very carefully how much space each will realistically need, and how often it will be used. Make sure you separate *real need* from *desire*. Cost is also a consideration, and there is not much sense in coming up with a complex design if you cannot afford it. Work out how much you are prepared to spend and investigate what materials are available. And never forget that the garden needs to look good as well as being a functional space.

Maintenance is also a key consideration at the design stage. The amount of money and/or effort and expertise needed to keep it in first-rate condition should be clearly thought through. Try to fit maintenance requirements around your own lifestyle, and avoid being too ambitious.

HOW DETAILED DO DRAWINGS NEED TO BE?

The amount of detail needed ultimately depends upon the complexity of the design and the types of features you use. Hard landscapes and constructions, such as walls, need to have accurate estimates of the amount of materials required. Ponds and other water features also need estimates for the amount of liner material and the quantity of excavated earth. If your drawings are simple but your ideas are complex, it can lead to problems. Equally, there is little point in making extensive and elaborate plans if you simply intend planting a few extra roses.

If you are wary of this design stage, you can always enlist the help of a professional designer. Check the fee, and while it may seem costly, note that a professional will often find solutions that you hadn't considered. Even if you do employ a designer, try to complete as much of the design stage as you can. If drawing is not your strong point, then survey the garden in note form and make your wish list. It will help the designer to understand your needs and, ultimately, result in a design that is tailored to your taste. Remember that even when someone else draws it for you, it is still your garden and so must always meet your own needs.

Left: *Employing a professional garden designer can be costly, but the results are often well worth the additional expense.*

MAKING A PLAN

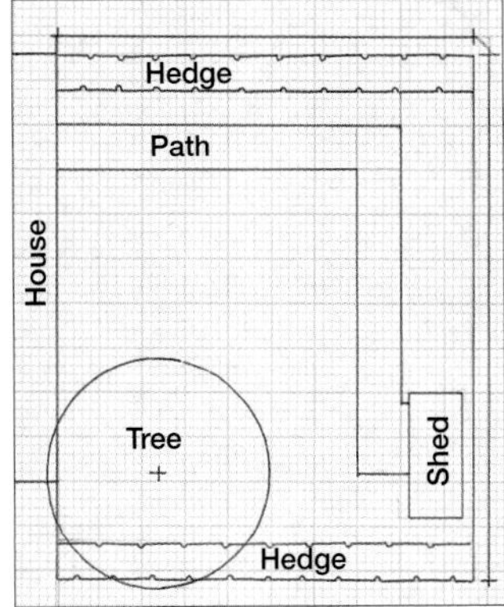

1 *Before beginning your plan, a survey of the area is required. The survey needs to be drawn to scale on graph paper, with all the important features included, for example paths, outbuildings, hedges and any tree with its dimensions shown in outline.*

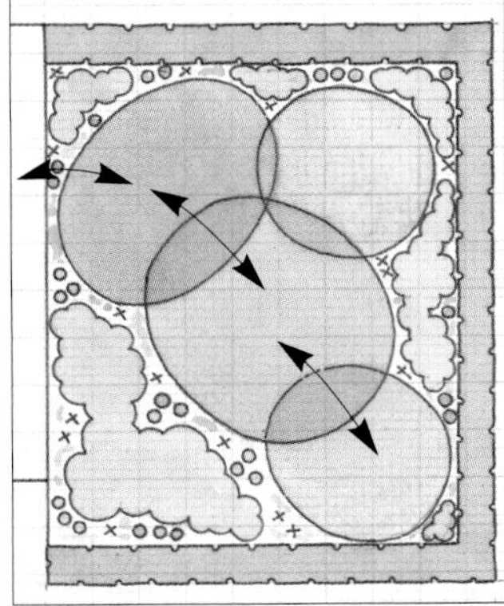

2 *Redraw the boundary lines of the garden on new graph paper, omitting any feature not required. Divide the garden space into zones according to the list of essential and desirable features required. Movement around the garden is shown using arrows.*

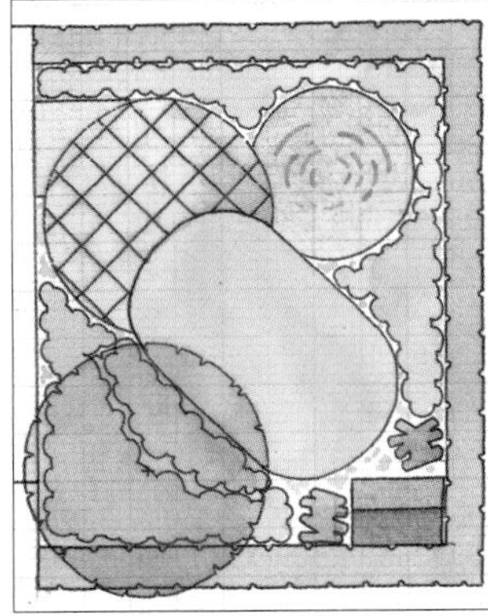

3 *At this stage, the design progresses by working the different zones created into a formal sketch. The sketch shown here is of an informal garden displaying flowing lines and curves. Try out a few different sketch ideas.*

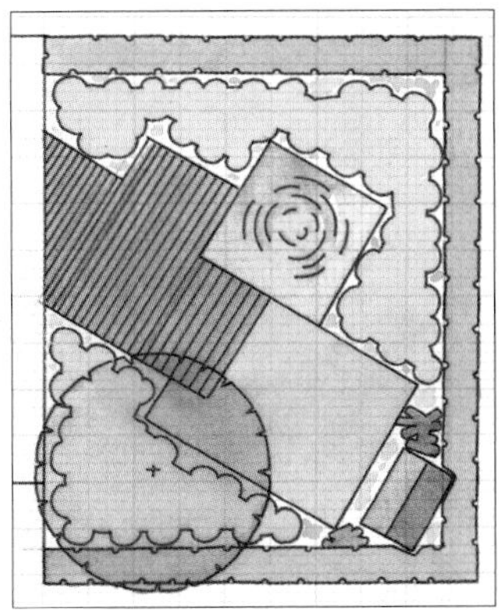

4 *This is an alternative sketch idea for the same area. Again, the different zones created here have been sharpened up into different areas, e.g. pond, grass. This sketch is very formal and uses straight lines and right angles to give this effect.*

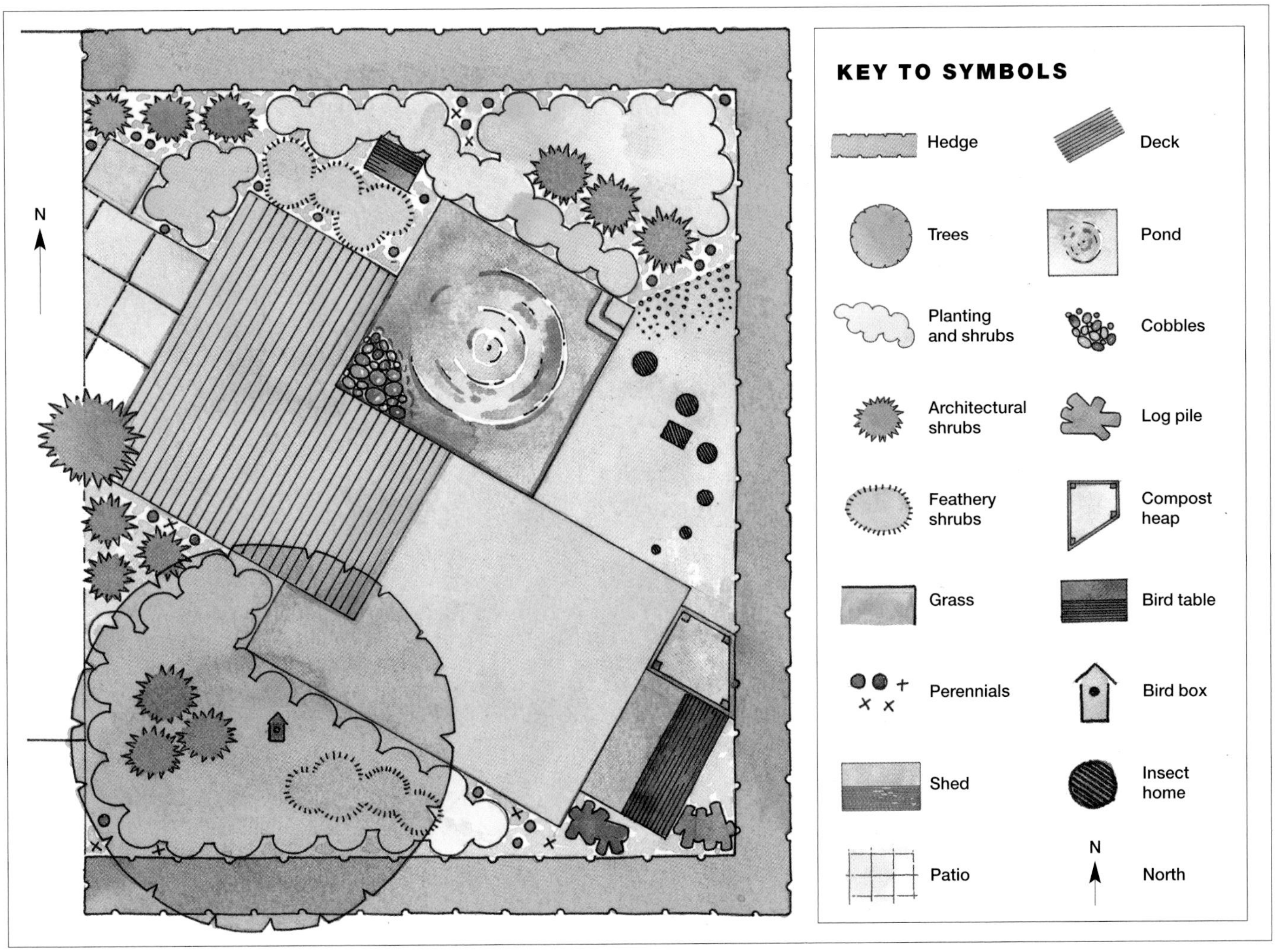

N

KEY TO SYMBOLS

Hedge
Deck
Trees
Pond
Planting and shrubs
Cobbles
Architectural shrubs
Log pile
Feathery shrubs
Compost heap
Grass
Bird table
Perennials
Bird box
Shed
Insect home
Patio
North

5 *Once you have had a few attempts at sketching ideas using the zonal areas, place them side by side and try to envisage which would be the best use of the available space to meet your needs. Once you have chosen the final sketch, it can be drawn up neatly using recognized symbols to indicate what each part represents. Colouring the drawing is not essential, but it is very effective.*

A LARGE COUNTRY WILDLIFE GARDEN

Large country gardens offer a wealth of possibilities for wildlife, having plenty of space for both a range of features and a wide variety of species. While a large garden is not inherently more useful in terms of wildlife than a smaller one, it does enable you to mimic nature with a mosaic of different habitats. Many more species are likely to be resident in your garden rather than just paying a casual visit.

Above: *Larger country gardens can accommodate forest trees, such as this oak, which are fantastic wildlife habitats.*

USE OF SPACE

A large space also allows you to let your imagination run freely. The bigger the space, the less limit will be placed on the inclusion of sizeable features such as trees. This does not mean, however, that designing a large garden is simply a matter of including every possible feature and deliberately making it big. As with any living space, it should be carefully tailored to your needs. It is also vital that your own personal space for leisure, relaxation, socializing and play is clearly defined. Decide how much of the garden is for your own use, and if any areas are exclusively for wildlife.

Scale must be carefully considered, with each chosen element being designed in relation to the space in which it is placed.

Above: *Art and sculpture in the garden can create an extremely ornamental feel to an area without affecting the different types of wildlife species that are attracted.*

A wildlife pond, for instance, should be neither too small and insignificant – for the space or visiting wildlife – nor too large and overpowering for the whole scheme. Indeed, a series of smaller, linked ponds and bog gardens may work better than one large pool with its considerable maintenance requirements.

Remember, too, that open expanses will attract certain species, such as ground-feeding birds, but this must be balanced with more confined spaces for shyer creatures. Use the space wisely in relation to all the other features in the garden, and ensure that habitats are linked and merge to allow the maximum diversity and plenty of escape routes between different areas.

ATTRACTING WILDLIFE

Large gardens often attract and can support large numbers of individual animals, and understanding where they will congregate may affect your choice of where to site the different areas. By placing flower borders and feeding stations near the house you'll be able to watch wildlife from indoors, but don't forget to make more secluded areas both for feeding and shelter, particularly if you are likely to use the area near the house for your own purposes on a regular basis.

ORNAMENTAL FEATURES

Features such as sculpture and willow tunnels can be added to the wildlife garden to improve its aesthetic appeal. Another design tip is to repeat features. This can be seen in this design, where trees surrounded by woven grass seats are used throughout the garden and are linked by the eye to aligning habitat entrances.

Left: *Lawns create space in a garden and link areas together. Ground-feeding birds use lawns to forage for insects and grubs.*

LARGE COUNTRY WILDLIFE GARDEN

A design on this scale has the scope to contain some well-manicured ornamental borders, while still allowing room for a wilder, more secluded area. While smaller gardens may have to mix fruit and vegetables with ornamental plantings due to lack of space, separate fruit and vegetable gardens are featured here. This design has been divided into smaller areas, but they are all linked up by the use of hedges and interconnecting borders to provide continuous cover for the resident wildlife.

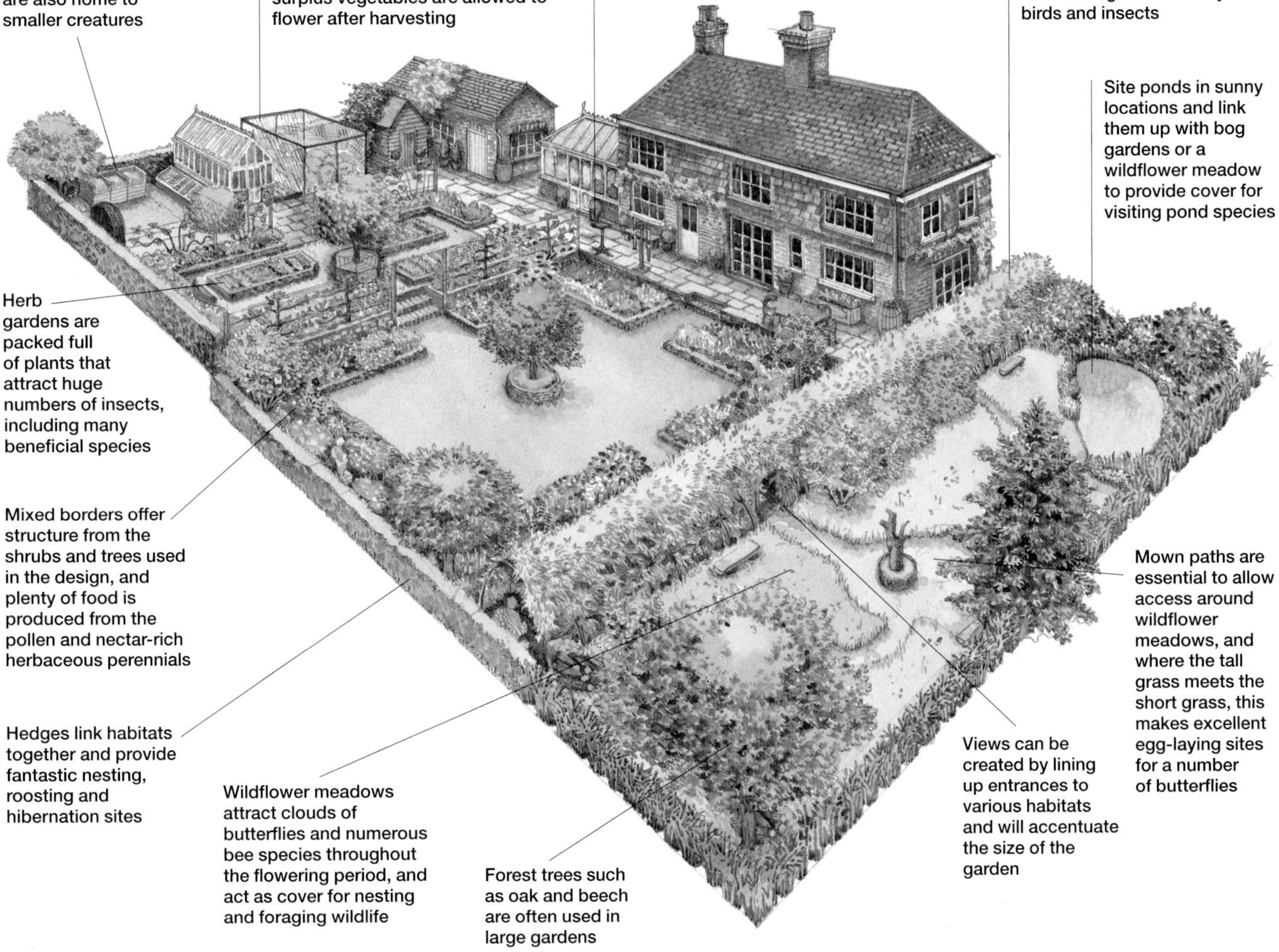

Compost bins are essential for recycling plant matter and are also home to smaller creatures

Fruit and vegetable gardens are beneficial to wildlife if the excess fruits are uncovered for wildlife and surplus vegetables are allowed to flower after harvesting

Position bird feeders near a window to observe the visiting species easily

A willow tunnel is a great feature in a large garden and will also act as a roosting and feeding site for many birds and insects

Site ponds in sunny locations and link them up with bog gardens or a wildflower meadow to provide cover for visiting pond species

Herb gardens are packed full of plants that attract huge numbers of insects, including many beneficial species

Mixed borders offer structure from the shrubs and trees used in the design, and plenty of food is produced from the pollen and nectar-rich herbaceous perennials

Hedges link habitats together and provide fantastic nesting, roosting and hibernation sites

Wildflower meadows attract clouds of butterflies and numerous bee species throughout the flowering period, and act as cover for nesting and foraging wildlife

Forest trees such as oak and beech are often used in large gardens

Views can be created by lining up entrances to various habitats and will accentuate the size of the garden

Mown paths are essential to allow access around wildflower meadows, and where the tall grass meets the short grass, this makes excellent egg-laying sites for a number of butterflies

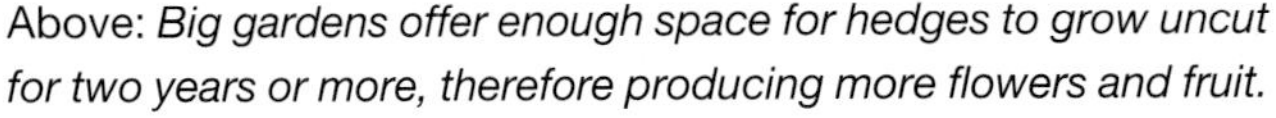

Above: *Big gardens offer enough space for hedges to grow uncut for two years or more, therefore producing more flowers and fruit.*

Above: *In a large garden, a pond can be linked to a bog garden. Together, these habitats will support many amphibians and reptiles.*

AN URBAN WILDLIFE GARDEN

The main problem faced by wildlife in an urban setting is that it will always be in close proximity to people. Add to that the dangers posed by pets – dogs and especially cats – and the garden suddenly seems a precarious space for wildlife to survive in. Despite these hardships, clever design can overcome some of the dangers and many "urban" creatures become surprisingly habituated to the people who "share" their home.

Above: *Bird tables and feeders will attract birds into your garden from surrounding gardens and the neighbouring countryside.*

NEIGHBOURING INFLUENCES

Despite such drawbacks, domestic gardens are often rich in wildlife. This is usually because many adjoining gardens combine to create a larger super-habitat. Of course parts of this area will be more useful than others, and if you choose the right features for your own patch you can benefit your own wildlife while enjoying the visits of other creatures from the surrounding areas.

USE OF SPACE

As with any domestic space, the golden rule is to decide how much of the space is for your needs, and which areas are to be devoted to wildlife. In a smaller space, however, such lines become blurred and you may need to compromise in order to find as near-perfect a solution as possible. Lawns are a prime example because most people use the space on the lawn for both play and relaxation. But there is no reason why such a space cannot also benefit wildlife, and a medium to short, clover-filled flowering lawn will instantly help wildlife without the need to keep off it. In addition, a corner of the lawn can always be left for naturalized bulbs and the grass allowed to grow long.

ATTRACTING WILDLIFE

Hedges and wildlife borders can also be included in most gardens, where they will provide valuable cover for many species

Left: *Hawthorn, sometimes classed as a small tree, is ideal to use as a large shrub in a restricted urban space. It provides both structure and food for wildlife.*

Below: *A winding path in a narrow space makes a garden look wider than it really is. The dense borders provide valuable cover.*

Above: *Water is vital for the survival of resident or visiting wildlife. Create drinking shallows for smaller creatures to drink from.*

and, if there is space, a small tree can even be included. Ponds and water features are often a big attraction for many species, and even a modest pool can make quite an impact. Not only will it act as a watering hole, but it will be a crucial breeding site for amphibians and aquatic insects.

Right: *Climbing roses provide excellent sites for roosting insects and birds feeding on pests such as aphids. Varieties that produce hips, which are good food for birds, will produce plenty of pollen for insects too.*

URBAN WILDLIFE GARDEN

Although they vary in size, nearly all urban gardens will be large enough to include a variety of different habitats. The resident and visiting wildlife found in a built-up area is strongly influenced by the surrounding gardens and habitats. Therefore, if your garden has neighbouring large trees or a pond, it may not be necessary for you to include these in your own design. Although the design pictured here looks like any well-designed ornamental garden, it contains all the vital ingredients for a classic wildlife garden.

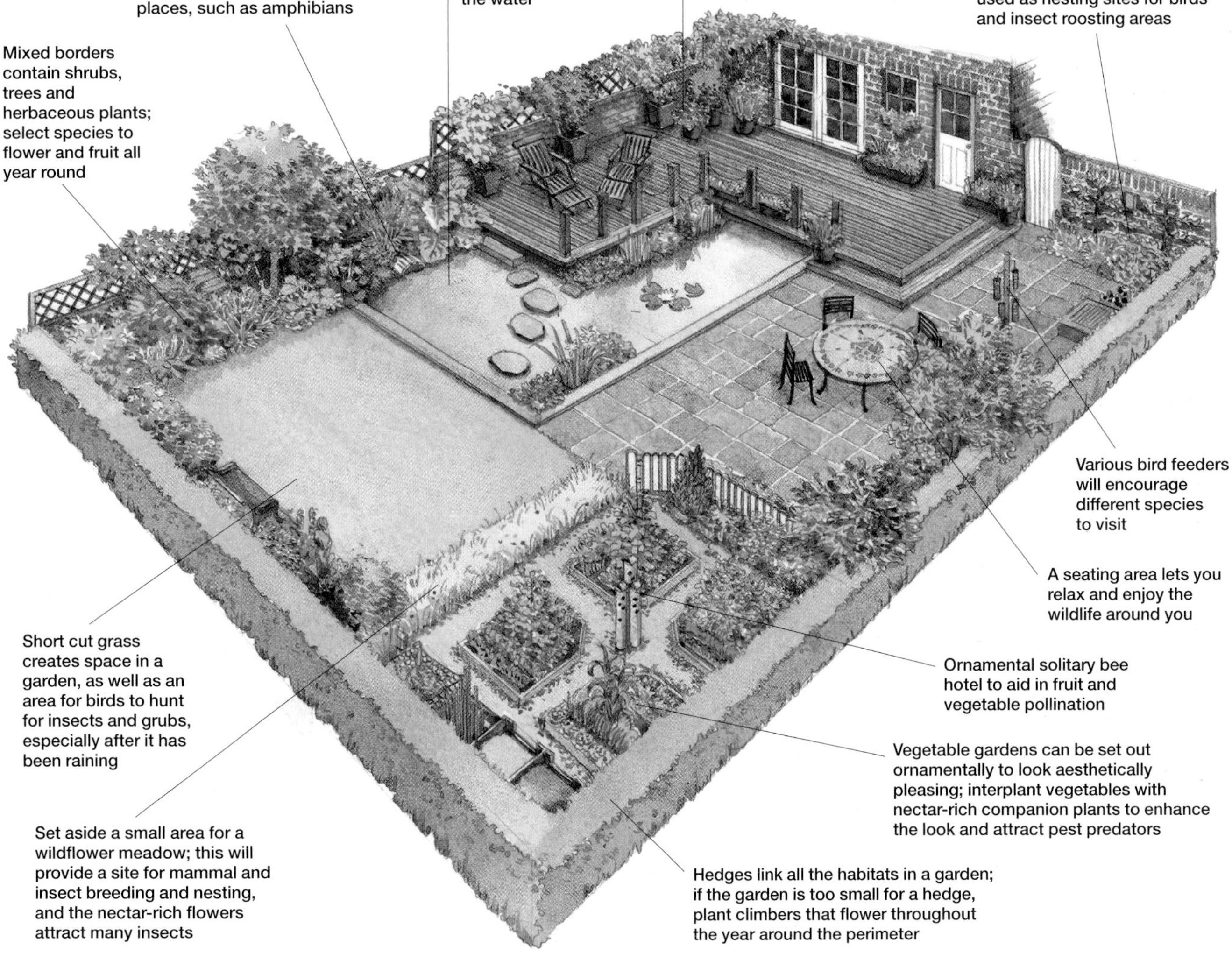

A bog garden is a transitional area between the water and dry land, and is used by creatures that like damp places, such as amphibians

An ornamental pond with a slope ensures that wildlife can enter and exit the water

Pots and containers provide seasonal colour and good quantities of nectar and pollen for insects

Wall shrubs and climbers can be great sources of nectar and pollen for insects and fruit for birds; they are often used as nesting sites for birds and insect roosting areas

Mixed borders contain shrubs, trees and herbaceous plants; select species to flower and fruit all year round

Various bird feeders will encourage different species to visit

A seating area lets you relax and enjoy the wildlife around you

Short cut grass creates space in a garden, as well as an area for birds to hunt for insects and grubs, especially after it has been raining

Ornamental solitary bee hotel to aid in fruit and vegetable pollination

Vegetable gardens can be set out ornamentally to look aesthetically pleasing; interplant vegetables with nectar-rich companion plants to enhance the look and attract pest predators

Set aside a small area for a wildflower meadow; this will provide a site for mammal and insect breeding and nesting, and the nectar-rich flowers attract many insects

Hedges link all the habitats in a garden; if the garden is too small for a hedge, plant climbers that flower throughout the year around the perimeter

A COURTYARD WILDLIFE GARDEN

Small gardens can be fantastic areas for wildlife. Courtyards are often devoid of birds and animals, but with the careful use of containers, hanging baskets and window boxes, you can easily grow a diverse range of plants, which in turn will attract a surprisingly large range of wildlife. While your garden may not be a permanent residence for all these creatures, it will prove to be a valuable and much appreciated food and drink stop.

Above: *Wildlife in a courtyard garden is easily observed due to the lack of space. Create seating areas to relax and enjoy this.*

USE OF SPACE

To ensure that a courtyard garden is fit for wildlife, tackle it in three dimensions. Avoid thinking exclusively about the space that is available on the ground. Many plants that are attractive to wildlife are perfectly at home in containers, and a little imagination can work wonders. Walls are relatively unattractive places for many species of wildlife, but can easily be improved by attaching a trellis and allowing climbers to grow up and over them. This will provide shelter for many species and, in the case of flowering and fruiting species, a valuable food source. Hanging baskets, wall and window boxes are also very useful ways of improving the appearance and wildlife value of the garden, while avoiding the need to use up too much of the ground space.

Above: *Water can be provided for birds in small gardens by hanging up bowls or attaching containers or troughs to a wall.*

PROVIDING WATER

Water is often in short supply in towns, and you may not have space for even a small wildlife pool, but you should endeavour to provide a constant source of fresh water for visiting creatures. This can be as simple as a shallow bowl or birdbath, or a small, raised, wildlife pool. A permanently planted water feature can be a mistake, however, if it is too small and shallow because it can easily become a breeding ground for mosquitoes. If this is likely to be a problem, add a small bubble fountain to keep the water moving.

DESIGN TIPS

Smaller gardens are harder to design as most of the space can be viewed at any one time. Vertical interest is needed to lead the eye away from the enclosed space, and will give the feeling of a larger area. This can be done with the use of trees or by installing a pergola and growing climbers up the frame to help draw the eye upwards. The pergola structure should be strong and the design simple so the area doesn't look too busy. Another tip is to avoid furniture that is bulky. Instead, select light and airy furniture such as wrought iron or teak as it will appear to take up less space.

Planting also plays a crucial part in giving the garden a larger look. Select cool colours such as blues and purples as this will give the illusion of the border being further away. Limit the number of different types of plants to avoid having the area look too busy. By incorporating these simple rules for gardening in a confined space your area will definitely give the illusion of being larger than it really is.

Left: *A small garden can become lush with vegetation in a short space of time, and can create a wonderful wildlife paradise.*

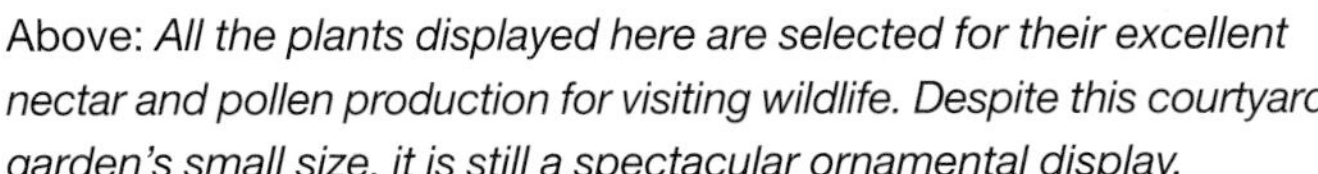

Above: *All the plants displayed here are selected for their excellent nectar and pollen production for visiting wildlife. Despite this courtyard garden's small size, it is still a spectacular ornamental display.*

Above: *A pergola in a courtyard garden creates an enclosed area. It also creates cool, shady areas within a garden if climbers and wall shrubs are grown up and around the structures.*

COURTYARD WILDLIFE GARDEN

Small courtyard gardens can be teeming with wildlife if a variety of different features are introduced. Much of the nectar and pollen production in a courtyard garden will be found in hanging baskets and containers. If you can remove an area of paving, a small mixed border can be created, otherwise plant up shrubs and trees in pots and arrange to create the same effect. Water can still be added in the form of a small fountain or a hanging saucer to tempt resident and visiting insects and birds.

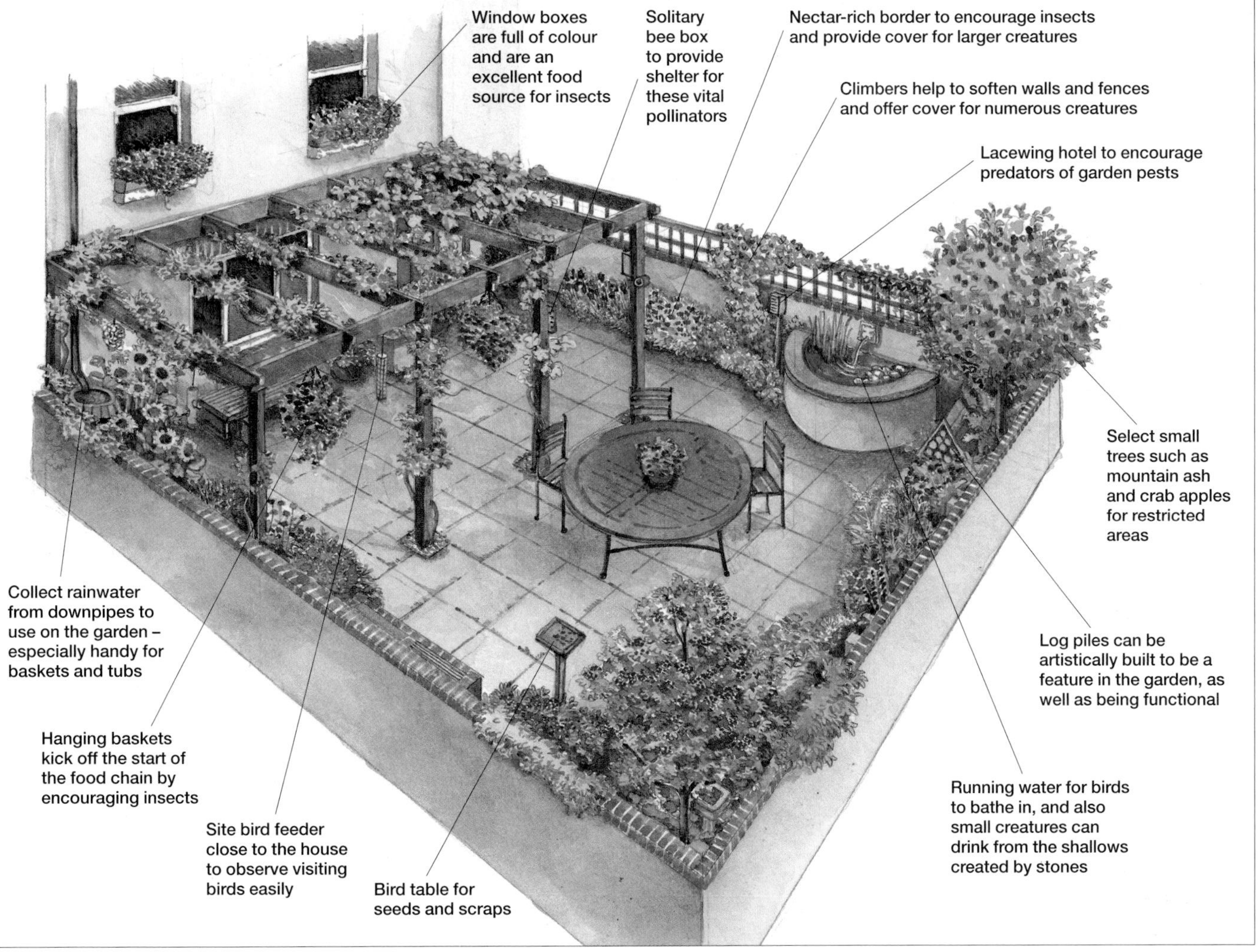

Window boxes are full of colour and are an excellent food source for insects

Solitary bee box to provide shelter for these vital pollinators

Nectar-rich border to encourage insects and provide cover for larger creatures

Climbers help to soften walls and fences and offer cover for numerous creatures

Lacewing hotel to encourage predators of garden pests

Select small trees such as mountain ash and crab apples for restricted areas

Log piles can be artistically built to be a feature in the garden, as well as being functional

Running water for birds to bathe in, and also small creatures can drink from the shallows created by stones

Collect rainwater from downpipes to use on the garden – especially handy for baskets and tubs

Hanging baskets kick off the start of the food chain by encouraging insects

Site bird feeder close to the house to observe visiting birds easily

Bird table for seeds and scraps

A WILD GARDEN

Wild gardens offer potentially the closest substitute to a natural habitat and, if designed properly, can be a wonderful place. However, the decision to build a wild garden should not be taken lightly, nor should it be thought of as a low-maintenance option, becoming completely disorderly and chaotic. It is still a garden, and the term "wild" could equally be replaced by "naturalistic". Regular maintenance is still required, especially in habitats such as the wildflower meadow.

Above: *In dappled shade areas, a mass of spring bulbs such as wild garlic offers a welcome early supply of nectar for insects.*

NATIVE OR EXOTIC PLANT?

Wild gardens differ from other styles of wildlife garden primarily because they use only plants that are native to the area. It is precisely because of this that more traditional gardeners sometimes deride them, regarding them as little more than weed patches. But many native plants are not only supremely beautiful, but are well adapted to the site and soil conditions of the area.

Thankfully, recent years have seen a reversal of the traditional form of gardening, with native plants now being commonly seen in an ornamental setting. With a little imagination they can form an immensely attractive display. Always avoid plants that are known to be invasive, however, because there are always less troublesome, attractive alternatives. Native plants also offer certainty that they are excellent choices for the local wildlife in terms of their food value. Always choose a range of species to flower, and provide food, over as long a period as possible.

Above: *Wildflower areas are more accessible if paths are mown through following natural "desire lines". Several species of butterfly lay their eggs alongside the mown paths.*

MAINTENANCE

When it comes to maintenance, most native plant species are no different from other garden plants. In fact your main focus should be on being untidy. Fallen plant debris harbours many overwintering insects, and those dead flowers in the borders are often a rich source of seed for birds in the winter. The only real difference in making a wild garden is that you will have created a refuge for a whole host of interesting creatures using a rich diversity of native plants, many of which are becoming increasingly rare in the wild.

Left: *This well-balanced pond is packed full of hidey holes by the use of wood, pots and plants for insects and amphibians to seek shelter, hide and hibernate in.*

Right: *Many species of butterflies are attracted to wild gardens, where they feed on nectar from flowers found in the wildflower meadows, and several lay their eggs in the edges of long grass areas.*

WILD GARDEN

A design for a wild garden has to be as well thought out as a formal design. Care should be taken to include as many different habitats as possible, especially wildflower meadows and deciduous trees which are renowned for the number of creatures that are associated with each. Short cut grass areas are kept to a minimum and standing deadwood extends proudly in this type of garden.

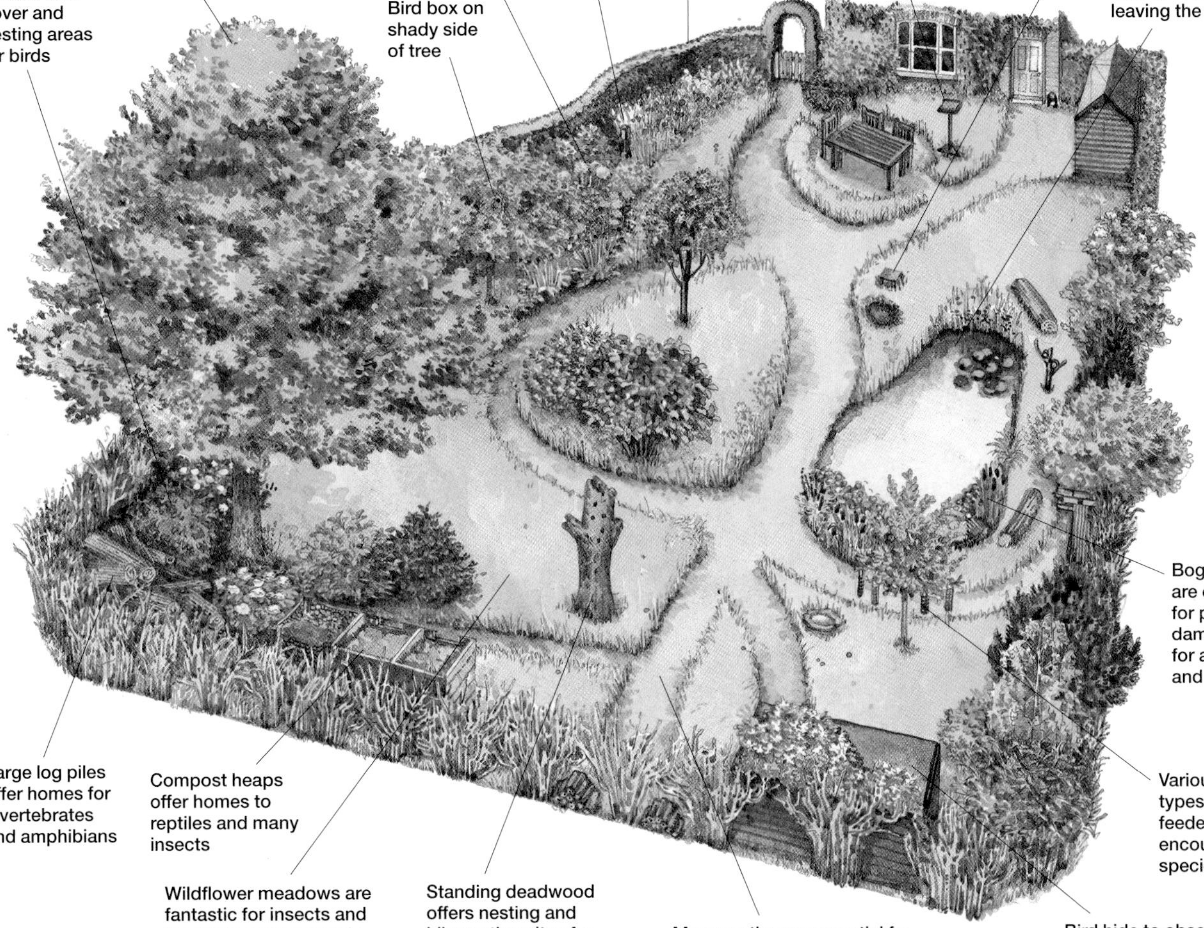

Large deciduous trees ensure a good litter layer in the soil

Nectar-rich border to attract insects

Lacewing hotel attracts predators of aphids

Hedging links all areas of the garden

Bird table ideally sited close to the house as kitchen scraps are put out daily

Ground feeder to attract birds

Pond surrounded by vegetation to protect creatures entering and leaving the water

Shrubs offer cover and nesting areas for birds

Bird box on shady side of tree

Bog gardens are essential for providing damp cover for amphibians and reptiles

Various different types of bird feeders will encourage more species to feed

Large log piles offer homes for invertebrates and amphibians

Compost heaps offer homes to reptiles and many insects

Wildflower meadows are fantastic for insects and the birds and mammals that feed on them

Standing deadwood offers nesting and hibernation sites for many creatures

Mown paths are essential for access around the garden

Bird hide to observe the wildlife visiting the feeders

Above: *Water lilies provide an ideal landing pad for damseflies, dragonflies and frogs to bask on.*

Right: *Allowing short grass to regenerate naturally can result in areas abundant with cow parsley.*

A BEE BORDER

Bees are one of nature's busiest creatures and superb pollinators, and without them many plant species would dwindle and, ultimately, become extinct. Fortunately, many very showy plant species will attract and serve bees well by providing nectar to make honey and pollen to feed developing grubs. Most gardens will have space for a bee border; it will be a great asset and, once you have one, you can enjoy the gentle hum of bees all summer long.

Above: *Bumblebees may have long or short tongues, and the shape of a flower dictates which type is able to access the nectar.*

WHY ARE BEES SO IMPORTANT?

The hum of bees visiting a border rich with flowers is one of the true delights of the summer. Plants are pollinated by bees when they gather nectar from the flowers, though wild bees and honeybees also collect pollen. Pollen is a vital food, used to feed the developing bee grubs, and is gathered with the nectar. To feed bees, then, you'll need a mixture of nectar- and pollen-rich plants.

DECLINE OF NATIVE SPECIES

Urbanization and changes to farming practices have resulted in the destruction of native flowers that provide both nectar and pollen, and consequently many wild species of bee have declined. This trend has to be reversed, and gardeners can help.

Bees – particularly species such as the long-tongued bumblebee – are choosy about which flowers they visit, most needing deep flowers with abundant nectar. Both the flowers and bees are reliant on each other's continued existence, and the loss of one bee species often has wider consequences than many people realize, with several plant species being affected as a result. Gardeners are in an excellent position to slow, and even reverse, this decline by growing plants that are suitable for these important wild bee species.

FORAGING BEHAVIOUR

Bees forage for a wide range of flowers, and the main thing that you need to promote is a variety of flower shapes. Different bee species have favourite shapes according to their size, weight and mouthparts. In addition, many large, cultivated forms of flowers no longer resemble ancestral forms, and are inappropriate for bees because they have trouble foraging from them. Old-fashioned cottage-garden varieties are usually the best option. In general, simple, unmodified flowers usually have most nectar, although the bees cannot easily distinguish between them and double flowers or cultivars that are poor in nectar.

DESIGNING THE BORDER

The trick is to plant a range of species, and mix them with attractive native wildflowers. Choose a range of plants to flower, and feed the bees, over a long period. This is especially important for bumblebee colonies, which generally only store a few days' worth of food and are much more vulnerable than honeybees to food

Below: *Choose a range of flower shapes when designing a border, as different species of bee will prefer a certain size or weight of flower to land and forage on.*

Below: *Bees such as the honeybee collect pollen in sacs on their rear legs. This activity not only pollinates the flowers but also makes an ideal food for their developing larvae.*

shortages caused by a scarcity of flowers or poor foraging weather. The bumblebees need constant access to nectar-rich plants throughout spring, summer and autumn.

Early season, nectar-rich plants are vital for newly emerging females. The female solitary bees often appear in mid- to late spring and, having mated, they then prepare the overwintering nest for next year's brood. Bumblebees, on the other hand, are social insects, and the females that emerge from hibernation in early spring are called queens. They must find and establish a nest – often a disused mouse burrow – and find enough food to mature the eggs and rear the first batch of workers. Consequently, early flowering plants play an extremely important role in ensuring the survival of these colonies and the species in general, so always include a few.

In the design shown here, the needs of both long- and short-tongued bees have been considered, as has the flowering season. From early to mid-spring, short-tongued species can forage on the cotoneaster whereas the long-tongued species will be attracted to the flowering currant (*Ribes sanguineum*) and the gorse (*Ulex europaeus*). Later, in spring and early summer, the short-tongued bees will be helped by the roses and any remaining flowers on the cotoneaster, while the long-tongued bees will delight in the foxglove (*Digitalis purpurea*), the perennial pea (*Lathyrus latifolius*), columbine (*Aquilegia vulgaris*) and red clover (*Trifolium pratense*).

From midsummer until early autumn the short-tongued bees will continue to visit the climbing rose, *Rosa* 'Mermaid', borage (*Borago officinalis*), the Japanese angelica tree (*Aralia elata*) and traveller's joy (*Clematis vitalba*). The long-tongued bees will visit catmint (*Nepeta* x *faassenii*), the giant thistle-like *Echinops nitro*, and honeywort (*Cerinthe major*), with *Hebe salicifolia* and the bellflower (*Campanula latifolia*) feeding a wide range of species at this time.

Above: *The selection of single flowers for a border is vital in a bee garden as the many petals in the make-up of a double flower will hinder access to pollen and nectar. Old-fashioned varieties and cottage-type plants are among the best flowers to do this.*

BEE BORDER

The plants selected in this design for a bee border are ornamental as well as rich in nectar and/or pollen. A range of annuals, bulbs, perennials, shrubs, climbers and trees have been selected to flower from spring right through until autumn, offering food throughout the seasons when bees are active.

1 *Trifolium pratense* – Red clover
2 *Salvia nemerosa* – Wood sage
3 *Cotoneaster horizontalis* – Herringbone cotoneaster
4 *Ceanothus impressus* – Santa Barbara lilac
5 *Digitalis purpurea* – Foxglove
6 *Lathyrus latifolius* – Perennial pea
7 *Hebe salicifolia* – Hebe
8 *Campanula latifolia* – Bellflower
9 *Aquilegia vulgaris* – Columbine
10 *Nepeta* x *faassenii* – Catmint
11 *Echinops nitro* – Globe thistle
12 *Cercis siliquastrum* – Judas tree
13 *Rosa* 'Mermaid' – Rose
14 *Ribes sanguineum* – Flowering currant
15 *Monarda didyma* – Bergamot
16 *Cerinthe major* 'Purpurascens' – Honeywort
17 *Sedum spectabile* – Ice plant
18 *Ulex europea* – Gorse
19 *Rosa canina* – Dog rose
20 *Clematis tangutica* – Clematis
21 *Aralia elata* – Japanese angelica tree
22 *Borago officinalis* – Borage
23 *Cirsium rivulare* – Plume thistle
24 *Eschscholzia californica* – California poppy
25 *Alcea rosea* – Hollyhock
26 *Allium giganteum* – Ornamental onion
27 *Perovskia atricifolia* – Russian sage
28 *Agastache foeniculum* – Anise hyssop
29 *Limnanthes douglasii* – Poached egg plant
30 *Phaseolus coccineus* – Scarlet runner bean

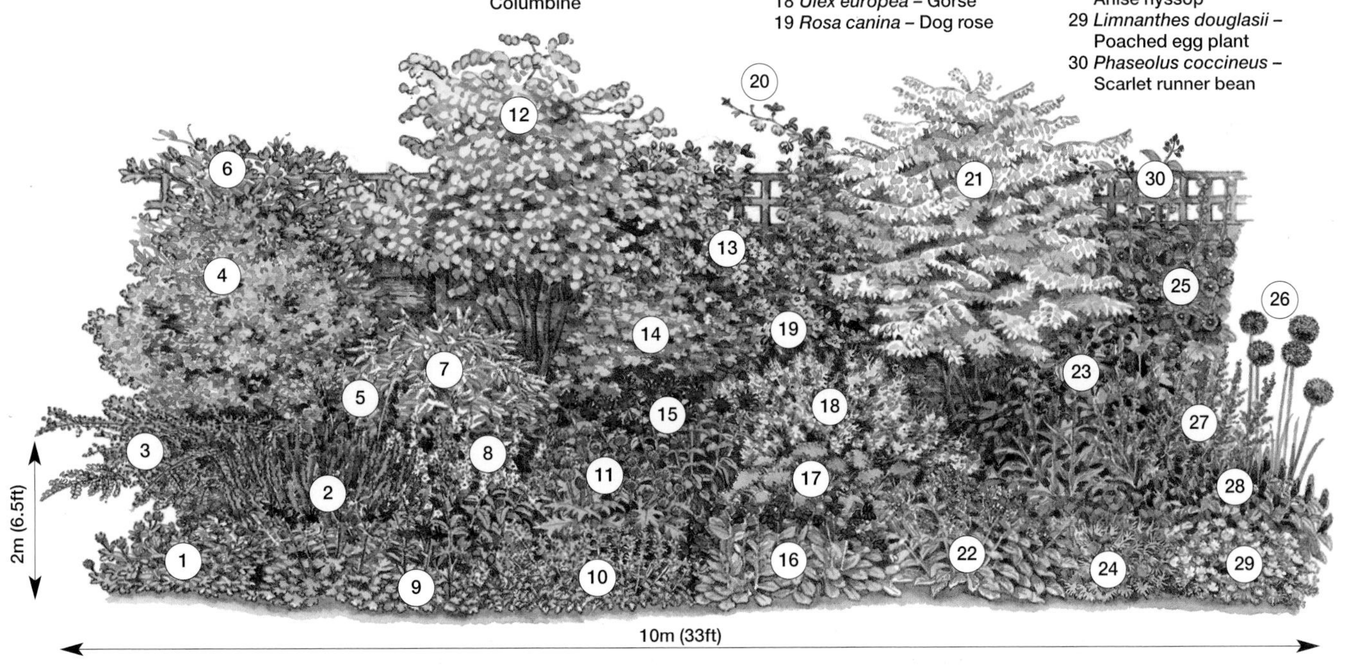

A BUTTERFLY BORDER

Butterflies are the true aristocrats of the insect world – they have inspired poets and are the epitome of a warm summer's afternoon. They are frequent visitors during the summer, attracted by the rich concentration of nectar offered by garden flowers. Attracting butterflies is generally quite easy, although it does require some planning. Find out which butterflies are native to your area and research their feeding preferences, the places where they prefer to see out bad weather, and what their larvae feed on.

Above: *Butterflies prefer single-flowering dahlias, such as the Collerette Group, rather than the showy blooms of other dahlia types.*

UNDERSTANDING LIFE CYCLES

Although showy adults are the prime attraction, the plants also need to support the larvae, or caterpillars. They are essentially a long, worm-like eating machine that must consume a prodigious amount of leaves, or other vegetation, to get enough energy to change (or metamorphose) into the adult butterfly. Unfortunately, the idea of a border full of tatty plants that have been munched by caterpillars is too much for most gardeners. The trick is therefore to grow a few of the more showy food plants, but so spread them out that if they are devoured by caterpillars they won't be so obvious. Also keep any clumps or patches of the less attractive food plants, such as nettles or brambles, in more out-of-the-way places, and remember that many species have caterpillars that feed on grasses. Making a long-grass area for wildflowers is a useful addition to your border.

Adult butterflies, on the other hand, are almost entirely nectar-feeding, although a few – depending on the species or season – may feed on fermenting fruit, manure and carrion. Most will also land on moist, muddy ground to get a drink of water and top up their mineral salt intake.

DESIGN AND PLANT SELECTION

Any site for a butterfly border must have good shelter and receive plenty of sun. The majority of flowers that attract butterflies are clump-forming or shrubby, make excellent subjects for a mixed border, and provide a striking display for you and the butterflies.

Adult butterflies need plenty of nectar to give them energy, and a good butterfly border should provide nectar from spring to autumn. Adult butterflies have mouthparts shaped into a long, coiled tube called a proboscis into which they force blood, straightening it out so that it can probe into flowers. They then suck up the nectar, and that's why good butterfly plant species often have narrow, tubular flowers.

The colour of the flowers can also be important, with most butterflies preferring blue, mauve, yellow and white. They do not see red as well as we do, but they can see ultraviolet light that is present on many flowers, guiding them to the nectar. Butterflies also seem to be attracted to areas with large masses of a single colour, or closely related colours, rather than to borders with many mixed colours. They also have a well-developed sense of smell from their antennae, which is why so many butterfly-attracting plants also have a sweet fragrance, increasing their appeal. If you visit a nearby garden where butterflies are plentiful, make a note of which butterflies are present, and which species visit which plants.

Make sure that any design for a butterfly border has a long flowering season to maximize its appeal to the greatest possible number of species. And provide a wide range of plants because all habitats thrive on diversity (stagger groups of wild and cultivated plants through the border). In the design shown here, spring-flowering species include holly (*Ilex aquifolium*), which

Below: *The monarch butterfly is a truly amazing insect that will migrate thousands of miles as part of its yearly life cycle.*

Below: Buddleja davidii *is aptly named the butterfly bush because the large panicles of its small tubular flowers are frequented by many butterflies.*

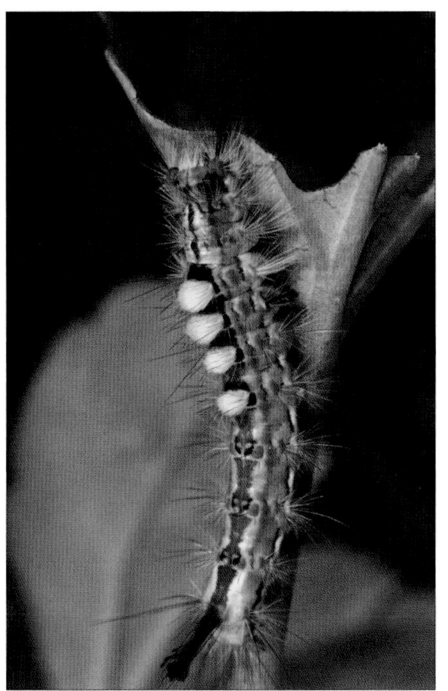

Above: *The caterpillars of some butterflies and moths store toxins. As a result, they have brightly coloured bodies or hairs to warn off any would-be predators.*

is also the food plant of the holly blue butterfly caterpillar, candytuft (*Iberis amara*) in mild areas, the alder buckthorn (*Rhamnus frangula*), which is also the food plant of the brimstone butterfly caterpillar, and, towards the end of spring, *Escallonia* 'Langleyensis'.

In summer – the prime time for many butterfly species – buddlejas, candytuft, sweet scabious (*Scabiosa atropurpurea*), *Verbena bonariensis*, red valerian (*Centranthus ruber*), hemp agrimony (*Eupatorium cannabinum*), heliotrope (*Heliotropium arborescens*) and *Escallonia* 'Langleyensis' all provide a feast of nectar. Autumn is also important for many species of butterfly that overwinter as hibernating adults. Nectar is provided by *Aster* x *frikartii*, ivy (*Hedera helix*), dahlias and the ice plant (*Sedum spectabile*).

Where space is limited, just grow a few nectar plants beside some woody ones to provide butterflies with shelter during bad weather and at night. And because butterflies bask in the sun, often early in the day, place a large, flat stone in full sun. Also note that adult butterflies cannot drink from open water, so provide a patch or tray of wet sand or soil to which you have added a pinch of rock salt. Finally, a butterfly-feeding station is a useful border addition. If you have fruit trees, leave some produce to rot on a feeding table where late-emerging butterflies can feed.

Above: *The meadow brown butterfly is a frequent visitor to garden flowers but requires an area of long grass to breed successfully.*

BUTTERFLY BORDER

In order to attract butterflies, a border needs to contain a range of large or flat flowers for the insects to visit. In addition, it is vital that you choose plants so that some of them will be in flower for as long a period as possible. Spring and autumn are especially important times for overwintering species because nectar is often scarce then.

1 *Lotus corniculatas* – Bird's foot trefoil
2 *Aster* x *frikartii* 'Mönch' – Aster
3 *Ilex aquifolium* – Holly
4 *Colletia hystrix* – Crucifixion thorn or barbed wire bush
5 *Hedera helix* – Ivy
6 *Dahlia* Collerette Group – Dahlia
7 *Heliotropium arborescens* – Heliotrope
8 *Iberis amara* – Candytuft
9 *Scabiosa atropurpurea* – Scabious or mourning bride
10 *Buddleja* 'Lochinch' – Butterfly bush
11 *Humulus lupulus* – Hop
12 *Rhamnus frangula* – Alder buckthorn
13 *Verbena bonariensis* – Tall verbena
14 *Sedum spectabile* – Ice plant
15 *Origanum vulgare* – Oregano
16 *Centranthus ruber* – Red valerian
17 *Hedera helix* – Ivy
18 *Buddleja alternifolia* – Fountain butterfly bush
19 *Eupatorium cannabinum* – Hemp agrimony
20 *Escallonia* 'Langleyensis' – Escallonia
21 *Anchusa azurea* 'Dropmore' – Anchusa
22 *Zinnia elegans* – Zinnia
23 *Polygonum bistorta* 'Superbum' – Snakeweed
24 *Origanum majorana* – Marjoram
25 *Hebe* 'Great Orme' – Hebe
26 *Phlox paniculata* – Summer phlox
27 *Dianthus barbatus* – Sweet William

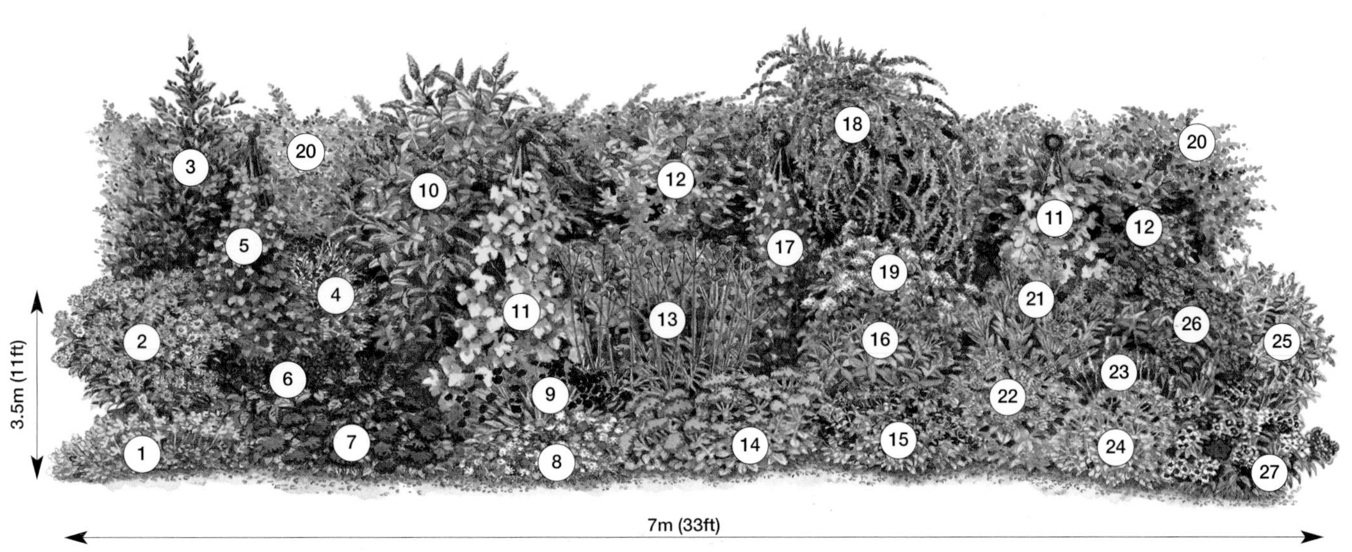

A BIRD BORDER

Birds are an absolute delight in the garden, both during summer for their sweet songs and useful habit of eating garden pests, and in winter when their bright plumage helps brighten up dull days. It's during this winter period that they most need our help, and a border, planted with birds in mind, can be a real lifeline, providing a diverse array of foods, including seeds, berries and even the odd overwintering insect hiding among the vegetation.

Above: *Blue tits are common garden birds in Europe. They rely on seeds and small fruits to see them through the winter.*

WHAT IS A BIRD BORDER?

A bird border doesn't have to be wild or overgrown, but can look attractive all year round. There are few absolute rights or wrongs when you plan one, and growing a wide variety of plants to attract wildlife in general will offer garden birds food and shelter, helping them both survive winter and feed their hungry fledglings the following spring. Think of your bird border as a roadside café, a place where birds can feed and rest before moving on.

CHOOSING A SITE

It is usually best to set aside a quiet area for a bird border because some species are much more sensitive to disturbance than others. The ideal backdrop might be a hedge or berrying shrubs. If planting against a fence or wall, clothing them with climbing plants and shrubs can turn them into a "living boundary", and might well provide cover and nesting sites. Bird borders can be made on any scale with even a small one proving useful, although the more space and diversity you can devote to such a feature, the better.

CHOOSING THE RIGHT SPECIES

Depending on where you live, it is often best to include a range of native plants in your border, and you should try to include as many different kinds as possible. In the example shown here, a formal backdrop has been created by using a hedge made of yew (*Taxus baccata*), although beech (*Fagus sylvatica*), holly (*Ilex aquifolium*) and hornbeam (*Carpinus betulus*) are equally effective, all providing good shelter for birds.

Below: *Barberry is an ideal plant to include in a bird border, offering both spring protection from predators as well as a rich crop of autumn berries.*

If space permits, try a less formal hedge of native shrubs, pruned on only one side in alternate years to provide an excellent source of food and nectar, as well as nesting and shelter.

Trees are also extremely useful, although large forest species – such as oak (*Quercus*) – are often too large for most gardens. If choosing trees for a town garden, make sure you use smaller examples like the ones shown in this design. Mountain ash (*Sorbus aucuparia*), holly (*Ilex aquifolium*) and the crab apple (*Malus* 'Red Sentinel') provide perches and shelter, and an excellent food source when in fruit.

A range of shrubs will provide cover from predators and the worst of the weather. Native species might come top of the list, but more importantly consider a range of evergreen and deciduous types to give variety and hiding places in winter. The barberry (*Berberis thunbergii atropurpurea*)

Below: *The song thrush is an example of a bird species that is carnivorous in the summer but switches to berries and seed during the dormant winter months.*

is an attractive semi-evergreen whose thorny branches offer protection to smaller birds from the likes of cats. Firethorn (*Pyracantha coccinea*) offers similar protective cover for larger birds, and both have berries that can be eaten over winter. The Oregon grape (*Mahonia aquifolium*) is a slightly shorter, evergreen, prickly leaved shrub with berries that ripen in summer, while both elder (*Sambucus nigra*) and blackcurrant (*Ribes nigrum*) are deciduous species that attract many insects and bear summer berries.

Ideally, in addition to these woody plants, you should aim to plant a range of annual and herbaceous plants. Natives are very useful but, if you want a more ornamental look, choose a range of showier species that will attract insects in spring and summer, and later produce good seed heads to help feed small songbirds.

Lastly, you might want to leave some space in your border for a birdbath and feeders, providing food supplies when natural sources run low.

Above: *The shy jay is an occasional visitor to the urban garden. It will take a range of foods, including insects, seed and fruits.*

Above: *The greater spotted woodpecker usually feeds on wood grubs and other insects, but occasionally eats fruit in winter.*

BIRD BORDER

This type of border needs to provide a range of food throughout the seasons. The plants are chosen to either attract insects or bear fruit in the summer, or to be rich in seeds and/or fruit in the winter months. It also includes a range of trees, shrubs and smaller herbaceous plants.

1 *Polygonum bistorta* – Common bistort
2 *Artemisia vulgaris* – Mugwort
3 *Helianthus annuus* – Sunflower
4 *Sorbus aucuparia* – Rowan
5 *Berberis thunbergii atropurpurea* – Barberry
6 *Achillea millefolium* – Common yarrow
7 *Oenothera biennis* – Evening primrose
8 *Lavandula angustifolia* – English lavender
9 *Ribes nigrum* – Blackcurrant
10 *Sambucus nigra* – Elderberry
11 *Pyracantha coccinea* – Firethorn
12 *Ilex aquifolium* – Holly
13 *Angelica sylvestris* – Wild angelica
14 *Amaranthus caudatus* – Love-lies-bleeding
15 *Myosotis arvensis* – Field forget-me-not
16 *Mahonia aquifolium* – Oregon grape
17 *Malus* 'Red Sentinel' – Crab apple
18 *Taxus baccata* – Yew
19 *Dipsacus fullonum* – Teasel
20 *Solidago virgaurea* – Golden rod
21 *Lunaria annua* – Honesty
22 *Viburnum opulus* – Guelder rose
23 *Tanacetum vulgare* – Tansy
24 *Melissa officinalis* – Lemon balm
25 *Ribes uva-crispa* – Gooseberry
26 *Cotoneaster horizontalis* – Herringbone cotoneaster
27 *Fragaria vesca* – Wild strawberry

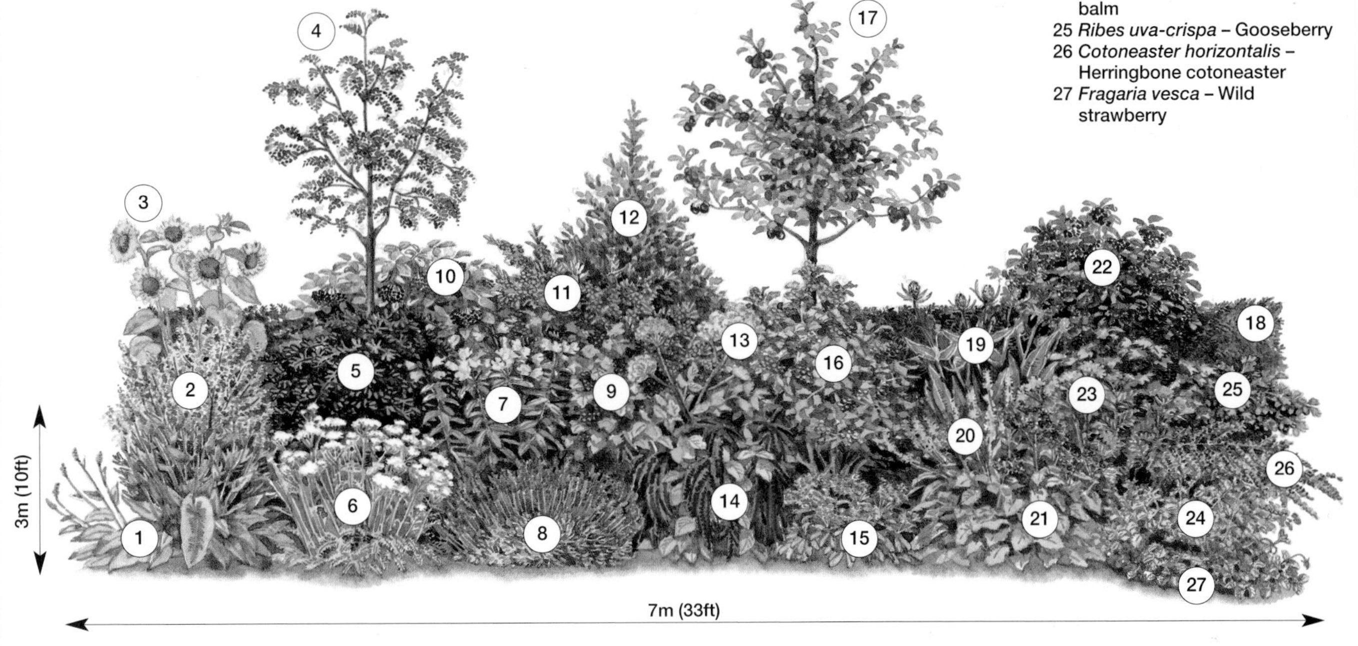

GARDEN HABITATS

To provide for the needs of wildlife in your garden, you must first understand where that wildlife lives. Garden habitats may be extensive in the case of woodlands, while others may be as small as a piece of rotting wood within the same woodland, or can be found in the narrow space between two flat stones in a wall. All of these habitats are important and to support the widest range of wildlife your garden should aim to have as many of them as possible. Once you understand the nature of different habitats, large and small, you can start to replicate them in your own garden.

Left: *Flower-rich grasslands are a superb wildlife habitat and a wonderful garden feature during the summer months.*

Above: *Water is not only essential for wildlife but can also be a habitat in itself, supporting visiting and resident wildlife.*

Above: *Woodlands are extensive habitats that often contain many smaller habitats within, supporting a wide range of species.*

Above: *Even the narrow dark recesses of a drystone wall can provide a habitat for a range of creatures, such as hibernating newts.*

GRASSLANDS

These windy, partly dry habitats are dominated by grasses, with trees and bushes few and far between. Almost a quarter of the Earth's land surface is grassland and, in many areas, grassland is the major habitat separating forests from deserts. In gardens, most grassland areas consist of lawns, and these often bear little resemblance to their wild counterparts. With just a few changes to the way we maintain our lawns, however, we can transform them into superb wildlife habitats.

Above: *Grasshoppers were once common but many are now threatened as their habitat is lost mainly due to grassland management.*

GRASSLAND OR LAWN?

The commonest use of grass in the domestic garden is on a lawn. These manicured features mimic grassland in certain respects but, in many ways, the traditional lawn is quite different from its wild counterpart. In its close-cropped, well-tended state, a lawn might look good to humans but as wildlife habitat it doesn't offer much. Changing a lawn from what is effectively a green desert to a thriving wildlife habitat often involves little more than reducing the amount of mowing, and outlawing the use of fertilizers, pesticides and weedkillers. This will have an almost immediate benefit for wildlife, but it may take some years before the full effects appear. And the time saved maintaining it can be spent more usefully elsewhere in the garden.

Above: *Spring and summer are the most spectacular time for meadows. Flowering reaches its peak at this time and the sight is truly stunning.*

THE IMPORTANCE OF LONG GRASS AREAS

There is a simple truth where grass in your garden is concerned. If a lawn is less frequently mown and not walked on wherever possible, it soon becomes richer for wildlife. Indeed, long grass habitats are some of the most useful undisturbed areas in the garden and are very simple to provide. Where space is limited they may be restricted to strips of uncut grass alongside a hedge, or around the base of a tree, or if space allows they can form more extensive areas.

Whatever the size of a long grass area, they are an important, sheltered habitat and may provide respite or even residence for a range of creatures. Insects such as bumblebees or other wild bees often like to nest in longer grass, while grasshoppers or the caterpillars of moths will feed on the grass leaves and other creatures such as spiders and beetles move in to eat them. Small mammals including shrews make good use of these areas, both to hunt for food and to hide from predators, and many birds such as finches and sparrows may search the area for seeds to eat.

Above: *The combination of dazzling flowers and brightly coloured insects makes a grassland a wonderful place to visit.*

Above: *Buttercups, once a common sight in pastureland, have become rarer with the intensification of modern-day agriculture.*

FLOWER-RICH GRASSLAND

Lawns that are converted into a wildflower meadow can be an important refuge for declining wildflowers, and are an excellent habitat for many insects and spiders. Lawns facing the sun are especially useful, attracting solitary bees and butterflies, and plants

Left: *Traditionally, garden lawns were kept short by mowing and although this keeps the grass healthy, it results in a poor wildlife habitat.*

Right: *Even when you intend to let the grass grow, short cut paths allow access and create a contrast that is useful to butterflies. Some species lay their eggs alongside the paths.*

such as clover (*Trifolium*), knapweed (*Centaurea*), trefoil (*Lotus*), and vetches (*Anthyllis, Coronilla* and *Hippocrepis*) are excellent food plants that provide nectar for long-tongued bumblebees.

TYPES OF WILDFLOWER LAWN

In nature, grassland is a rich and varied habitat that is moulded by the effects of geography, climate, soil and, in many cases, human intervention. Choosing the right type of grassland for your needs will depend on all these factors. Where you live will automatically decide the first three, but the last factor is mostly your choice, and depends on what you want in the garden.

Short grass or downland turf is most commonly seen in temperate regions. It is usually the result of grazing sheep, and the consequent short-cropped turf contains a multitude of flower species. It is the closest model to the modern garden lawn, and can be maintained by regular (if infrequent) cutting by a mower on a high setting.

Hay meadows are a traditional way of managing grassland for the hay that is cut in the summer months and stored for animal fodder. The long grass frequently harbours many species of wildflower during spring and early summer, creating an extremely pretty artificial habitat. Traditional forms of management often resulted in poor soil that reduced the vigour of the grasses and favoured the growth of wildflowers. Sadly, modern intensive agriculture has seen a severe decline in these habitats and consequently in many wildflower species. Wet meadows or flood meadows are largely similar to hay meadows, except that they are subject to seasonal flooding, usually in winter, and consequently harbour different species. All types of meadow can be established in gardens, but they need to be situated carefully and cut during the summer months, when they are not that attractive. Also note, they can be hard to establish on lawns that have been previously well fertilized.

Prairie is a term used to describe the vast areas of flower-rich grassland that once clothed North America, and is similar to the European steppe. The soils are often richer than those found in artificial meadows, and they are often full of wildlife and colourful flowers, many of which have become familiar plants. The effect is potentially much easier to establish in most gardens because it depends on rich soil, with similar mowing regimes to those used in meadows.

Marginal grassland is often used to describe remnants of grassland plant communities that occur on field margins, roadsides or waste ground, and which have been marginalized. They are often a last, vital refuge for native flower species and their dependent wildlife that were formerly common in that area. The effect can be duplicated in a garden at the base of a hedge, or by leaving an occasional space. All you need do is cut it back every year or two in late winter.

TYPES OF GRASSLAND

With such a wide distribution, grassland occurs in many different forms. The commonest types can be mimicked in a garden and provide excellent wildlife refuges.

Wildflower meadow These rich flower habitats are the result of traditional management of grassland to gather hay crops. The constant removal of hay creates a poor soil.

Pasture or downland Grassland was often maintained by the constant grazing of livestock. This results in short grass that is rich in low-growing herbs.

Water meadow Sometimes called flood meadow, these are very similar to hay meadows but are flooded on a seasonal basis and so harbour different plant species.

Prairie and steppe These vast swathes of grassland formerly covered large areas of the USA and Eurasia. Their rich soil supports many species of plants and animals.

Marginal grassland This simply refers to remnants of formerly extensive natural grassland and is often seen in field margins or roadsides.

Above: *Amphibians such as toads spend much of their life on land in damp areas, but they always return to water to breed.*

WETLANDS, PONDS AND BOGS

A wildlife garden would not be complete without a pond because it provides a habitat for some species and a much-needed drink for other residents and visitors. This, with its aesthetic appeal, makes it a worthy addition to any design. Even where space is too limited for a pond, the smallest patch of water can be useful and a damp corner of the garden can provide a habitat for wetland flowers.

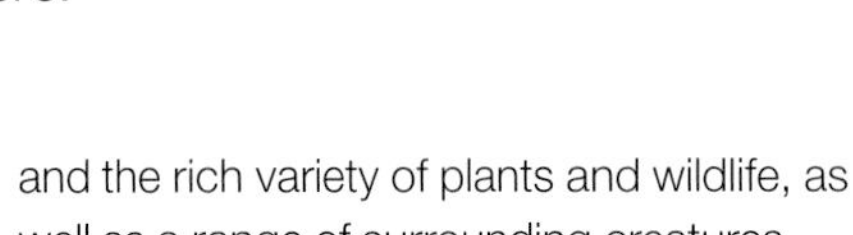

WETLANDS

This general term is applied to areas that are wet or marshy. The term includes both seasonally and permanently wet areas often existing as a complex mosaic of wet ground and open water, including rivers, streams and natural ponds. The natural fertility of these areas means that they are often drained for agriculture or dwellings, and the rich variety of plants and wildlife, as well as a range of surrounding creatures, are often critically endangered as a result.

Below: *Even a relatively small area of water can be an attractive garden feature, which results in a surprisingly diverse habitat for numerous species of plants and animals.*

WHAT IS A POND?

The term is surprisingly vague, and there is no clear distinction between a large pond and a small lake. The average garden pond is relatively small, often supporting a wide range of wildlife. In fact a well-designed pond can attract more variety of wildlife than any other single feature in the garden. It provides a breeding space for amphibians, such as frogs and toads, and a whole host of insects, such as dragonflies, that spend part of their life here. In addition, it is the sole habitat for a range of other creatures, from water snails that spend their life beneath the water to pond skaters that spend most of their life on the water surface.

Ponds should be shallow at one end to provide a bathing area for birds and a watering hole for small mammals, and have wet, muddy margins to attract insects needing a drink. Ponds also provide a unique visual focus, and have a restful quality that is hard to match.

Above: *Ponds are full of interest, often revealing curiosities such as this empty dragonfly larva case in the summer.*

Above: *Pond dipping is a good way to assess what wildlife you have in a pond. It is a great way to interest children in wildlife.*

POND PLANTS

Plants are essential to the health of any small area of water, enabling the habitat to achieve a correct water balance and provide surface cover on otherwise open water. Without them the water would, over time, probably start to resemble a thick pea soup, as algae – small, mostly microscopic plant-like organisms – will start to grow prolifically and ultimately colour the water the same as their own bodies. Plant leaves have the double action of absorbing both carbon dioxide and minerals from the water, which in turn starves the algae. Many natural bodies of still or slow-moving water have extensive cover of floating plants and their sides are also shaded by larger, bank-side or shallows vegetation. In a garden pond it is easy to recreate this by ensuring that there are plenty of submerged plants, about half of the water surface is covered with foliage and that the margins have plants in them that are capable of surviving immersion in shallow water in order to achieve this balance. This will keep water clear and will also make the pond attractive for a whole host of fascinating creatures that come to visit or live there.

BOG GARDENS

Usually specially constructed areas, bog gardens provide permanently waterlogged soil. They are often made in conjunction with a pond, and can support a range of fascinating plant species that would normally be found in wetland habitats. Bog gardens are an important element of any mosaic, and can be a vital refuge for many semi-aquatic species, such as amphibians, which will relish the cool, damp shelter.

PLANTS FOR WETLANDS

Wetlands naturally contain both open water and wet ground, and the plants that live in these places are often adapted to occupy a particular situation.

Marginal or emergent plants Plants that have roots and sometimes stems that grow in shallow water but with shoots, leaves and flowers above the water surface.

Oxygenators Plants that have adapted to live beneath the surface are called oxygenators, due to their role in enriching the water with oxygen.

Water lilies and deep-water aquatics The roots of these plants are submerged, the leaves are on the surface of the water and their flowers are either found on or above the water surface.

Free-floating plants The leaves and stems are free-floating and are found on the water surface. The roots are submerged and the flowers grow on or just above the water.

Bog plants Plants that prefer to grow in permanently wet or waterlogged ground. Some marginal species can also be grown as bog plants.

POND PLANTINGS

Ideally, a pond profile will include shallow areas as well as deeper areas of water. In the deeper reaches, the vegetation consists of plants that are capable of living permanently under water or those with roots that send up leaves which in turn float on the surface. Shallow water will support plants capable of tolerating waterlogged conditions and the remainder are free-floating on the surface.

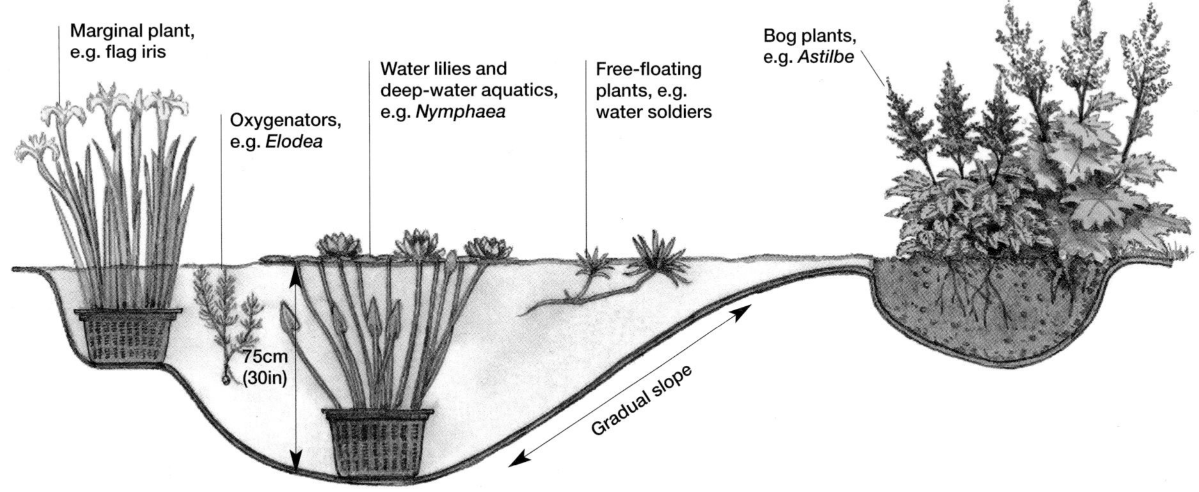

HEDGEROWS

Widely used as boundaries and dividing features in landscapes for centuries, hedges are important habitats for many creatures. Some hedges are relics of former habitats, meaning quite simply that they harbour species found in prior woodland cover, and may even be the oldest remaining feature in the area. Properly managed, they provide a great opportunity for wildlife to find shelter and food, and are home to many once common and often beautiful wildflower species.

Above: *Hedgerows are often rich in seed- and berry-producing shrubs that provide an ideal food source for overwintering birds.*

WHAT IS A HEDGE?

A hedge can be defined as a boundary of closely planted woody shrubs or trees. The earliest known use of the word dates back to the Anglo-Saxons (though hedges would have been grown before that), being derived from the Saxon *hæg* or *hag*. The Saxons used hedges as a way of defining ownership of land, but their hedges were not the same as those we know today, being more like a rough fence, only loosely clipped and often containing as much deadwood as living material. They used many species, such as hawthorn (*Crataegus monogyna*) – haw also means hedge in Old Saxon – and briar roses.

In centuries past, people exerted less pressure on wildlife and hedges were just another place for animals to shelter and forage. With increased land clearance, intensification of agriculture and a growing population, however, habitats dwindled and hedges became a refuge for many native species. In this way ancient agricultural hedges are a tangible link with the wildlife that once inhabited the woodland edge and open spaces across many areas, containing a rich variety of animal life and a multitude of plant species, both woody and herbaceous. Hedges are often a prime habitat in their own right.

THREATS TO TRADITIONAL HEDGEROWS

The intensification of agriculture in recent decades, coupled with the introduction of large machinery, has meant that many areas traditionally managed using hedgerows as part of the rural landscape have been transformed beyond recognition. Machines work more efficiently in large fields, and hedges were seen as taking up valuable land that could produce crops. In addition, hedges in the United States contained a lot of barberry (*Berberis*), and this was identified as the alternative host species of the wheat rust *Puccinia graminis*, which is a serious fungal disease of wheat.

The net effect of this was that farmers on both sides of the Atlantic were encouraged to remove hedges and in doing so this rich and vital habitat was removed from these landscapes. In the case of European hedges, the rich legacy of over a thousand years was lost in some cases and it left wildlife in a precarious position. Gardens became one of the few places where hedges remained common and as such they are an invaluable wildlife resource.

Left: *Some hedgerow species, such as this hawthorn, have abundant spring blossom that is attractive to a wide variety of insects.*

Above: *Even where a more formal effect is required, you can choose a species well suited for wildlife, such as this hornbeam.*

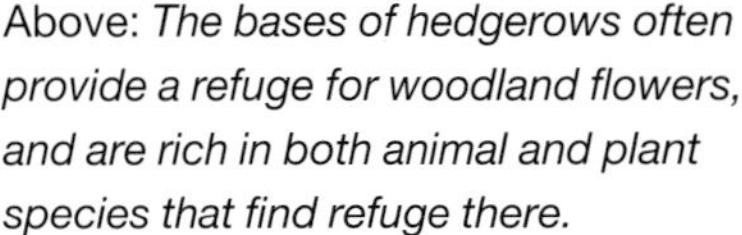

Above: *The bases of hedgerows often provide a refuge for woodland flowers, and are rich in both animal and plant species that find refuge there.*

Above right: *Hedgerows often provide an excellent habitat for climbing plants, such as this ivy. Climbers add to the diversity of the habitat, attracting more species.*

GARDEN HEDGES AND WILDLIFE

The modern approach to hedges, especially in garden settings, has been to cultivate a tight-cropped and controlled shape with many closely planted specimens of the same species. But while highly decorative, they have limited appeal to wildlife. Some species are able to find shelter in the dense growth, but the range of species is limited, as is the likelihood of finding much food.

The answer often lies in planting a mixed, native hedge. Remember that a mosaic of plant species will favour a wider range of wildlife. Choose plants that provide food in the form of nectar-rich flowers and berries for overwintering birds. Hawthorn (*Crataegus*), wild roses (*Rosa*), holly (*Ilex*), hazel (*Corylus*) and elder (*Sambucus*) are good all-round choices. Also try barberry, cotoneaster and pyracantha, which produce lots of berries for the birds.

Resident birds may also appreciate the hedge for shelter, and even breeding, which is why wildlife hedges can't be trimmed in the nesting season, from early spring to late summer. Human impact can be further lessened by cutting back (not too tightly) only one side of the hedge on alternate years. Ideally, hedges should be pruned in late winter so that wildlife can take advantage of the insects, fruits and buds during the cold months, and again in summer and autumn.

Hedgerows are especially important habitats because they share key characteristics with two other habitats – woodlands and open fields – providing corridors for wildlife, and allowing species to disperse and move from one habitat to another. Always allow the hedge bottom – the portion where the base of the hedge adjoins another habitat such as grassland – to become overgrown with grasses and flowers. The bottom is characteristically the dampest and most fertile area, and often proves to be the part richest in wildlife. Plants also find it difficult to spread across open fields, and "travelling" along the base of a hedge is their only realistic option.

Below: *Honeysuckle is a good example of a hedgerow climber that is both useful for wildlife, such as moths and birds, and is also ideal as an ornamental plant.*

TYPES OF HEDGE

Hedges are quite diverse in nature, partly as a result of what they are used for but also because of their maintenance.

Mixed hedges Quite simply, a mixed hedge is one where the intention is to grow a range of species and provide a habitat that has the maximum species diversity, and is most like a natural woodland edge.

Single-species hedges These hedges are common, especially in gardens, where their intention is to provide a consistent backdrop or feature. They can be useful for wildlife provided that a suitable species is chosen.

Formal hedges Found in highly manicured gardens and cut with a smooth face, the high frequency of their cutting and general absence of flowers or fruits mean that formal hedges are less useful for wildlife.

Informal hedges As the name suggests, these are hedges where the cutting regime does not entail frequent cuts or a smooth face or finish. They can be planted as single- or mixed-species hedges.

Dead hedges These are barriers that consist of dead branches and twigs that are firmly staked in place. Climbers are allowed to ramble through them and provide excellent shelter.

WOODLAND

An important feature of many landscapes, woodland provides a rich and varied habitat for an abundance of wildlife species. Woodland varies greatly, depending on where it grows and the tree species within it. In many cases, it is a product of the way in which it has been managed, due to the importance of timber to humans. In a few areas, however, natural undisturbed woodland still exists, and this is one of the most diverse habitats found anywhere on the surface of the earth.

Above: *Rodents, such as this wood mouse, are common and important in woodlands as food for larger predators, including owls.*

WHAT IS A WOODLAND?

There are still vast areas of the Earth's surface covered with trees. They are highly variable, although some generalizations are possible.

Almost all woodlands are structures with a number of layers of different plant species. The tallest and most dominant form the canopy. This can either be closed, in the case of dense woodland, or more open, with sunlight penetrating between the trees. Beneath the canopy is a layer of less dominant tree species, called the understorey, and beneath that is a layer of smaller, woody plants and immature trees called the shrub layer. The ground is covered to a greater or lesser extent with a layer of herbs. The soil is continuously enriched by the decomposing leaves, shed from the trees either throughout the year, in the case of evergreens, or in autumn with deciduous trees.

TYPES OF WOODLAND

Broadleaved woodland is dominated by trees with wide, flat leaves. There is considerable variation between such woodlands in different locations in respect of the wildlife and dominant plant species that they contain. The most obvious kind is the temperate, deciduous woodland found in cool, rainy areas with trees that lose their leaves in autumn in order to survive the cold, dark winter weather. They occur mostly in the northern hemisphere, in North America, Europe and Asia, with smaller areas in South America, Africa and Australia.

Above: *Taking a long time to die, trees often become full of deadwood, which in turn provides a habitat for other creatures.*

Left: *Trees are very large, long-lived plants that form a dense shady habitat beneath them. Ground-cover plants only grow in spring before the trees form leaves again.*

Above: *Fallen leaves and seed coats often naturally form dense layers on woodland floors. These slowly break down to release nutrients for trees and other plants.*

Coniferous woodland mostly grows in the northern parts of North America, Europe and Asia, and covers more of the Earth's surface than any other habitat – around 17 per cent of the Earth's land area. The trees are mostly adapted to a cold, harsh climate and a short growing season.

Temperate rainforest grows in areas with warm summers and cool winters, and can vary enormously in the kinds of plant life contained. In some, conifers dominate, while others are characterized by broadleaved evergreens. They are mostly restricted to coastal areas, with some coniferous woodlands having trees that reach massive proportions. They are mostly found in the north-west Pacific, south-western South America, New Zealand and Tasmania, with small, isolated pockets in Ireland, Scotland, Iceland, south-western Japan and the eastern Black Sea, and despite their relative rarity they are some of the most amazing natural habitats and home to some of the world's most massive trees.

Above: *Clearings in woodlands, such as this one alongside a path, are often the richest area in terms of wildlife and plant species.*

TRADITIONAL WOODLAND MANAGEMENT

In many areas where woodland once formed extensive cover, much has now been removed and the vast majority that remains has long been managed by people. Despite the loss of ancient "wildwoods" the remaining managed woodlands proved to be excellent habitats, whose exact nature depended upon the system of management employed.

Coppicing is one such traditional method of woodland management, by which young tree stems are cut down to 30cm (1ft) or less from ground level to encourage the production of new shoots. This is done repeatedly through the life of the tree and results in a habitat that repeatedly transforms from a clearing into a woodland habitat. Many familiar woodland flowers and associated animals are well adapted to coppicing. Pollarding is a similar operation but involves cutting the branches from a tree stem 2m (6ft) or so above ground level. Pollarding was mostly practised in wood-pastures and grazing areas where cutting above head height protects the new shoots from being damaged by browsing animals.

Below: *Branches and even whole trees naturally fall on to woodland floors and decompose over a long time, providing a rich habitat for many species.*

THE BEST TYPES OF WOODLAND FOR WILDLIFE

The ability of woodland to support wildlife varies considerably. The age of a woodland and the variety of plant species it contains all have their part to play, as does the way in which it has been managed. Generally, open woodland, especially when deciduous, is more accessible than closed woodland to species that browse and graze, and it tends to be richer in ground-level plants.

The woodland floor is often rich in species that feed on decaying plant matter, and deadwood is also important for many insect species that live in rotting wood. Where the greatest concentrations of wildlife occur will vary greatly according to the type of woodland, but the richest areas always tend to be those that border other habitats, for example at the woodland margins. The latter is the easiest to recreate in a garden.

TYPES OF WOODLAND

Woodland covers vast swathes of the Earth and with such a wide distribution that it has assumed many forms, all of which are excellent wildlife habitats.

Deciduous woodland This type of woodland is most common in the northern hemisphere, where it once formed vast, uninterrupted swathes of cover. The leaves fall each autumn and its floor is rich in spring flowers.

Evergreen broadleaved woodland This habitat is often more characteristic of hotter or drier climates and while often rich in species, it casts deep shade beneath the leaves.

Coniferous woodland In high latitudes and altitudes with long, cold winters, conifers often form extensive woodlands, characterized by a range of highly specialized wildlife and plant life.

Pasture woodland Areas were once managed for both grazing and timber production with the result of a light, species-rich woodland of pollarded trees set in grassland.

Savannah Occurring in hot countries where natural grazing results in a mixture of light woodland cover in grassland, the resulting habitat is described as woodland savannah.

Below: *Deer browse and graze in woodland, and their activities create clearings among the trees. These clearings favour other smaller species of wildlife, such as invertebrates.*

SOIL HABITAT

To most of us, garden soil is simply a medium in which we grow plants. Indeed, the very word "soil" is often equated with dirt. It may come as a surprise, then, that the soil in your plot is one of the most diverse habitats you are ever likely to encounter. It is not only the place that plant roots must reside, but also home to a huge range of species, many of which, though invisible to us, are essential to all plant growth through their role in decomposition and nutrient cycling.

Above: *The earthworm is an essential recycler of nutrients, and it also aerates the soil in many different habitats.*

THE ULTIMATE HABITAT?

What do a worm, cow, human and daisy have in common? They are all soil organisms. Creatures that depend on the soil for their food or habitat can be defined as soil organisms or soil dwellers. While we do not live within its confines, our survival does depend on it.

WHICH ORGANISMS INHABIT THE SOIL?

The most obvious examples of soil life are those seen with the naked eye. Apart from plants, we often recognize some as being important – worms being taken as a sign of soil fertility, for example. But there are many others that are so tiny that, despite being just about visible, they often go unnoticed, with countless millions more microscopic creatures, arguably the most important ingredients of all garden life.

Below: *Centipedes, often overlooked in gardens, are voracious predators of many smaller soil organisms, and they help to provide a balance in the habitat. They are mostly harmless, although larger, warm-climate species can bite.*

MICRO-ORGANISMS

These organisms are extremely important to plants because they actually control the flow of nutrients. Some form a part of the nutrient cycling process for carbon, sulphur and nitrogen, all of which are essential elements in plant growth. Other micro-organisms are an important means of removing chemical pollutants that might otherwise build up in the soil. Microbes are also a food source for a vast array of larger soil organisms and form the start of many food chains. Their role in decaying dead material means that they can be seen as the driving force of the entire garden habitat.

Despite their huge importance, though, barely 1 per cent of the total soil volume is made up of microbes; compare this to the 5 per cent volume of plant roots and 10 per cent dead organic matter. The microbes make up for this, though, in sheer weight of numbers with around 90 million bacteria alone in just $1cm^3$ ($0.4in^3$) of average, healthy, mineral soil. Bacteria also reproduce rapidly when compared to the larger organisms, and are generally concentrated where there is food (decaying matter), adequate water and, for most species, oxygen. In general, this limits them to the top 30cm (1ft) of topsoil, where they live with tree and plant roots. This layer occurs naturally in all soils over time, and is familiar to gardeners through its darker colour and, often, quite different character to the subsoil immediately below.

In common with any habitat, soil is a complex community that takes a long time to develop. It is not static, and its balance often shifts to match a change in conditions. While it is resilient, it could lose the diversity of life contained if it is not cared for properly, causing problems for the larger plants and animals that ultimately depend upon it for their well-being.

SOIL LIFE AND PLANT ROOTS

Almost all plants must live with their roots in the soil and it is precisely because of this that we sometimes fail to understand the significance of this habitat. The most noticeable parts of the garden are what we see: the leaves, shoots, flowers and produce that our gardens provide for us. Roots, however, are just as vital, and the dark mysterious habitat they occupy is critically important for the whole plant.

Right: *The harvestman, often seen in gardens, appears spider-like but is actually more closely related to scorpions. It runs rapidly over the soil surface, preying upon any smaller creatures it encounters. Larger species such as this are often met with suspicion or even revulsion by gardeners, but they are essential creatures that help maintain a natural balance.*

Left: *Ground beetles are extremely important predators of many garden pests, such as slugs. They thrive in the litter layer that lies on top of undisturbed soil, and their numbers can often be severely reduced as a result of frequently cultivating the ground.*

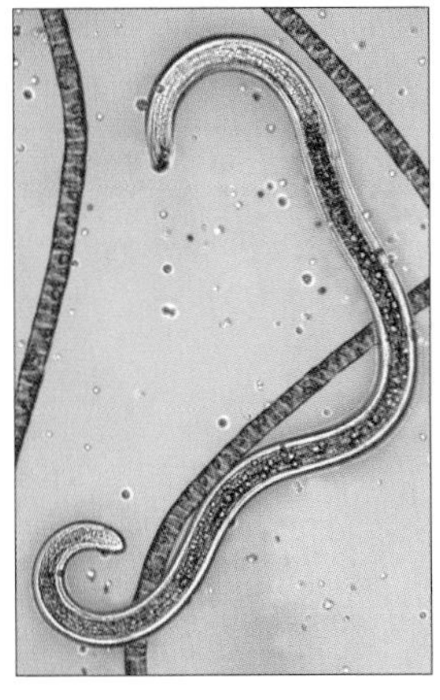

Plant roots have long exploited the soil and have struck up marvellous interactions with many other soil-dwelling life forms. Leguminous plants in the pea family, for example, make special nodules for a bacterium called *Rhizobia*, which collects nitrogen for the plant. Many forest trees also have roots that form close associations with fungi, called *Mycorrhizae*. The tree provides the fungus with sugars and in return for this food the fungus supplies vital mineral nutrients from the soil. This relationship is called a symbiosis and helps to show just how complex soil habitats are.

Above left and above: *Slugs are often regarded as the scourge of gardens, but many species depend upon them as a food source. The slug (above) has been attacked by soil-living nematodes (above left) that naturally parasitize them. The actions of nematodes ultimately establish a balance.*

SOIL LIFE

Much of the life in the soil is unseen, either because it's so small or because it is buried. Microbes are an extremely important part of the soil, through which all essential life-giving elements must pass at some stage.

Bacteria, fungi and algae

Unicellular, and almost always invisible unless they are species that form extensive colonies, bacteria, fungi and algae are the most common organisms found in the soil, and there may be billions surrounding each plant. While a few may cause damage to plants, the vast majority are benign or even essential, by virtue of their ability to break down and cycle or recycle essential nutrients needed to support healthy plant growth.

Earthworms, spiders and insects

While these species are frequently large enough to be seen, they often remain out of sight unless disturbed during cultivation. Many such creatures are important in the early stages of recycling nutrients and, while some may attack plants, the vast majority are important in maintaining the balance within the complex soil food web. Pesticides that target some species often wreak havoc at this level.

Plants, trees, birds and mammals

With the exception of plants, it's all too easy to imagine that these have no direct link with the soil. In all cases, though, they depend on the soil either directly or indirectly as a source of essential nutrients, and their actions (whether feeding or otherwise) often modify the soil.

Far left: *Roots depend on a healthy soil habitat because good soil aids the release of nutrients that the plant needs, thus promoting its healthy growth.*

Left: *Many types of fungi are essential in the soil, not only because of their ability to decompose dead plant matter, but also because many species set up intimate associations with plant roots, supplying minerals to the plant in return for sugar.*

Above: *Fungi, so often neglected or forgotten in gardens, occur in many colours and forms, and can be very beautiful.*

MINOR HABITATS

There are lots of habitats that you can easily build into your garden that will encourage a whole host of common animal species. Most are easy to create and can form decorative or unusual features. Essentially, by thinking about these smaller, less obvious living spaces, you can favour a wide range of species that might otherwise have difficulty finding a home. These creatures will add to the diversity of your garden and, in certain cases, might even return the favour by eating a few garden pests.

NEW LIFE FROM OLD

Deadwood is an incredibly important part of a woodland ecosystem, and there is a whole host of species that are specialists in eating and decomposing it. A rather overly fastidious streak in many gardeners, however, often deprives species of this habitat. The easiest way to remedy the problem is by retaining and even making a feature of some deadwood.

Probably the easiest way of helping deadwood species is to make a small log pile, positioned in an out-of-the-way, shady and preferably damp part of the garden. The thicker the logs the better and, unless you have a ready source to hand, you may have to buy them. Pile them up and add some thinner prunings and leaves from trees and old shrubs to avoid too many gaps. Then plant a few ferns, ivies and other plants to grow through and over the wood, thereby softening its appearance. Gradually, these rotting logs will attract many species, including fungi, insects and other invertebrates that, in turn, will attract small mammals, amphibians and possibly reptiles, who may also decide to take up residence in its dark recesses.

Left: *Deadwood is an important habitat for many species of insects and is naturally very common. It can be made more decorative by sculpting the top.*

Below: *A drystone wall can be a highly decorative feature in a garden, with small dark recesses that provide cover and hibernation places for small creatures.*

If you don't have the ideal spot for a woodpile, try making a dead hedge. This traditional feature dates back to the Middle Ages and involves driving two rows of stakes into the ground, and binding the sides with loosely woven hazel or willow to hold the structure together. Once the framework is made, the void is filled with deadwood. Start by putting the largest material at the base, with lighter material – brush and leaf litter or even lawn clippings – towards the top. You can easily make it more attractive by planting vigorous climbers, such as honeysuckle (*Lonicera*), to ramble through it, with more flowers being planted at the base on the sunny side, or ferns if it is shady. Dead hedges can be used as boundaries or garden divisions, and with luck will attract nesting birds. They can be surprisingly long-lived features, and if climbers become established they actually become more of a "live" feature than a "dead" one, combining the best features of both.

Right: *Dead hedges are made from pruned branch material which is woven between stakes that are driven into the ground. They provide good cover for many species.*

LITTER LAYERS

This refers to the loose layer of dead material that builds up on the soil, particularly in woodlands or around garden plants in the winter months. Traditionally, the litter was removed in early winter to prevent the spread of disease and, although there is some merit in this, it has the greater disadvantage of removing a valuable habitat for many predatory insects. Beetles, in particular, are very fond of a layer of decaying matter over the soil, and the litter can also help support several larger predators, such as shrews and hedgehogs. Adding a deep layer of well-rotted compost or bark will avoid most of the disease problems, while helping to create a useful habitat, and may also improve the soil.

WALLS

The two main kinds of wall are rock piles and drystone. Both are a valuable habitat for a range of species, and are especially useful features for hibernating reptiles and amphibians needing a cool, shady retreat. The dark recesses between the stones are also ideal for beneficial creatures such as spiders, parasitic wasps, solitary bees, centipedes and ground beetles.

The rock pile is easily made, and is best constructed using rough-hewn, flattened pieces of stone. In many places drystone walls were a traditional way of utilizing local stone when making boundary walls. They offer the same benefits as a rock pile but are usually more aesthetically pleasing, and can be used in a more formal design. They look simple to make but can be tricky for the beginner, and are often best left to a specialist if you want a neat and tidy look in a more formal setting.

Below: *Leaf litter naturally harbours a range of species, many of which perform a useful role as beneficial garden predators.*

Bottom: *Rock piles are an excellent refuge for many species, including reptiles and amphibians. It is best to site them in a cool shady area, under a hedge or shrub.*

BURROWS

Many creatures make burrows, ranging from the tiny, in the case of some insect species, to larger excavations of mammals and other vertebrates. Bumblebees often occupy a disused mouse burrow, for instance, and a shortage of mice and voles can seriously hamper their nesting efforts. If you know that an area is being used by burrowing animals of any description, leave them undisturbed, as any attention might cause them to move elsewhere.

Below: *Many animals use burrows, including larger mammals such as badgers and rabbits. Bumblebees often colonize empty mouse burrows in long grassland.*

HABITAT LOSS

The loss of habitats is the single most important danger to wildlife, affecting not only single species of animal or plant but entire ecological communities. Every living creature needs a place to live, find food and reproduce. The loss of a habitat eliminates these possibilities, and many species now face a bleak outlook. Few parts of the world have not been altered, damaged or destroyed, mostly by human intervention as we occupy land for building, agriculture and extracting natural resources.

Above: *Leisure activities such as golf require playing areas that can result in the loss of habitats for wildlife.*

CAUSES

Humans have always altered their environment according to their needs, but modern technology has accelerated this process to unprecedented levels. Serious damage can now be inflicted very quickly.

There are so many demands on Earth for space; space to build roads and towns, to grow food, and for work and play. This problem is amplified by the huge increases in population over the last 200 years. Larger populations need ever more resources and, often, natural habitats suffer as a consequence.

WHICH HABITATS ARE MOST THREATENED?

Deforestation is the greatest concern, with over half the Earth's forests having disappeared already. The great European forest, which once spread from the west coast of Ireland to Siberia, has all but vanished, and many other forests are disappearing at an alarming rate thanks to agriculture and timber felling. Although forests can recover, and even be harvested in a sustainable way, the rate of loss is currently 10 times higher than the rate of re-growth.

In addition to deforestation, the drainage of wetlands, grubbing up of hedgerows and ploughing up of ancient meadows for agriculture contribute to habitat loss. Even the clearing of too much deadwood from managed woodland can affect the ecology, removing habitats for the grubs and beetles that form an important link in the food chain. No wonder many species are now classified as being under threat in terms of their long-term survival. It is likely that some were never particularly numerous in the first place, and extinction is a natural part of evolution – without it there would be no room for new species – but the current rates of extinction are far above those at which such species can be easily replaced.

HABITAT FRAGMENTATION

This process occurs when large, natural areas are broken up into smaller fragments or islands of habitat. Habitat fragmentation often happens in the course of urban development, oil and gas exploration and extraction, and the conversion of land to agricultural use. Habitats may be left intact, but they may be too small to support viable populations of some species, particularly those that occupy and defend territories. Inbreeding often results, and, without the influence of genetic diversity obtained by breeding with other populations, species may disappear even though their habitats remain.

Left: *Deforestation for timber has accelerated in the last century, and many habitats are now severely threatened as a result.*

CLIMATE CHANGE

Likely to have a considerable impact on most or all ecosystems in the 21st century, it is very likely that changes in climate patterns will alter the natural distribution range for many species or communities. If no physical barriers exist, it may be possible for species or communities to migrate. Forest or grassland, for instance, may move towards higher latitudes (i.e. nearer each of the respective poles) or to higher altitudes following changes in average temperatures. There is nothing new about this, and at the end of the last ice age (12,000–10,000 years ago) many plant communities moved quickly north in response to the rapid global warming that followed. The real danger to these habitats arises in most cases, however, where natural or artificial barriers prevent or limit this natural movement of species or communities. Many nature reserves and protected areas have been surrounded by urban and agricultural landscapes that will prevent the migration of species – especially plants – beyond their current artificial boundaries.

WILDLIFE CORRIDORS AND REFUGES

To help mitigate the effects of the loss of habitat, many scientists and conservationists urge the development and conservation of connecting patches of important wildlife habitat. These corridors, if planned correctly, allow wildlife to move between habitats, and also allow individual animals to move between groups. Often roads, urban developments, agricultural land and, of course, gardens can be designed in such a way that new wildlife habitats are created. It's always best to protect unspoilt habitats, but sympathetic design can help some of our most beautiful and vulnerable wildlife.

MAJOR CAUSES OF HABITAT LOSS

Without doubt, human activites have resulted in the most serious loss of habitats. While many of these are essential to our own well-being, they are not always done with wildlife in mind, this taking a "back seat" in favour of economic concerns.

CAUSE	EFFECT

Human population growth

This places incredible stress on ecosystems. Some estimates put the global population at around 10 billion by the end of the 21st century. More people means more development, a greater chance of "exotic" (non-native) plantings, more demand for energy, water and ultimately more pollution resulting from these and other activities. The more of us there are, and the greater level of development we achieve, the greater the demand is likely to be upon the already dwindling natural resources around us.

Agriculture

Agricultural development is a major threat to natural biodiversity (the total diversity of life), particularly the modern intensive agriculture that is now practised increasingly in both developed and developing nations around the world. In many developed countries, native grasslands have nearly disappeared beneath an onslaught of ploughing and grazing, and the development of water resources for both agriculture and urban use has also fragmented many freshwater habitats.

Urbanization

Estimates predict that by the year 2032, more than 70 per cent of the Earth's land surface is likely to be destroyed, fragmented or disturbed by cities, roads, mines and other infrastructure of human civilization (a figure presently at around 50 per cent). Many wild animals are routinely poisoned in suburban situations, and still more are killed by traffic. The footprint of environmental damage often stretches far beyond the confines of the city itself, often having even international consequences in its demand for resources.

CAUSE	EFFECT

Water use

With population expansion comes increased demand for fresh water. For some, this is a basic need to survive, raise crops and livestock. Increased development, however, often means that water use per individual rises as water is needed for industry, domestic use, sewage and of course industrial-scale agriculture to support the population. Rivers being dammed to provide new lakes can have disastrous consequences for wildlife both downstream of the dam and by habitat loss in flooded valleys.

Road construction

An ever-increasing threat stemming from population growth is the increase in roads. More traffic means more collisions with wildlife, especially where new roads are built through habitats such as forests, where animals are unaccustomed to the dangers of vehicles. There is also an increased risk of toxic spills and air pollution, to say nothing of the resulting influx of people into formerly unoccupied areas, often resulting in new developments that might ultimately lead to the wholesale destruction of formerly pristine habitats.

Pollution

Urban development brings a whole range of problems, most of which are inextricably linked with the ones described above. In cities, however, all of these problems invariably become more concentrated, particularly when development is rapid and areas become very over-crowded. The most immediate issue is that of habitat loss as land is developed for industry and habitation. The resultant vehicle and factory pollution, toxic waste and the problems of refuse and sewage disposal that inevitably follow such development all cause major harm.

CREATING WILDLIFE HABITATS

Nature is a mosaic of many different types of habitat that create a rich and varied tapestry across the landscape. Grassland gives way to woodland and wetland, and it is where these different habitats meet that we see the greatest diversity of wildlife. Gardens give the opportunity to help a wide range of wildlife for the same reason, since domestic gardens are also capable of supporting several habitat types, often in close proximity. By creating and managing garden features as potential habitats, gardens can become wonderfully rich in wildlife.

Left: *Naturalistic borders, rich in flowers, are excellent places for many species of wildlife to feed, breed and make their home.*

Above: *By adopting a new cutting regime in the lawn, you can incorporate bulbs, such as this cyclamen, as a food source.*

Above: *Water is an essential part of any wildlife garden, and can prove to be a highly ornamental feature visited by many species.*

Above: *Hedges provide dense cover for nesting birds and act as a corridor for wildlife that needs to seek food over a large area.*

Above: *Wildflower meadows offer both a habitat and a food source for bees, and are wonderfully ornamental in early summer.*

ESTABLISHING A WILDFLOWER MEADOW

Any area of long grass is a valuable habitat, and by simply letting an area of existing lawn grow long, you will provide cover for many insects and small animals, as well as greatly enhancing both the look and diversity of the area. Wildflower meadows and flowery lawns are actually easier to make than you might think. You can add wildflowers by re-seeding an area or by planting pot-grown plants into existing grass.

CHANGING AN EXISTING WILDFLOWER LAWN

The first step in transforming an existing lawn is to think about what you want it for, and how much you want to change. If it is important to keep the same amount of lawn, the simplest approach may be to change to wildlife-friendly maintenance. Alternatively, reduce the area of short cut lawn to a minimum, with wildflowers.

Assuming that you intend to keep some lawn, the simplest change is to let flowering plants colonize it. Reduce the frequency of cutting, and stop fertilizing, using pesticides and weedkillers, and watering it. The initial effect may be hard to see, but low-growing, broadleaved plants will soon begin to get a foothold. Even allowing areas on a clover-rich lawn to have a flowering break for a week or two will help the bees.

MAKING NEW WILDFLOWER LAWNS

Most grassland wildflowers grow best in full sun and open spaces with minimal root competition from trees, so choose your site accordingly. New lawns are best grown from seed that can either be bought ready mixed or you can mix your own. Ideally, the mix will produce about 60–80 per cent grass coverage, with the remainder being wildflower. The seed mix is sown sparingly –

PREPARING THE GROUND AND SOWING WILDFLOWER MEADOWS

1 *Start the project by marking out the area you intend to convert to a wildflower meadow. It is best to use a rope or hose to establish flowing lines and curves.*

2 *Once you have finalized where the edge of the meadow is to be, cut the line in the existing turf using a half-moon edging iron, following the line made by the rope.*

3 *Lift the existing turf, ensuring that you dig deep enough to remove all grass plants. Plants growing in wildflower meadows prefer nutrient-poor substrate and little topsoil.*

4 *Once the turf has been lifted and removed, lightly cultivate the whole area with a fork, before raking it to produce a light, crumbly seed bed ready for sowing.*

5 *Mix the wildflower seed into the grass seed prior to sowing. This will make it easier to distribute evenly. Lightly sow the mix at a rate of 15g/m² (½oz per sq yd).*

6 *The grass and wildflower seedlings will soon emerge, and the light sowing rate ensures that the grass does not swamp the less vigorous wildflowers as they develop.*

PLANTING WILDFLOWERS INTO EXISTING GRASS

1 *Set out small wildflower plants grown in pots, and, once positioned, cut out and remove a plug of turf before planting.*

2 *The wildflower plants, once planted into the turf, have a head start and are able to compete with the surrounding grass plants.*

to avoid the grasses out-competing the wildflowers – at a rate of about 15g/m^2 (½oz per sq yd), or less.

You can also make an existing lawn richer in flowers by over-seeding in autumn with a mix of wildflower seed. To over-seed an area, cut the grass as low as possible and rake away the debris, leaving bare patches of soil. The seed is mixed with some fine, dry sand, particularly in the case of fine seed, and is thinly sown over the bare patches and then raked in lightly.

The results from over-seeding can be quite variable, and many gardeners prefer to plant out pot-grown wildflowers directly into an existing lawn. Mow the lawn early in the season and scrape or use bare patches for planting into. Arrange the young plants in groups of three to nine for the best effect and maximum chances of success. Once planted, the lawn can be mown on a high setting every two to three weeks in the first year to reduce the competition from grasses. The following year, the lawn can be mown less.

MAINTAINING A WILDFLOWER LAWN

The amount of time and effort a wildlife lawn needs will vary, depending on what you want. Shorter lawns need little change to their maintenance because the basic method of mowing remains the same, albeit less frequent.

Long grass is trickier, not least because it can be a fire hazard during dry weather. Always site an area of long grass at least 6m (20ft) away from buildings or other combustible items. A buffer zone of conventional lawn can be made more attractive by cutting the first strip of lawn next to the tall grass on the highest mower setting, and reducing this by one setting on each consecutive strip so that the longer grass blends in gradually.

Also, mowing a margin between long grass and features such as flower beds means that the grass will not collapse on to it following rain or storms. If you have a large lawn, mow a path through it so you can watch the wildlife without having to trample on the tall grass. Frequently mow areas you want to keep as paths, preventing long grass from developing and animals from sheltering there, and possibly getting killed by a lawnmower.

Hay and water meadows are usually best cut after they have stopped flowering, although if space allows you can try leaving some areas of long grass uncut until late winter to provide shelter and hibernation sites for insects and other grassland species. When you do cut the grass, remove all the clippings, usually after letting them lie for a day or two to let any wildlife escape, and then dispose of them elsewhere.

TOP PLANTS FOR A WILDFLOWER MEADOW

Choosing flowers for a wildflower lawn will depend on which species are native to, or will succeed best in, your area. The suggestions below give ideas for how some plants can be used; it is possible to substitute other species according to your local area.

SHORTER GRASS

Cowslip (*Primula veris*)
An ideal plant for areas of grass that are cut somewhat infrequently, it is suited for hedge bottoms and attracts a number of insects that feed on the abundant nectar in late spring.

Harebell (*Campanula rotundifolia*)
The diminutive harebell is extremely widespread in the wild, being found across much of the northern hemisphere. It is ideal for dry sites where its flowers attract bees.

Red clover (*Trifolium pratense*)
A pea family member with round, red flowerheads that are a real favourite with bees, due to the copious nectar that they produce. Often included in agricultural mixes of grass seed because of its ability to fix nitrogen in the soil and enhance grass growth.

LONG GRASS

Field scabious (*Knautia arvensis*)
One of the most nectar-rich of meadow flowers with pretty blue-mauve pincushions on branching stems throughout summer and well into autumn, when its seed is often eaten by birds.

Ox-eye daisy (*Leucanthemum vulgare*)
This quick-spreading, pretty perennial produces an abundance of yellow-centred, white daisy flowers in summer. Many daisy flowers – including coneflowers (*Echinacea*), tickseed (*Coreopsis*) and asters – are suited to long grass.

Wild carrot (*Daucus carota*)
This wild ancestor of the cultivated carrot has a delicate filigree head of dainty flowers that appear in summer, and are an excellent source of food for hoverflies, butterflies and a range of other species.

Cowslip

Red clover

Field scabious

Wild carrot

MAKING A WILDLIFE POND

Ponds are a real boost to wildlife gardens, being a watering hole for land-living animals as well as a complete habitat for others. They are relatively easy to construct, but need to be properly sited and designed for them to be useful habitats. A little care and attention at the planning stage can ultimately lead to a feature that will look good and boost the wildlife potential of your whole garden.

Above: *Frogs and other amphibians need water in order to breed, and they are highly dependent upon garden ponds for this.*

CHOOSING THE RIGHT SITE

Use an attractive, sunny place, sheltered from the prevailing wind. Try to avoid a site that is shaded by trees because they will not only cut out light, but their leaves will drop into the water, enriching it with mineral nutrients and organic debris. This promotes green water and blanket algae in the warmer, sunnier months.

In any garden where a water feature is planned, child safety is of paramount importance. If there is any risk that young children might fall in, consider delaying your plans until they are older. Children love water and the wildlife it attracts, but you should always weigh up the risks.

THE SHAPE AND SIZE OF A POND

As a general rule, 4m² (43sq ft) is the minimum area needed to create a balanced environment, with marginal shelves at least 25cm (10in) wide to support containers of emergent plants. Create the outline using sweeping curves with no sharp bends; a figure of eight or a kidney shape is often the best idea for smaller ponds. Then draw a rough cross-section of the pond to check how much depth you will get for your width. Aim to get at least 60cm (2ft) and ideally 90cm (3ft) or more in the deeper reaches to benefit a range of wildlife. The slopes should drop at a rate of one-third of the equivalent distance travelled across the top to assure stability.

CHOOSING A LINER

For small ponds, moulded or fibreglass pools can be used but they are limited in terms of design, and do not always look particularly natural. A flexible liner, such as butyl rubber, is generally considered the best (if most expensive) option, although UV stabilized PVC can be a cheaper alternative. Both these materials are prone to puncture, and particular care must be taken to line the hole with soft sand and/or an underlay, such as old carpet (made of natural fibres), to avoid this. The liners are easy to lay, and can also be used when creating bog gardens.

HIDING THE EDGE

Both flexible and rigid liners need to be hidden if you want to promote a natural effect. There are many ways of doing this.

A cobbled edge is easily achieved by setting some large stones or cobbles into a bed of sand/cement that has been laid on the liner, both below and above the eventual water surface on a shallow slope. The stones form a firm base, and other loose stones can be piled on and between them with the gaps providing sheltering space for small animals, while also providing a gently sloping "beach" for larger animals to approach the water and drink.

A drystone wall, or alternatively a loose rock pile set on a mortar base on the liner, just below the water, can act as a retaining wall for nearby planting, with the niches

CREATING DRINKING SHALLOWS

1 *The shallow areas of ponds are important to allow animals to drink, but they can become muddy traps for smaller creatures and offer little protection or shelter for visitors.*

2 *Start by placing some larger stones or rounded rocks both in the shallow water and on the bank, arranging them in small groups of varying sizes to create a natural-looking effect.*

3 *Once the larger stones have been placed, the spaces between them should be filled with round cobblestones to create both shallow stony pools and drier beach areas.*

4 *The finished effect is very ornamental, and the strong shoreline provides hiding places for smaller creatures as well as a basking area and safe drinking site for pond wildlife.*

between the stones providing excellent shelter for amphibians and reptiles. Walls or rock features are always best placed at the back of the pond so that they create a reflection on the water surface.

A planted edge is also an option with a "planting pocket" being built on the liner. This involves running the liner about 10cm (4in) above maximum water level, and then burying it in the soil around the edge. It provides a simple and natural effect, with the overhanging plants hiding the edge, but the liner will show when the water level drops, and there is always the added danger of damaging a flexible liner when mowing or gardening near the pond.

Concrete or stone slabs laid on a sand/cement bed over the edge of the liner are a somewhat formal solution, but are very practical if you want to view the water up close. Try to avoid this all the way around, though, as very small animals, such as young frogs, may have difficulty climbing in and out over the stone edge.

PUTTING IN A BUTYL LINER FOR A POND

1 *Start by marking out the outside edge of the pond using stakes or canes, and then mark out the locations of any shallow margins with spray paint.*

2 *Once marked out, begin digging the pond, starting with the deeper areas first, before digging out the margins and finalizing the edge of the pond.*

3 *Once you have excavated all of the pond to the required depth, establish the slopes on the side of the pond and the planting shelves within it.*

4 *To gain nicely smooth sides to the excavated pit, line the whole of the base and sloping sites with graded stone-free sand, fabric or old carpet.*

5 *Carefully lift the liner over the pit. Don't drag it because sharp stones may puncture it. Secure the corners using bricks or stones and start to fill the pond with water.*

6 *As the liner fills with water, it will mould to the shape you have excavated. Once the pond is nearly full, cut the edge of the liner, leaving a generous overlap.*

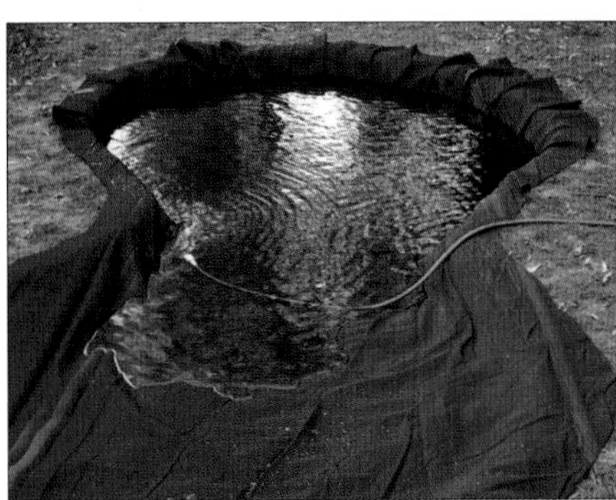

7 *As the water level continues to rise, fold the liner to create an even finish and avoid any unsightly creases across the pond bottom or sloping sides.*

8 *Once the water is almost up to the top, bury the edges of the liner by cutting and then lifting the turf edges of the pond and laying it under the cut turf.*

9 *The new pond can now be filled to the brim, then planted with various wetland species and drinking shallows created by using varying stone sizes.*

Above: *Water lilies, such as this* Nymphaea alba, *are a beautiful addition to any garden pond. Frogs are often seen on the leaves.*

PLANTING PONDS AND WATER FEATURES

Naturally occurring ponds and wetlands are rich in plant life, much of which is specially adapted to grow in waterlogged ground, shallow water or even under the water surface, where it plays a vital role in the aquatic habitat. There are many forms of these plants, including some highly ornamental species, and by including a good range of them in your pond, you will improve both the look and habitat value of this essential garden feature.

CHOOSING POND PLANTS

Surprisingly, new ponds can seem initially quite stark and lifeless. Plants provide the magic to bring them to life and, once surrounded by vegetation, the whole feature becomes more attractive to us and the wildlife.

To create a natural look, you could put a layer of soil on top of the liner for plants to root into, and creatures to hide in. This has the disadvantage, however, of introducing nutrients that can cause algal growth, and often means that you must be prepared to cull the plants regularly because aquatic plants can spread rapidly and choke the pond. Most people minimize the problem by using special aquatic plant containers that curtail excessive growth.

Most pond plants are perfectly happy in clay loam. Provided you ensure that the soil used is free of pesticides or pollutants most heavy types are fine, but the best idea is to buy a proprietary brand. The planting of most aquatic plants is the same as for other potted plants, but the soil needs to be firmed down a little more than usual, and it is a good idea to spread gravel and/or cobbles on top of the soil to keep the pot stable and keep the soil in the pot. The best time for planting is late spring as the water warms up. Don't give plants a shock by plunging them into icy water.

There are three different types of plant that you need to attract wildlife. All are essential to a healthy pond because they constitute the range of habitats needed to support a diverse wildlife community.

Oxygenators spend the whole year submerged, and they supply a steady infusion of oxygen, which is needed by the aquatic creatures that breathe through their gills. Oxygenators often grow densely and serve as egg-laying sites, nurseries and cover for many aquatic animals.

Deep-water aquatics have roots and stems in the deeper reaches, but with floating leaves and flowers. They are especially important because they help to shade the water from too much sunlight in summer. Too much light entering the water can cause algae to become a problem, and ideally you need to cover about half the surface of the pond with these plants. Water lilies (*Nymphaea*) are a big favourite, being very decorative, relatively easy to grow and available in a wide range of colours and sizes. Other plants are also available, and you must ensure that the species chosen are not too vigorous for your pond size. A few species are entirely free-floating and include duckweed (*Lemna*), water fern (*Azolla*) and water hyacinth (*Eichhornia crassipes*), but they can be very invasive and are best avoided.

Marginal or emergent plants grow in shallow water at the edge of the pond and offer shade and cover for animals, while greatly enhancing the visual appeal. They are used by dragonflies and nymphs to crawl out of the water and pupate. Many species of marginal plants are equally at home in a bog garden, and careful planting in such situations can help hide the division where the water stops and the bog garden starts, thereby enhancing its look.

FILLING A POND BASKET AND PLANTING IT UP

1 *Pond plants are best planted in specially made crates. These are lined on the base with gravel and filled with specially formulated compost.*

2 *Once the base is covered with stones and soil, put your plants in the crate and fill around the remaining gaps with more of the aquatic compost mix.*

3 *When the compost is up to the height of the top of your plant root ball, dress the compost surface with more gravel to help keep it in place.*

4 *The pond plants should quickly establish in their new surroundings and will soon send up new shoots and flowers above the water surface.*

RENOVATING A BOG GARDEN

1 *Thoroughly weed the bog garden, taking special care to remove all the roots of any persistent perennial weeds or unwanted plants.*

2 *Retain any useful specimens and dig in some organic matter to enrich the soil. Take a note of bare areas to calculate numbers of new plants needed.*

3 *Dig over the whole area to be planted, then set out the new plants and decide the best arrangement before planting them in their final positions.*

4 *Once the area is planted, give the garden a thorough watering to help the plants settle in. Take a note of all species planted in case replacements are needed.*

Above: *Small sections of oxygenating plants, such as this* Elodea, *can be tied with a stone and placed into the pond to grow and start to oxygenate the water.*

BOG GARDENS

Mimicking areas of marshy ground found in wetland areas, bog gardens are closely associated with ponds, lakes or streams. They are ideal cover for amphibians as the soil in these areas is permanently wet, and the plants that grow there have a great deal in common with marginal plants, with many species being equally at home in either as a result. This need for permanently wet ground means they are lined in a similar way to a garden pond. Bog gardens make an ideal accompaniment to a garden pond and are often constructed at the same time.

PLANTS USUALLY BEST AVOIDED

These plants can become invasive in a garden pond and, if they escape into the wild, can become a severe problem in natural ponds, lakes and waterways. Avoid using them in favour of native species or non-invasive plants.
Note: If these plants are already in the pond, dispose of them carefully to prevent their spread.

- Australian swamp stonecrop (*Crassula helmsii*)
- Fairy moss (*Azolla filiculoides*)
- Floating pennywort (*Hydrocotyle ranunculoides*)
- Parrot's feather (*Myriophyllum aquaticum*)
- Curly waterweed (*Lagarosiphon major*)
- Kariba weed (*Salvinia*)
- Water hyacinth (*Eichhornia crassipes*)
- Water lettuce (*Pistia stratiotes*)

TOP PLANTS FOR WILDLIFE PONDS

There are various types of wetland plants. They are split into categories to make it easy to select the correct plants for different areas of the pond or wetland.

MARGINAL/EMERGENT PLANTS

- Flowering rush (*Butomus umbellatus*)
- Water forget-me-not (*Myosotis palustris*)
- Marsh marigold (*Caltha palustris*)
- Yellow flag (*Iris pseudacorus*)
- Watermint (*Mentha aquatica*)

WATER LILIES/DEEP-WATER AQUATICS

- Water lily (*Nymphaea alba*)
- Water hawthorn (*Aponogeton distachyos*)
- Japanese pond lily (*Nuphar japonica*)
- Yellow floating heart (*Nymphoides peltata*)
- Golden club (*Orontium aquaticum*)

Flowering rush

Marsh marigold

Water lily

Golden club

OXYGENATORS

- Curled pondweed (*Potamogeton crispus*)
- Hornwort (*Ceratophyllum demersum*)
- Milfoil (*Myriophyllum spicatum*)
- Pondweed (*Elodea* spp.)
- Water starwort (*Callitriche stagnalis*)

FREE-FLOATING PLANTS

- Water soldier (*Stratiotes aloides*)
- Lesser duckweed (*Lemna minor*)
- Water lettuce (*Pistia stratiotes*)
- Water fern (*Azolla filiculoides*)
- Bladderwort (*Utricularia vulgaris*)

Hornwort

Pondweed

Water soldier

Water fern

PLANTING A WILDLIFE HEDGE

The best wildlife hedges usually consist of mixed species that provide nesting sites, year-round cover, flowers, berries, and areas at the base where wildflowers can flourish. Single-species hedges provide less variety, but may still be useful if managed properly. Wildlife hedges are a real boost to a wildlife garden providing cover for a range of animals whilst linking other habitats nearby.

Above: *Birds, such as this linnet, find cover and a food supply in a well-managed wildlife hedge that is not cut too frequently.*

CHOOSING A HEDGE

When deciding what sort of hedge will most benefit the wildlife in your garden, you must also consider your needs. If it has to double as a security hedge or barrier, or if you need a certain height, then check the plants' possible dimensions. Also note that a wildlife hedge will not be frequently pruned, and can grow both tall and wide in a single season.

The most wildlife-friendly hedge includes a range of four or five species in varying numbers. The exact species will vary considerably according to the conditions, but any plants chosen should always be compatible in their maintenance requirements when grown as a hedge. Start by walking around your neighbourhood, looking at the hedges and seeing what plants are growing well. Try to choose at least half of your plants from locally indigenous species because they'll often be most valuable to native wildlife, and if possible, when looking at other hedges growing locally, make some notes about the range and types of wildlife they attract.

A single-species hedge can be very useful, if only because all the plants will have similar maintenance requirements. For plants that flower and set fruit, you could try fuchsia, escallonia or barberry, all of which attract bees. Traditional agricultural hedges mainly consist of up to 80 per cent of one species, such as hawthorn (*Crataegus*), but will usually also have a diverse mixture of other trees and shrubs. This creates a variety of blossom, berries and scent with a range of niches that make such a hedge the best choice for wildlife. If you have a large garden, in the right setting, this type of hedge may be appropriate, but for a typical suburban semi-detached or terraced house, a single-species hedge may be more aesthetically pleasing.

PREPARATION AND PLANTING

When planting a wildlife hedge, prepare the soil properly beforehand. Dig a trench at least 50cm (20in) wide, and mix plenty of organic compost and a general fertilizer such as blood, fish and bone at around 50g (2oz) per m^2 (sq yd). Refill the trench and allow it to settle for a couple of weeks before planting.

Hedges are usually planted as either single rows of plants, about 30cm (1ft) apart, or as staggered, double rows with

SETTING OUT AND PLANTING A HEDGE

1 *Start by levelling your previously prepared ground, using a rake to ensure that there are no rises and dips along the length of the row.*

2 *Consolidate the ground to make sure there are no void spaces in the soil by lightly treading the area with a flat foot rather than a heel.*

3 *Rake the ground level, either with a rake or using the back of a fork, as shown here. It is best to start planting into level ground.*

4 *Using a spade to make a planting pit, slide the roots of the plant down into the hole, ensuring they are all covered.*

5 *Using a heel of a boot, make sure the young plant is firmly planted, with no air spaces around the stem.*

6 *To protect the stems from rabbits, place guards around them. These also shelter the young plants from wind.*

CUTTING A HEDGE

1 *Once the hedge begins to outgrow its setting, it must be cut. This is preferably carried out before or after the nesting season.*

2 *Set out a line of canes every couple of metres (7ft) or so to mark the line that you want to cut, thereby producing a good face.*

3 *Before cutting the top, set out a string line to mark the desired height and ensure that a straight line is maintained.*

4 *Even for neat wildlife hedges, the finished cut should not be too tight as it will still preserve a somewhat informal look.*

the same distance between the plants and rows. When planting, peg out a line of string to keep the hedge straight. Some species – beech (*Fagus*) and hawthorn (*Crataegus*), for example – are best planted at a 45-degree angle to encourage thick growth at the base. With other species this isn't necessary.

To stimulate dense, twiggy growth, trim off one-half to two-thirds of the total height of the hedge and then, for the first two or three years, remove at least half of the new growth during the winter period. Mulch the base of the rows annually, and apply an organic feed just before you do this.

MAINTAINING YOUR HEDGE

Once established, trim your hedge every second or third year, but avoid doing so when birds are nesting. The ideal time is in late winter, making nuts and berries available to birds and mammals for the longest possible period. Try cutting opposite faces of the hedge in alternate years where space is restricted, or if a slightly more formal shape is desired, because this will produce some flowers and fruit each year.

The best shape for a wildlife hedge is an "A" shape because the sloping sides allow light and rain to reach the bottom of the hedge. An established hedge, say four to five years old, can often be enhanced by planting climbers such as honeysuckle (*Lonicera*), roses (*Rosa*) and clematis. Take care, though, because planting climbers before the hedge is well established can easily result in the hedge being overwhelmed and strangled. You can also plant hedgerow wildflowers at the base to provide extra cover for birds and mammals, and additional food for other wildlife.

TOP HEDGE PLANTS FOR WILDLIFE

Any hedge has potential as a wildlife habitat, but the species described here are among the most useful to the widest range of creatures.

Alder buckthorn (*Rhamnus frangula*)
A thornless tree with five-petalled, green-white flowers, it's visited by many insects and is characteristic of hedges growing on damper soils, especially those on former marshes. The flowers are followed by pendulous red berries that turn black in autumn and are eaten by rodents.

Blackthorn (*Prunus spinosa*)
Also known as sloe, the flowers of this thorny plant attract early bees and butterflies, while the leaves support many moth and butterfly caterpillars. The whole plant supports over 150 species of wildlife. It doesn't like heavy shade but withstands strong winds, making it a good plant for coastal areas.

Hawthorn (*Crataegus monogyna*)
Frequently used for hedges in northern Europe, with several other species being used as small garden trees. Hawthorn is very important for wildlife, and can host at least 150 insect species with many songbirds and finches readily nesting in it, the berries being another attraction.

Hazel (*Corylus avellana*)
This well-known plant, also called hazelnut or cobnut, supports at least 70 insect species in addition to woodpeckers, squirrels and small rodents that are attracted to the nuts which ripen in late summer and early autumn. It is best left untrimmed for at least two seasons if you want to get any nuts.

Sweet briar (*Rosa rubiginosa*)
Also known as the eglantine rose, the leaves and stems of this European species have a brownish-red tint and the whole plant forms a dense mass. Bright pink flowers from late spring to early summer give way to bright red hips. The leaves have a fruity scent when rubbed because of the sticky, brownish glands on the underside.

Wayfaring tree (*Viburnum lantana*)
This small, attractive shrub is naturally found on chalk and limestone soils, and sports bright red berries in autumn that later turn black, preceded by clusters of scented white flowers in late spring and early summer. White, silky hairs coat the undersides of the leaves and young stems.

Blackthorn

Hawthorn

Hazel

Sweet briar

PLANTING TREES AND SHRUBS

Trees and shrubs form the essential framework of any garden, and provide cover for a wide range of animals, as well as nesting sites that are well above the ground and safe from ground-dwelling predators. The secret to success lies in careful ground preparation, stock selection and planting. Trees and shrubs are among the most rewarding plants you can grow, needing little or no maintenance once established.

Above: *Birds often rely on trees as nesting sites for their chicks. Holes in trunks are also used by insects, mammals and amphibians.*

SELECTING PLANTS

Always choose trees and shrubs that are vigorous, healthy and suitable for the site conditions or intended usage. They should always be free from any obvious signs of damage, pests or disease. If you are buying bare-rooted stock, make sure that the roots never dry out before planting, and keep them covered at all times – even a couple of minutes left exposed to cold or drying winds can cause a lot of damage. You should plant them as soon as possible; if the soil is frozen or waterlogged, plant them in a temporary bed of compost, at a 45-degree angle (heeling in), and keep them moist until you are able to plant them out.

PREPARING THE GROUND

Despite what is written in many books and guides, organic additives such as compost can be a mixed blessing if they are incorporated into soil at planting time. An enhanced soil mix does improve the soil but also causes the plants to become "lazy". Quite simply, the roots like it better than the

PLANTING AND STAKING TREES

1 *Container-grown trees should be thoroughly watered an hour before you intend to plant them or soak really dry ones overnight.*

2 *Clear any weeds and cut any suckers coming from the roots as these may slow the trees' top growth and root establishment.*

3 *Once you remove the pot, tease out any encircling roots to encourage root spread in the soil and to prevent root-balling.*

4 *Dig the planting pit and ensure that it is deep enough for the root-ball, checking this by lying down a spade or fork on its side.*

5 *Backfill the pit, firming the soil with a heel every 8cm (3in) to make sure it is well planted and contains no large air pockets.*

6 *Drive the stake in at an angle to avoid damaging the roots. Face the stake into the prevailing wind for stronger root growth.*

7 *Secure the stem of the tree using a tie, nailed on to prevent movement. Choose one with a spacer to stop the stem chafing.*

8 *The tree should remain staked for around one year, during which time the tie must be regularly checked and loosened.*

MULCHING A TREE

1 *Young trees growing in short or long grass are often slow to establish due to the competition from the surrounding plants.*

2 *Start by removing the turf around the tree. Create a cleared circle around the stem of the tree that is 1m (3ft) in diameter.*

3 *Thoroughly water the ground and then apply an even layer of mulch to a depth of about 5cm (2in) on the cleared circle.*

4 *The tree must be kept clear of weeds and competing vegetation for around 4 or 5 years. Water thoroughly in drought conditions.*

surrounding soil and circle round as if in a pot of compost resulting in an unstable "corkscrew" growth pattern known as girdling. Avoid this by applying organic matter across the surface after planting. This is much more like the natural situation and encourages many insects including ground beetles. Apply fertilizers only if really needed, after planting but before mulching.

WHEN TO PLANT

Plant deciduous species during early winter, when they are dormant. Evergreens, on the other hand, tend to do well if planted either in early autumn or late spring. Trees and shrubs growing in containers can be planted throughout most of the year, provided that the ground is kept sufficiently moist, although they too will generally establish best in the cooler months. Never plant when the soil is frozen, excessively dry or waterlogged, as this may damage the roots and lower stem. Make planting holes big enough, allowing a quarter to a third of the diameter again of the root spread. Check that the plant is at the same depth as it was before; placing a spade across the hole is the easiest way. As a rule of thumb, the topmost root should be about 1cm (½in) below the soil level.

STAKING AND PROTECTION

Large shrubs and trees require staking, to prevent them blowing over in their first season. Smaller, more vulnerable stock is protected by putting it in a tree or shrub shelter that helps stems thicken, promotes rapid upward growth and protects plants from rodents and sometimes deer attack.

TOP TREES FOR WILDLIFE

If you have the space, trees are a valuable feature for wildlife, and by choosing the species carefully, you can greatly enhance the wildlife potential of a garden.

Apples and crab apples (*Malus sylvestris*)
They are a familiar fixture in many gardens, and have enormous potential for wildlife. The older trees are best, supporting a diverse array of insects on the leaves and stems. The buds are eaten by some birds as is the fruit. The tree is of most use to wildlife if it is left largely unpruned.

Oak (*Quercus robur*)
While this long-lived tree has outstanding wildlife value, it is too large to grow in all but the largest garden. There are over 600 species, enjoying different climates, and some are the richest habitat trees available for insects, mammals, plants and birds.

Pine (*Pinus sylvestris*)
Pines are among the best conifers for wildlife, offering a source of seeds that are taken by birds and squirrels and dense crowns that are used by nesting birds such as owls. An excellent choice for dry soils, although they eventually grow quite tall.

Red mulberry (*Morus rubra*)
The mulberry produces berries throughout the summer that are eaten by at least 40 different bird species and makes an ideal tree for moist, fertile soils. Keep it clear of paths and patios as the fruit can be messy.

Rowan (*Sorbus aucuparia*)
A medium-sized tree that is well suited for the smaller garden, with numerous closely related species and cultivars. Rowan generally supports species that visit the tree, but don't make it their permanent habitat. Insects love the flowers, while birds (especially thrushes) often feed on the attractive, bright red berries.

Southern beech (*Nothofagus alpina*)
A fast-growing and, eventually, quite large forest tree, only worth growing in a big garden. In many places it supports large numbers of species that feed on the nuts and live in the tree, especially in the gnarled bark of older specimens.

Crab apple

Oak

Pine

Southern beech

CREATING WOODLAND EDGES

Woodland edges are found where forest gives way to another, more open area, and are potentially the most productive habitats for providing food for wildlife. In addition, such environments offer a whole host of shelter and breeding sites for species usually restricted to wooded areas, and while many gardens are too small for true woodland, the edge is much easier to recreate than you might think.

Above: *Squirrels often spend a great deal of time on woodland margins, searching for food in the trees and on land.*

VALUE OF THE WOODLAND EDGE

Woodland is most diverse at its edges, either at the tree-tops or adjoining another habitat. Here, species from both areas meet and share the space and its exact nature is largely dependent on the adjoining habitat. Often this is grassland or cultivated land but, equally, it could be marsh or open water. Either way, the woodland produces an abundance of growth each year during the growing season. This leads to a rich organic layer deposited over the soil that produces very fertile ground, both within and just beyond its limits. Most gardens, even relatively large ones, do not have room for an area of naturalized woodland, but you might be able to accommodate a group of several small or medium-sized

Above: *Woodland edges are home to a great abundance of flowers, such as this blackberry, which thrive in dappled shade areas.*

Left: *Where trees and shrubs give way to grassland, the mosaic of different habitats is naturally rich in plant species and wildlife.*

REMOVING A TREE STAKE

1 *Start by removing any nails that were used to secure the tie to the stake, then unbuckle the tie. Do this carefully and avoid pulling at it as this may damage the bark of the tree.*

2 *Gently loosen the tie by feeding the belt through the spacer block that was used to prevent the stem from chafing on the stake. Check the stem for signs of damage.*

3 *Remove the stake by gently rocking it back and forth until it can be pulled upward. If it is too firmly in the ground it can be cut off with a saw, taking care to avoid the stem.*

TOP WOODLAND EDGE PLANTS FOR WILDLIFE

Woodland edges are naturally rich in flowering and fruit-bearing species, many of which provide a vital food resource for a rich variety of visiting wildlife species.

CANOPY PLANTS

Apples and crab apples (*Malus*) Deciduous, small, shrubby, spring-flowering tree with abundant round, fleshy, apple-like fruits that follow large, cup-shaped, white, pink-flushed flowers that attract bees. A food source for many insects and birds.

Rowan (*Sorbus*) Includes the familiar rowan or mountain ash *Sorbus aucuparia*, which becomes heavily laden with bright red berries in late summer and early autumn. A versatile genus that boasts many species and cultivars.

Box elder (*Acer negundo*) A small, usually fast-growing and fairly short-lived maple whose winged seeds are sometimes eaten by birds and other animals. Its sugary sap is sometimes eaten by squirrels and songbirds.

THE SHRUB LAYER

Rose (*Rosa*) Roses can be extremely attractive shrubs. If possible, plant a wild species and choose single flowers over double types as these are best for visiting insects. The hips that follow the flowers are often eaten by birds.

Rubus An important group of wildlife shrubs that includes the common blackberry (*R. fruticosus*). Care should be taken when choosing this as it can become very invasive. Many other species and cultivars are good garden specimens.

Viburnum An extremely varied group of plants that includes a wide range of species and hybrids, with good wildlife value and an attractive appearance. Choose varieties with berries, such as the guelder rose (*V. opulus*) to feed birds.

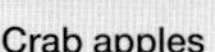
Crab apples

Rowan

Rose

Viburnum

trees, which will support many insect species and provide perches for birds. Even if space is limited, shrub borders fulfil some of the role of a woodland edge, and, if managed correctly, hedges can also attract woodland-edge species.

THE IDEAL SITE FOR A WOODLAND EDGE

Choose a strip along an edge of the garden facing the sunniest direction. This means you'll minimize shade on the rest of the garden while the woodland-edge bed gets the benefit of sunshine that will widen its appeal to a greater range of species. Alternatively, make it face the afternoon sun. This will, of course, cast shade on your garden in the morning, but this need not be a problem. The plants often benefit most from the warmer afternoon sun, especially in the cooler seasons. When choosing a site for your border, don't forget to discuss your plans with neighbours, whose gardens may be affected by shade. A wall or a fence is the ideal back boundary for your woodland edge because it can provide support for some of the climbing plants.

PLANTING AND MAINTAINING A WOODLAND EDGE

You should plant a woodland edge so that there is a general increase in height from the front to the back of the area or border, thereby allowing light to reach all the plants. The tall plants at the back are called the "canopy edge" plants. In a narrow border, you will need around one canopy tree for about every 5m (17ft). Choose smallish, sun-loving woodland trees, particularly those that bear berries. The plants in front of this are the shrub layer, with the herbaceous layer forming the smallest layer at the front. Growing under the canopy trees, these layers can include both sun-loving and shade-tolerant plants because the canopy trees cast very little shade on the bed. There is always room for variety, though, and many smaller, more shade-loving plants, such as early perennials and bulbs, can easily be planted among the taller woody plant species.

Rather surprisingly, managing an area of your garden like a woodland edge takes far less time and work than you might imagine. Once planted, you just need to keep the area well watered until everything is established. You should also keep an eye on the border for the next few years, making sure that no one plant is dominating and smothering the others. Eventually, though, the area should need little or no maintenance.

Below: *Planting a mixture of trees and flowering shrubs in narrow strips mimics the edge of a woodland. You should remove tree stakes after one year.*

ESTABLISHING CLIMBING PLANTS

Above: *Hoverflies are attracted to the nectar of flowering climbers, and their larvae are good for controlling aphids during summer.*

The vertical dimension of a garden is where many species – especially birds – make their nests, usually in the dense twiggy growth of a hedge. Climbers are an ideal way of providing some of the benefits of hedges where the space or setting does not permit hedge-planting. They are versatile and include some of the most beautiful flowering plants, many of which attract a wide range of wildlife.

CLIMBERS AND WALL SHRUBS

One of the many reasons for planting climbers is that they can provide a way of screening or covering an unsightly object. In nature, climbers piggy-back, usually on woody species, to get up to the light. They often grow rapidly and some species are extremely ornamental. Wall shrubs are often used for the same purpose, although they are sprawling or scrambling species that do not actually climb, and must be trimmed and supported against a fence or wall to encourage vertical growth.

Climbers and wall shrubs are ideal where a hedge is not feasible. They can easily be trained up walls and fences, for example, and can even be grown in large pots on a patio. Climbers can also be used with hedge plants, where they can grow as they would in the wild, scrambling through the branches of a woody plant. Be sure to choose a good range of plants (where space permits) to provide plenty of flowers and berries.

TYPES OF CLIMBING PLANTS

Climbing plants are generally classified according to the way that they climb, which will affect the type of support required.

Self-clinging climbers can cling to sheer, vertical surfaces by attaching themselves to a support. They might use adhesive pads at the end of tendrils, like the Virginia creeper (*Parthenocissus quinquefolia*), or small adhesive rootlets on their stems, as in the case of ivy (*Hedera helix*).

Twining plants cannot climb up a flat surface and require wires, a trellis or the branches of another plant for support. Their tendrils (small, cord-like appendages) reach out and wind around narrow supports (a wire or slim branches) in the case of the pea family, whereas others, such as the clematis, curl specially adapted leaf-stalks around supports. Most species, however, are vines like the honeysuckle (*Lonicera periclymenum*), which twines its stems along and around supports.

Scandent, scrambling, rambling and trailing plants, on the other hand, are not strictly speaking climbers at all. They are usually referred to as wall shrubs, and all of them send out long stems that reach up to a support. Some, including climbing and rambling roses, have thorns or spurs that provide extra means of holding on to the support, though they usually need tying to a trellis or horizontal wires.

PLANTING CLIMBERS AND WALL SHRUBS

Once you know how your climber or wall shrub grows, you will need to fix a support. This should always be done before planting so that you don't damage the roots. Once you have done this, you can prepare the ground. Because the soil near walls or fences is often poorer than the surrounding garden, dig in plenty of organic matter, such as leaf mould, garden compost or well-rotted manure.

Left: *Even in a formal setting, such as this yew hedge (*Taxus baccata*), a climbing* Tropaeolum *adds variety, contrast and a nectar source for visiting species of wildlife.*

Above: *Climbers, particularly evergreens, make excellent screens and can both clothe and soften walls, sheds or other outbuildings in a relatively short space of time.*

Above: *A trellis uses very little space in the garden and makes a wonderful support for twining and flowering climbers.*

When planting climbers near walls, always remember that the foundations may extend out into the garden. In addition, many building walls can be very dry at the base, particularly if overhung by the roof, and if you intend growing a climber here plant it 45cm (18in) away from the wall, sloping the roots away from the house towards the open garden, where the roots can spread, drink and feed. Fences and lower walls tend to be less problematic, but you should never plant climbers right against the base of either. Climbers can also be grown in containers if they need winter protection or if they are grown on patio and roof gardens. In almost all cases, you will need to provide some initial support, even if you choose a self-clinging species.

TOP CLIMBING PLANTS FOR WILDLIFE

Climbers are mostly very quick and easy to grow, offering both the chance to help wildlife and a covering for unsightly or bland walls and fences in the garden.

Clematis A large and varied genus of woody-stemmed perennial climbers, often with beautiful flowers, followed by prominent, feathery seed heads that hang on through winter. Although some species are rather vigorous, they are easily controlled by pruning and make ideal garden plants. The seeds are eaten by birds, and the flowers are a good nectar source for moths, hoverflies and bees. The seed heads are used by breeding birds to line their nests.

Honeysuckle (*Lonicera* spp.) Naturally found in hedges and woodlands, this woody climber has clusters of highly scented yellow, tubular flowers flushed with purple and red, appearing from midsummer to early autumn, that attract moths. Twining stems are reddish when young but become brown and woody with age, climbing around stems and branches of other plants. Bright red berries form in clusters after flowering, and are attractive and long-lasting, provided they are not eaten by birds.

Ivy (*Hedera helix*) This vigorous evergreen climber, found in woodlands and hedges, on banks and walls, is an excellent wildlife plant, arguably one of the most important for a garden. Large specimens offer shelter, nesting sites and food for birds, and it is also the food plant for many species of moth. It flowers rather late in the season, and as a result can offer nectar to a huge range of insects late in the year when most other sources are becoming quite scarce.

Jasmine (*Jasminum officinalis*) Grown chiefly for its mass of highly scented white flowers that continue from midsummer to early autumn, this strong, twining shrub is a vigorous grower and needs plenty of room. It is usually best pruned annually to keep it tidy and mixes well with climbing roses (*Rosa*), honeysuckle (*Lonicera*) or clematis, although it looks equally good on its own. It is moth-pollinated and is most fragrant in the evening, when a single vine fills the whole garden with scent.

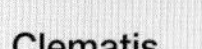

Clematis

Honeysuckle

Ivy

Jasmine

PLANTING A CLIMBING PLANT AGAINST A WALL

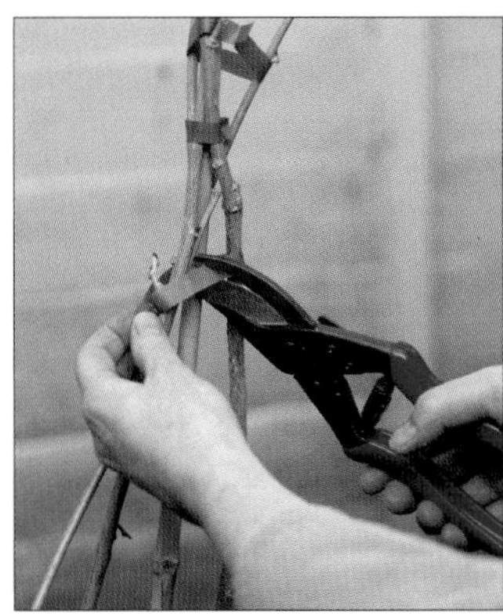

1 *Before planting, remove any ties or canes from the plant that would restrict growth, and remove any damaged growth with sharp secateurs or a knife.*

2 *Dig a hole 30cm (1ft) or more from the wall or fence to make sure that the roots will receive rainfall. Angle the shoots towards the climber supports.*

3 *Once properly positioned, backfill the hole, using the excavated topsoil, then firm the soil with your heel to ensure that the climber is well planted.*

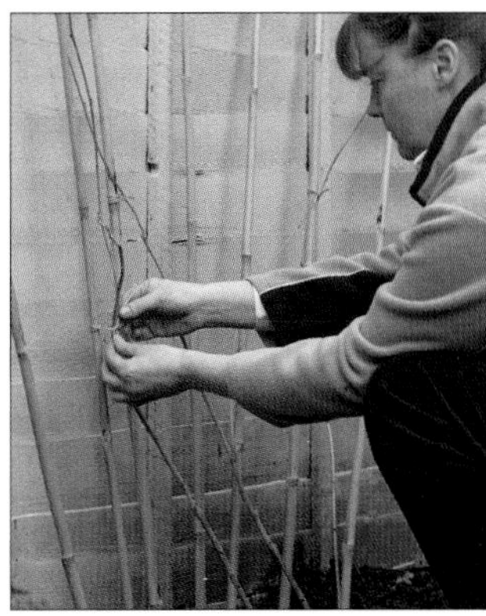

4 *Use garden twine to tie the climber stems to the supports. Water the plant in well. Keep tying it in and water in dry spells until it is well established.*

CREATING FLOWER BORDERS

A flower border full of nectar-rich plants is an essential feeding station to a variety of insects that in turn attract other wildlife to feed on them. Although beautiful summer borders are very contrived features, they provide both homes and shelters to various wildlife species, and so your choice of plants can have a significant impact. Quite simply, the greater the variety of plants you grow, the better.

Above: *A good range of nectar-rich flowers is the best way to attract butterflies, bees and other insects into the garden.*

PLANT SELECTION

Nectar-rich borders, full of plants chosen to attract bees, butterflies or even nectar-feeding birds, need a sunny, sheltered position. Ideally, plant groups of the same species in small blocks to create a pleasing effect and ensure that insects can find them easily.

Also choose plants that flower at different times to ensure a continuous supply of nectar throughout the growing season. Include plants that flower late or early in the season, using lady's smock (*Cardamine pratensis*), chives (*Allium schoenoprasum*), golden rod (*Solidago*) and borage (*Borago officinalis*), to attract bees and butterflies from spring to autumn. Regularly deadheading (removing the old, dying flowers) will help generate more buds and therefore wildlife. And note that plants that have been highly bred to produce large or double flowers are often far less suitable for wildlife, being poor in nectar, with bees in particular being unable to reach it in some highly cultivated forms. Concentrate on cottage garden plants or old varieties because they generally have flowers with simple structures, and their pollen and nectar is more readily available to foraging insects.

WILDLIFE VALUE

Once you start attracting insects into the garden, they will become food for other animals, including birds. The latter may be carnivorous for some of the year, but will appreciate seed left on the plants through autumn and winter. Many ornamental grasses, such as the garden cultivars of millet (*Pennisetum glaucum*), and annuals, like the sunflower (*Helianthus*), provide valuable sources of energy-rich seed at the end of the season for both resident and migratory birds. The tobacco plant (*Nicotiana*) has the added advantage of providing nectar-rich, night-scented flowers for night-flying insects, such as moths, which in turn provide food for bats.

The plants you choose for your initial design may be less effective in attracting wildlife than you hoped, so be prepared to modify your border, either by including spaces for annuals, or by trying different plants. When visiting other gardens in your area, make a note of any plants that attract large numbers of insects.

Left: *The abundant nectar of flowers such as this* Centaurea macrocephala *is an essential food for both domestic and wild bees.*

Below: *Flower-rich borders are wonderful for wildlife and provide a colourful summer spectacle and a winter retreat if left uncut.*

Above: *Birds occasionally visit flowers to access nectar from blooms such as this red hot poker. The visitor is rewarded with a rich, sugary drink from the tubular flowers.*

PLANTING A HERBACEOUS BORDER

1 *Dig over the whole plot using a digging fork and remove stones and any weeds, paying particular attention to the roots of perennial weeds.*

2 *Break down the larger clods using the tines of the fork, and remove any remaining plant debris, large stone or rubble to leave a level surface.*

3 *Tread over the whole area using "flat-footed" steps to get rid of any large air pockets and to ensure an even consistency across the whole bed.*

4 *Rake over the surface to give a level finish and to remove any remaining debris or stones from the soil before commencing planting.*

5 *Wearing gloves, apply an organic fertilizer rich in phosphates, such as bonemeal, to enhance the root growth and the establishment of the plants.*

6 *Before planting, finish off the bed preparation by forming an edge with a half-moon cutter and make a gulley between this and the prepared soil.*

7 *Thoroughly water the plants at least an hour before you plant them to give the plants time to take up water and allow the excess moisture to drain.*

8 *Use sand or grit to mark out the bed according to your plan and set the groups of plants out before planting them in their final positions.*

TOP PLANTS FOR FLOWER BORDERS

Flower borders are a mainstay of many gardens, providing both colour and interest throughout the summer months. Choose your plants carefully to ensure a long flowering season, and include a range of types to suit different insect species.

Coneflower (*Echinacea purpurea*) Large, daisy flowers attract many insects, and its seeds will feed visiting finches.

Fern-leaved yarrow (*Achillea filipendula*) Easy-to-grow perennial that attracts bees and many other insects in summer.

Heliotrope (*Heliotropium arborescens*) A highly fragrant, tender perennial notable for its intense, rather vanilla-like fragrance.

Honeywort (*Cerinthe major* 'Purpurascens') Unusual blue-green plant with mauve-purple flowers. Immensely popular with bees.

Sea holly (*Eryngium planum*) A coarse, thistle-like plant with flowers that attract many bee species in summer.

Tall verbena (*Verbena bonariensis*) Possibly the best butterfly-attracting plant, even exceeding *Buddleja* in this respect.

Coneflower

Fern-leaved yarrow

Heliotrope

Honeywort

Sea holly

Tall verbena

NATURALISTIC PLANTING

Many of us lead busy lives and the idea of low-maintenance, self-sustaining landscapes is an attractive proposition. In nature, plants fend for themselves, and ultimately, plant communities become stable and self-sustaining. Naturalistic or wild planting styles are becoming increasingly popular with landscape architects and the general public. Like many simple ideas, however, good naturalistic design needs careful implementing.

Above: *Thistles provide good height in the garden, giving it a naturalistic look and attracting insects such as this burnet moth.*

WHAT IS NATURALISTIC PLANTING?

Planting described as naturalistic has the appearance of a natural area (e.g. a prairie, woodland or wetland) and obviously differs from more traditional, structured designs. The layout of the plants is inspired by the patterns and groupings in the wild. It should not be confused with ecological planting, though, when plants are allowed to spread and seed so as to create a changing or dynamic plant community. Naturalistic planting is more structured and permanent than that, despite the apparent lack of artifice.

There are several ways that naturalistic planting arrangements can be laid out, with block planting and drifts being two of the best. Block planting is the most commonly used, and involves planting similarly sized groups of each species in irregular, repeating patterns. The groups of plants are arranged according to height and aesthetic qualities, such as foliage colour and texture. Drifts are much more variable in respect of size and shape, and have no obvious repetitive pattern. Small groups may repeat again and again, with larger, more occasional groups providing contrast and variety.

Even though you are trying to create a random effect, you should divide your plants into general categories according to habit and form. As a guide, a balance is readily achieved with tall, solitary, architectural specimens occupying 10 per cent of the total area, lower-growing, clump-forming plants occupying 40–50 per cent of the space, scattered irregularly, and the remainder filled with ground cover. This will give the balance of height and space that is needed. Avoid a random assortment of plants. Even if they are all planted in the right conditions and grow well, they still need an overall structure.

Naturalistic should never mean haphazard or formless. Always remember that a collection of choice plants arranged without thought is no more a garden than a collection of choice words, spread randomly across a page, is a poem.

Left: *Dry areas can be planted using a range of drought-tolerant plants to give a stunning display, especially with focal points such as this* Agave.

Below: *Despite their lower maintenance needs, naturalistic borders can be just as beautiful as more formal gardens, as well as providing a refuge for wildlife.*

THE BENEFITS FOR WILDLIFE

The exact benefits of the naturalistic effect are debatable because many traditional garden features may already provide the same results. However, the naturalistic garden is prone to fewer disturbances, particularly at soil level, making a more

complete garden ecosystem possible. The mosaic of flowers and plants is also an enticing place for a range of insects and birds, and the dense, packed summer growth will harbour many larger creatures.

THE BEST PLANTS

As with any type of garden, you should choose plants that are suited to your conditions. Remember that the plants in a naturalistic garden are going to be left to fend for themselves, and must compete with the other plants. Don't include too many species that spread very rapidly either by seed or vegetatively because they'll quickly take over, and destroy the effect.

Decide which type of habitat you are mimicking and choose the plants accordingly. Visit a similar wild place and take notes on the best types and mix of plants. Use species that you know attract wildlife, giving careful consideration to which species they attract at any given time.

MAINTENANCE OF NATURALISTIC PLANTINGS

Although the planting style is borrowed from nature, it is a contrivance relying on conventional horticultural techniques. Herbaceous plants will need a measure of weeding, particularly in the first couple of years, while woody plants will need some pruning. You may wish to lift and revitalize certain areas from time to time but, on the whole, it is a case of a little work done often that will ensure the best results and allow the plants to form a stable and self-sustaining community.

TOP NATURALISTIC PLANTS FOR WILDLIFE

Plants for naturalistic plantings must be tough and able to thrive with a minimum of maintenance. They often self-seed and so help retain a natural effect in the border.

Bog sage (*Salvia uliginosa*) This striking, tall perennial has blue flowers and is covered in bloom during late summer and autumn. In its native habitat, it grows in bogs and can therefore grow aggressively in wet soils. A popular plant with bees.

Carrot (*Daucus carota*) The wild form of this biennial plant, also known as Queen Anne's lace, is related to domesticated carrots, but has small white roots. Excellent for attracting butterflies and hoverflies.

Coneflower (*Echinacea purpurea*) This popular ornamental plant is quite tolerant of drier soils and produces a multitude of large daisy flowers in the summer. It attracts butterflies and bees.

Fennel (*Foeniculum vulgare* 'Purpureum') This cultivated variety is an excellent foliage plant with feathery leaves that contrast well with other plants. The flowers attract butterflies and beneficial insects.

Field scabious (*Knautia arvensis*) This summer-flowering perennial can form a small to medium-sized plant that is equally at home in a flower border or meadow, and it will readily self-seed. The flowers are attractive to a wide variety of insects.

Plume thistle (*Cirsium rivulare* 'Atropurpureum') An excellent choice due to its reliability, which, although related to the thistle, is not invasive. Its flowers are long-lasting and attract many insects, including beetles, butterflies and bees.

Solidaster (X *Solidaster luteus* 'Lemore') A naturally occurring goldenrod-aster hybrid, discovered in France during the early 20th century. Its pale, buttery blooms fade to nearly white and attract numerous insects.

Tall verbena (*Verbena bonariensis*) This tall perennial has purple cymes of flowers borne on tough, wiry stems from midsummer onward. It readily self-seeds, and the tiny individual flowers are very rich in nectar.

Carrot

Coneflower

Fennel

Plume thistle

CREATING A NATURALISTIC PLANTING

1 *Choose a variety of plants to fill the space and arrange them within the bed, ensuring that more vigorous ones are not planted too close to slower growing ones.*

2 *Once you have finalized their positions, place the plants into the prepared ground and firm them in using a heel to knock out any air pockets trapped in the soil.*

3 *After planting is complete, water the area thoroughly. Subsequent watering should be infrequent but deep, especially during dry spells in the summer.*

ESTABLISHING A HERB GARDEN

Herbs – encompassing any plants or trees with leaves or flowers that are used for food or medicine – are a great addition to the garden. They attract a wide range of insects, with many having the added advantage of being drought-resistant. A herb garden can therefore include trees, shrubs, ground cover, perennials and annuals. With such a range of material, there will always be some herbs that will suit your garden.

Above: *When in bloom, herbs – especially this oregano – are often very attractive to bees and other pollinating insect species.*

PLANNING YOUR HERB GARDEN

First, make a list of all the herbs you use in the kitchen or home. If a few favourite plants are just used on an occasional basis, it may be simpler to grow them in a few well-placed containers or in gaps in a flower border. Also consider the plants' site and soil preferences, and the levels of maintenance required. Fresh herbs are very useful, but remember that most are plentiful in short seasons, and planting too many will be a waste of time and effort.

SELECTING A SITE

Most herb plants require a site with well-drained soil and full sun for at least six hours each day. If your garden soil is clay, or if you live in an area prone to prolonged wet spells, you may need to make a raised bed

TOP HERBS FOR WILDLIFE

Herbs are excellent plants to use in any garden, and are notable for their ability to attract wildlife and, in particular, beneficial insect species. They can be grown in pots, herb borders or alternatively dotted in spaces among flower borders.

Basil (*Ocimum basilicum*) This annual herb is frost-tender and is usually planted out as a summer addition to the herb garden. It is highly aromatic and greatly valued by cooks; the flowers, borne later in the summer, attract bees, butterflies, and a few moths.

Bergamot (*Monarda didyma*) Perennial, more commonly known as bee balm because bees are so attracted to the scent of its vivid red flowers, it smells rather like the bergamot orange used to flavour Earl Grey tea. Bergamot's leaves can be used to make a refreshing herbal tea, and it is an attractive inclusion in any herb garden.

Chives (*Allium schoenoprasum*) This little perennial onion relative is arguably one of the best herbs for attracting bees when the flowers appear from early to midsummer. It is an adaptable and accommodating plant that is best grown in a sunny position, in moist, rich soil where it will rapidly form clumps and self-seed.

Hyssop (*Hyssopus officinalis*) A wonderful shrub for attracting butterflies, bees and hoverflies, and an ideal candidate for a low hedge in a herb garden. Can also be grown in stony areas where there is little soil. The flowers are violet-blue but also come in white and rose.

Lavender (*Lavandula angustifolia*) Very attractive shrub for bees, bumblebees and butterflies. It is often used to make low, informal hedges, and the seed is popular with many smaller birds, such as chaffinch, goldfinch and tits, during autumn and early winter.

Mint (*Mentha* spp.) Perennial mint is almost irresistible to bees, which are attracted to the lilac-pink flower spikes of many types, including peppermint, water mint and spearmint. It is one of the few herbs that likes moisture, but it can be very invasive so it is best grown in a bottomless pot sunk into the ground.

Oregano (*Origanum vulgare*) This perennial is popular with bees, small moths and a range of butterflies that take nectar from its small, whitish flowers. It makes an attractive groundcover plant, spreading rapidly without becoming too invasive, and grows best in full sun on well-drained soil.

Rosemary (*Rosmarinus officinalis*) This evergreen shrub likes a sunny, sheltered position and is especially good in a poor soil. Its clusters of mauve-white flowers are popular with bees, hoverflies and early flying butterflies. It is slow growing and ideal where space is limited.

Thyme (*Thymus* spp.) Despite its diminutive nature, shrubby thyme provides nectar for honeybees, bumblebees and butterflies, although golden and lemon-scented varieties are unpopular with butterflies. It is best when grown in large patches, and thrives in paths, walls and containers, or exposed or seaside gardens.

Basil

Bergamot

Chives

Lavender

Rosemary

Thyme

Right: *Herbs are often grown in specialist borders or gardens where their foliage and flowers create wonderful contrasts of both colour and fragrance.*

with good drainage or (more simply) plant the herbs in containers. If you do the latter, use a well-drained potting mix. A loam-based one is ideal, but can be expensive. Alternatively you can make your own potting mix, with one-third of well-rotted and friable organic matter (leaf mould or well-rotted compost is ideal) with one-third of grit, vermiculite or perlite, and a final third of sand or sandy loam if it's available.

Herbs grown in pots benefit from the free drainage, but will always need watering. Perennial herbs growing in the ground will become less prone to drought in their second and third seasons, but will need some water if it is dry in their first season. Annual crops will always be more drought-prone and need watering. When choosing a site, ensure that there is a reliable source of water close by.

PLANTING COMBINATIONS

Once you have decided what sort of herb garden you want, the next stage is to select the appropriate plants. Always ensure that those you select are suited to your soil type, climate and site conditions. If you are growing them in pots, for instance, group together plants that require the same conditions. Remember also that a herb garden should be as attractive as possible to complement the rest of the garden. Use plants that make pleasing contrasts of leaf texture or colour for the most striking effects, and include a diversity of species to ensure a wide range of flowering and fruiting times to create the maximum benefit for the wildlife.

HERBS IN THE REST OF THE GARDEN

Herbs are ideal candidates for existing flower beds, containers, or kitchen gardens where their abilities to deter pests and attract beneficial predator insects have long been recognized. Their ability to thrive in containers has led many gardeners to plant edible hanging gardens with fruit, vegetables and herbs in displays that are both attractive and delicious, and yet other herbs have gained merit as ornamental garden specimens in their own right, playing a central role in herbaceous or shrub beds.

PLANTING UP A HERB CONTAINER

1 *Start by choosing a large container and select a range of herbs of various sizes and habits, as well as a suitable potting mixture.*

2 *Cover the drainage holes at the pot's base with flat stones or crocks from a broken pot to stop the compost from leaking out.*

3 *Part-fill the pot until the largest specimen can sit on the surface with the root-ball about 2.5cm (1in) below the rim of the pot.*

4 *Put in more compost and place the smaller plants, checking they are similarly positioned below the rim. Remove pots before planting.*

5 *Fill the remaining gaps between the plants with compost, taking care not to over-firm it. Water the pot and top up with compost.*

6 *The finished decorative container can be placed on a patio along with other pots of herbs to create a mini patio herb garden.*

Above: *Try not to worry if caterpillars attack the green leaves of your vegetables, as visiting birds will soon pick them off.*

PLANTING VEGETABLE GARDENS

Offering an unusual alternative in wildlife gardens, vegetables can replace ornamental plants. They are often every bit as good as their ornamental counterparts for attracting wildlife, and have the added advantage of producing fresh food. Grow them in a kitchen garden or as elements among existing features, or if space is more limited, you could try growing them in hanging baskets or containers.

WHY GROW EDIBLE PLANTS IN A WILDLIFE GARDEN?

There can be few pleasures that compete with gathering your own fresh produce. Home-grown well-ripened fruit, and vegetables harvested when they are just right, are always more flavoursome than those you can buy. In addition, you know that they are free of pesticides and have not been produced at a cost to the environment. They also save on grocery bills, and you can grow unusual varieties not normally available to buy.

VEGETABLE GARDENS

Edible plants, particularly vegetables, grow best where they receive at least six hours of full sunlight a day, in a well-drained soil with a pH of 6–6.8. If part of your garden matches that description, then that is where you should put the vegetable garden.

Below: *A traditional vegetable garden is usually quite formal, with the crops planted in neat, ordered rows. Plant companion plants to enhance the aesthetics of an area and encourage beneficial insects.*

Growing vegetables is too big a subject to cover here in any depth, but there are a few things that you can do to improve a vegetable plot for wildlife. Avoid using pesticides, use companion plants (plants that encourage beneficial predators) to keep your plants pest-free, and always rotate your crops to prevent disease build-up. Herbs are a wonderful addition to the vegetable garden and help attract many wildlife species. In addition, the flowers of many vegetables are very attractive, so, if you have a few unused crops in the ground at the season's end, try leaving them for the wildlife.

POTAGERS

Also known as kitchen gardens, potagers gain their name from the French word for a soup of broth with vegetables (*potage*), and generally refer to a garden where vegetables are grown, along with herbs for cooking and medicine. The garden is usually made up of small geometric plots, each containing a variety of useful herbs, vegetables, and perhaps some flowers for daily use. The design is a hybrid of styles that rejects the need for neat rows of produce. The difference is that most, if not all, the plants contained are edible.

TOP VEGETABLES FOR WILDLIFE

Vegetables can attract a whole host of wildlife and, when included as a part of your summer displays, add contrast and interest to any border or container.

Blackcurrant (*Ribes nigrum*) This small to medium-sized shrub is not particularly attractive but has extremely good wildlife potential. The leaves attract many insects that feed on them and these in turn attract predators. Birds love the dark, sweet fruit that ripens in midsummer.

Carrot (*Daucus carota*) The familiar garden carrot may seem an unlikely candidate for attracting wildlife, but leaving the roots unharvested and allowing them to flower in the second year will attract a huge range of insects, including many beneficials, such as hoverflies, small wasps and a whole host of butterflies.

Globe artichoke (*Cynara scolymus*) The large flowers of this stately and unusual garden vegetable can be highly beneficial if you leave a few to mature, attracting a range of bees and beetles. The seed heads that follow are used as nesting and lining material by birds in late winter and are best left on the plant until spring.

Tomato (*Lycopersicon esculentum*) Attractive to a whole range of species, many of which we consider pests, although these in turn attract many predators. The yellow flower trusses are immensely popular with bumblebees, which are important pollinators, ensuring a good crop of fruit.

Blackcurrant

Carrot

Globe artichoke

Tomato

PLANTING UP A VEGETABLE HANGING BASKET

1 *Choose a large-sized basket and a range of herbs, vegetables, fruits or plants with edible blooms that will provide contrasting colours and shapes to one another.*

2 *Fill the basket to around two-thirds of its depth with compost, and incorporate a slow-release fertilizer, mixing it thoroughly before starting to plant.*

3 *Plant the upright specimens in the middle first and then place the trailing specimens around the outside of the container, angling them over the edge of the basket.*

4 *Space the plants evenly around the edge of the basket. Once you have finished the arrangement, fill up any remaining gaps between the root-balls with more compost.*

5 *The completed basket is now ready for hanging. However, do not water it until you have hung it up, because this will make it quite heavy and awkward to place.*

6 *Once the plants are settled in, they quickly grow, and the basket will become a striking feature, as full of contrast, colour and interest as any good floral display.*

MIXED PLANTING

If you don't want to devote all, or even a particular part, of your garden to edible plants, then the best way to start may be to consider a one-for-one substitution. This means replacing existing (non-edible) specimens with an edible counterpart. If you plan to plant a small ornamental tree, for instance, plant a fruit tree instead. When choosing a deciduous shrub, opt for a currant (*Ribes*) or hazelnut (*Corylus*), and replace herbaceous flowers with plants with edible blooms, such as daylilies (*Hemerocallis*) or chives (*Allium schoenoprasum*). Some plants, such as peppers (*Capsicum*), have very colourful varieties and can be grown beside flowers. Lettuces, radishes and other short-lived greens can also be tucked into gaps in the flower beds, and rainbow chard and ornamental cabbage are also excellent additions. You could also make a gooseberry hedge that, with its thorny stems, makes a secure barrier, and if you are building a pergola why not grow a grape over it?

Edible plants come in nearly all shapes and sizes, and can do the same job in your garden as ornamental plants.

CONTAINERS AND HANGING BASKETS

Try putting some pots of herbs on the patio, with basil and cherry tomatoes in a window box or hanging basket. The combinations are endless and, with a little imagination, even a small courtyard garden can become a fairly productive space.

Above: *Even a small patio can house an excellent range of edible plants in containers, and can look very attractive.*

PLANTING ROOF GARDENS AND PATIOS

Despite the limitations that the lack of open soil presents on roof gardens and patios, there are many ways of quickly planting up these spaces. Properly designed, roofs and paved areas can easily be transformed to provide a welcome oasis of calm and a source of shelter and food for many wildlife species, which would otherwise find these areas a harsh and unwelcoming place.

Above: *Hanging baskets are a good way of increasing the number of plants you can grow, especially when space is limited.*

WHAT IS A ROOF GARDEN?

Roof gardens are as varied as any other type of garden and, with a little imagination, can easily form an excellent wildlife-friendly space, largely helped by the exclusion of cats, dogs, foxes and rats. In their simplest form, they are described as a green roof. This refers to the roof of a building being partially or completely covered with vegetation and soil, or a growing medium that has been placed over a waterproof membrane. The greenery can be placed on both pitched and flat roofs, and many different designs and construction methods exist. They vary in their complexity, and the work is invariably best left to a specialist contractor. The plants are an alternative to tiles or other roof materials.

More complex designs can create a space for relaxation and leisure. They may simply involve planted containers, arranged to make a roof terrace (or sundeck) more pleasant. Others, however, may be far more elaborate, using feature plants that are quite

Left: *Perched high on top of a city building, this roof garden provides a welcome respite from the busy streets below.*

Above: *This garden chalet roof has been covered with sedum (stonecrop) to provide insulation and a good home for wildlife.*

PLANTING THYME THROUGH A PATIO

1 *This patio has been laid over an engineering membrane put in place to suppress weeds, and so needs scissors as well as a trowel to plant the thyme.*

2 *Clear the gravel mulch to the side to expose the fabric. Use scissors to cut a cross shape in the fabric, making a hole slightly larger than the plant.*

3 *Dig a hole using the trowel, and remove the soil. Place the thyme into the hole and backfill around the plant using some of the excavated soil.*

4 *Thoroughly water the thyme in using a watering can, doing this slowly in order to allow the water to soak into the soil beneath the membrane.*

tough because they must cope with the dry, windy conditions that often prevail. If you want a roof garden, the first priority is to get a structural engineer from a specialized firm to check that the structure can support it. Get a design drawn up by an expert.

PATIOS AND COURTYARDS

Unlike roofs, patios and courtyards are often very sheltered, and may be shaded by the surrounding buildings, which will influence your choice of plants. A sunny, sheltered area, on the other hand, will allow you to grow more tender plants than you could in the open garden.

Remember that the soil in a container drains more quickly than topsoil in the ground, and the plants you grow will require a rich potting mix to be at their best. You can mix your own blend but it is often easier to buy a proprietary brand specially mixed for the type of plants you intend to grow.

The new patio can seem rather stark in relation to the wider garden, but you can always link it to the rest of the design by using plants at the edge of the patio. Also try ageing the look of the patio by planting smaller, creeping plants, such as thyme (*Thymus*), in the cracks between the paving slabs.

If your outdoor space is especially limited, you can increase the number of plants by making use of the walls: mount hanging baskets and troughs on the walls, filled with trailing plants to create a third dimension. This will save ground space but doesn't compromise your wish to grow some plants.

PLANTING AN ALPINE TROUGH

1 *Choose a shallow, preferably clay trough and some free-draining compost and grit. Water the plants 1 hour before planting.*

2 *Mix some grit into the compost and cover the base with old bits of pot and a thin layer of compost before putting the plants in.*

3 *Fill the gaps between the plants using more compost mixed with grit; this will help with drainage. Ensure no air pockets remain.*

4 *Finally, dress the surface of the compost with a 1cm (½in) layer of grit to ensure that no water lies on the surface, as this will rot the basal growth of the plant.*

In addition to wall-mounted pots, you can also place a few annual or smaller perennial climbers in large pots near the wall. They will clothe the walls in greenery and flowers, and have the added advantage of providing food and shelter for many wildlife species. Try growing a twining plant, such as honeysuckle (*Lonicera*) or a jasmine (*Jasminum*), on a wall-mounted trellis, and watch the moths feeding there at night.

TOP PLANTS FOR CONTAINERS AND HANGING BASKETS

There are many plants that you can grow in containers that will attract wildlife to your garden. As a rule, smaller containers, and especially hanging baskets, are best when used for shorter term planting, and so generally suit annuals or tender plants best.

Bedding chrysanthemum (*Argyranthemum* spp.) This tender plant, covered in daisy-blooms all summer, attracts many insects.

English marigold (*Calendula officinalis*) The bright orange flowers attract a whole host of insects, including bees and hoverflies.

Indian cress (*Nasturtium majus*) Bees love the flowers. Prone to aphids, but these feed other predators. Make successive sowings.

Petunia (*Petunia* x *hybrida*) A good choice for attracting moths. Grow upright forms in summer tubs and trailing varieties in hanging baskets.

Tobacco plant (*Nicotiana sylvestris*) Attracts moths, and is richly fragrant from dusk onwards. Grow it in pots near the house.

Trailing lobelia (*Lobelia erinus*) The tender, trailing half-hardy types are ideal in summer baskets, where they attract many insects.

Chrysanthemum

English marigold

Indian cress

Petunia

Tobacco plant

Trailing lobelia

WORKING IN YOUR WILDLIFE GARDEN

A wildlife garden should always be enjoyed, and there are few better ways of doing that than by getting out and working in it. There is never really an "off season", and there is always something that needs tackling. The dormant season is the best time to design new areas and prune deciduous shrubs and trees, spring is the time to sow seed and realize your plans, summer is the time to check how the wildlife is responding, and autumn is the time for assessment and making plans for the future, so that next year's wildlife garden will be even better.

Left: *This ornamental compost bin provides a welcome view from the house, while still fulfilling the function of a traditional bin.*

Above: *A well-balanced garden can be a superb place to watch wildlife. A pair of binoculars will help you spot any shy species.*

Above: *Wildlife, such as this fox, will sometimes turn up when most unexpected, and can result in memorable encounters.*

Above: *A wildlife pond can be a source of wonder for children and adults alike, filled with fascinating wetland creatures.*

WATERING AND FEEDING

In order to keep your plants healthy, they will need both nutrients and sufficient water in the soil, and a lack of either may limit their growth. With a little careful thought and planning, though, you'll keep your garden plants healthy all year round. Knowing when and how much to water and feed your plants is an essential part of maintaining healthy plant growth throughout the whole season.

Above: *Plants growing in containers can be especially vulnerable to shortages of water and nutrients. Always make regular checks.*

TO WATER OR NOT TO WATER?

Using water wisely pays dividends for you, your garden and the wildlife. The simplest way to help conserve mains water is to install a water butt to catch the rainwater from your roof. It's much better than chlorinated tap water, and can be used to give plants a drink and top up the pond. Remember that it is no good having a garden rich in wildlife if this is achieved at the expense of other habitats, for example where dams have to be built.

Collecting rainwater can have its limitations, though, especially in drier locations, and it may be better if you use plants and features adapted to the local conditions. If you are planning a new garden or revamping an existing feature, check to see if the plants are drought-tolerant. Summer-bedding plants, for example, require a lot of water because they do not get sufficient opportunity to establish extensive root systems. Herbaceous plants can have the same problem in their first year but soon root deeper, and are more tolerant in subsequent years. Shrubs and trees may also be vulnerable in their early years but rapidly become better at surviving drought.

Above: *Hanging baskets and wall baskets need regular and careful watering to ensure they don't dry out, especially in summer.*

The rule of thumb, then, is only to water new plants and always avoid watering established plants unless they show signs of stress. Indeed, watering plants on a frequent basis encourages shallow root growth and actually weakens a plant's resistance to dry periods. If you must water, do so when it is cooler – during early morning or evening – to reduce evaporation, and avoid watering when it is windy for the same reason. Using mulches can also help.

Choosing large containers for patio plants will also help reduce water use because they retain moisture better than small pots. Furthermore, in order to reduce the rate at which water is lost, it helps to group pot plants together.

Left: *Rainwater butts are an ideal way to collect winter rain from glasshouses and sheds, ready for use in the summer months.*

Right: *Fertilizer applied early in the growing season can give a real boost to garden plants, which quickly take up the nutrients as the roots are very active at this time.*

Lastly, resist the temptation to water lawns in dry spells. Leaving a sprinkler on for an hour can actually use the same amount of water as a family of four uses in two days. Grass will slow its growth if left to grow a little longer and water demand will drop as a result. Longer grass also traps dew and reduces evaporation from the soil, making it more drought-tolerant, and the bonus for wildlife from flowers left in such a lawn, as well as the additional cover it provides, more than compensates for the loss of a green manicured sward.

FEEDING YOUR PLANTS

Plants require nutrients that are extracted from the air and soil, and if they suffer a shortage, there are generally two possible reasons. Either the nutrients are not available to the plant, invariably because of pH problems (in future, choose plants appropriate to the site), or there are few or no nutrients present. If that's the case, the problem is easily solved by applying a soil feed in a granular or liquid form. Alternatively, a natural source can be used to enrich the soil and encourage natural cycling of nutrients over a longer term. While the latter method should always be the preferred option, it does take time to work and, if your plants need an instant application, the quickest and easiest way is to use a liquid feed.

MAKING NETTLE TEA FOR YOUR PLANTS

1 *Cut some nettles from your nettle patch, choosing good, strong, young leafy stems. You may need gloves to protect your arms from the stings.*

2 *Place the nettles in a large container, packing them in tightly, then weigh the cut stems down with bricks. Fill the container with water.*

3 *Cover the container with a sack or old carpet to prevent evaporation and keep the smell in as the organic material starts to decompose and break down.*

4 *After 2–3 weeks, the resulting liquid feed is ready for use. It should always be diluted 10:1 with fresh water or mixed to the colour of tea before using.*

WATER-WISE GARDENING

Water is a valuable commodity and should be used wisely. To make best use of it, here are four quick tips.

Install a water butt This will collect the rainwater running off your roof to save water and money. It can be used instead of treated mains water, has the advantage of being naturally soft, is free of chemical additives and is ideal for topping up garden ponds.

Grey water This is waste water from household use that can be used in the garden. The most likely and least polluted source is bath water. Water from a washing machine or kitchen sink often contains grease, oils and chemicals that can adversely affect both your plants and wildlife.

Avoid using hosepipes and lawn sprinklers This particularly applies to those using mains water, and beware of using a fine spray because a lot of water is wasted – not all reaches the plants. Use a watering can instead, or attach your hosepipe to a water butt.

Don't water your plants too often Abstinence encourages them to make deeper roots and become more self-sufficient. Instead of watering a lawn, cut it longer than usual in dry periods. It may go brown for a while, but will recover as soon as it receives some rain.

PLANT NUTRIENTS AND FERTILIZERS

Plant nutrients are divided into two groups, depending on whether they are found in high or low concentrations. Those found in high concentrations, needed in large amounts, are known as macro or major nutrients; low concentrations, needed in relatively small amounts, are micro or trace elements.

MACRO OR MAJOR NUTRIENTS

NUTRIENT	SOURCES IN THE GARDEN
Nitrogen (N)	Abundant in the atmosphere but unavailable until "fixed" as nitrates by bacteria. Encourage availability by applying compost to soils or by applying a long-term feed, such as pelleted chicken manure, or fish, blood and bone.
Phosphorus (P)	Naturally occurs as mineral phosphates in soils but often with low availability in sandy, acidic and chalky ground. Present in bone meal, comfrey, horse manure and, to a lesser extent, pelleted chicken manure.
Potassium (K)	Often available in large amounts in the soil, although not all plants are good at taking it. Comfrey, horse manure and wood ash are good sources; nettles are especially good at taking up and storing potassium.

MICRO NUTRIENTS OR TRACE ELEMENTS

NUTRIENT	SOURCES IN THE GARDEN
Calcium (Ca)	Naturally abundant in the Earth's surface, although it is easily lost by leaching on certain soils, which tend to become acidic. Easily re-applied using ground limestone, comfrey, horse manure or bone meal.
Magnesium (Mg)	Magnesium is freely available in most soils but may be lost through leaching, or be unavailable in waterlogged or very limy soils. Apply a mulch of compost or Epsom salts if the deficiency is severe.
Sulphur (S)	Normally available in the soil, and replenished from rainwater or other atmospheric sources. A base dressing or a light dusting of flowers of sulphur can be applied if a severe shortage occurs.
Iron (Fe)	Iron shortage in chalky soils is due to lock-up by calcium and is difficult to avoid. Stinging nettles, compost, horse manure and blood and bone are good sources.
Manganese (Mc)	Tends only to affect plants growing in acidic soils, especially those in the cabbage family. Apply lime and top dress with compost, made from grass clippings.
Boron (B)	Can sometimes be lacking from sandy soil. Horse manure, compost and untreated sawdust are all good sources, although you can also apply borax in severe cases.
Copper (Cu)	Normally available in the soil, although sandy soils can become deficient. Stinging nettles, chickweed, horse manure, garden compost and untreated sawdust are all good sources.
Zinc (Zn)	Normally available in all but very sandy soils. Horse manure is possibly the best source, followed by compost and untreated sawdust.
Molybdenum (Mo)	Acidic soils can become short of molybdenum, and the cure is normally to apply lime and compost rich in grass clippings.

COMPOSTING

Turning your garden and kitchen waste into a compost heap is not only a great way to recycle these materials into the nutrients your plants need, but can also provide a miniature, frost-free wildlife refuge. Many creatures like to overwinter in the cool, dark safety of the decaying vegetation, and yet more find a rich source of food in its damp recesses. A compost heap also means you don't need to buy expensive soil conditioners, saving you both time and money, as well as helping wildlife.

Above: *A compost heap needs to be turned periodically to ensure all the plant material decomposes properly. Special turning tools can be bought for tall, narrow heaps.*

WHY RECYCLE WASTE?

The environmental impact of sending waste to landfill sites can be huge. Domestic gardens often generate huge amounts of waste that, if disposed of as landfill, does not rot but ferments, producing environmentally harmful substances such as methane (a greenhouse gas), and a toxic slimy substance called leachates. This is a pointless waste of one of the best resources your garden can generate.

Compost, made from plant waste, will reward you with rich, fertile humus to add to your garden soil or to use in pots. In addition, compost is full of mini-beasts that will provide a great feast for thrushes, robins and blackbirds, as well as predators of soil-borne pests. Furthermore, over winter, a compost heap is an extremely important feature of a wildlife garden, acting as a mini-wildlife refuge where insects, bacteria and fungi carry on the decomposition process, while providing a hibernation site for amphibians and hedgehogs.

WHAT TO COMPOST

Simply piling all your organic waste in a heap would ultimately result in compost, but the process might be inefficient and the results variable. Some gardeners take quite a scientific view of their composting, and construct heaps that generate heat and rot down very quickly (called "hot piles"). Wildlife gardeners, on the other hand, might take a more leisurely approach and allow the process to continue quite slowly, while providing a habitat for animals, using a method called the "cold pile".

Even if you take a slower approach, it is important to get roughly the right proportions of different materials to make the end product usable in the garden. In terms of composting there are basically two types of materials, referred to as "greens" and "browns". Green materials are mostly wet, soft, green and high in nitrogen. Brown materials are dry, harder, absorbent and high in carbon. You should aim for roughly

HOT PILE COMPOST BIN

A hot pile compost bin is the best method to use if you want compost in a hurry. A good mix of green and brown material is best for nutritional balance for microbes. Twigs at the bottom improve aeration. You should water underneath the pile before placing the twigs, and water brown layers as you add them. Nettles are included as a good natural compost activator, and old compost or soil will introduce natural decomposers to the new heap. A lid on top will keep out the rain and conserve heat.

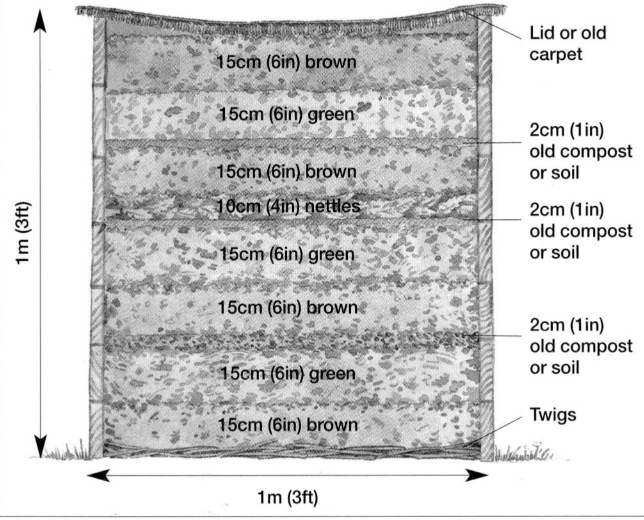

WHAT TO COMPOST, AND WHAT TO AVOID

You can compost almost anything that was once alive or part of a living organism, although not everything is necessarily ideal for handling. Adding a lot of coarse, woody material will significantly slow down the composting process, although it can be shredded first. Be sure to add around equal amounts of green and brown, and reject all items in the "Avoid" list.

GREENS
- Fresh plants
- Grass cuttings
- Raw fruit and vegetables
- Seaweed, algae and garden pond cleanings
- Tea leaves
- Urine and manure
- Weeds/nettles (avoid perennial weed roots)
- Wood/peat ash

BROWNS
- Coffee grounds
- Dry plant stems and twigs
- Egg shells
- Pet and human hair (takes a little time)
- Scrunched-up paper
- Straw and hay
- Torn-up cardboard (e.g. cereal and egg boxes, toilet-roll centres)

AVOID
- Barbecue or coal ash
- Grease, oil, cooked food scraps
- Meat or fish scraps
- Dog or cat faeces (they can contain dangerous pathogens)

BUILDING A BEEHIVE COMPOST BIN

1 *Take two square timber batons and lay them with the closest ends about three-quarters of the distance of the other. Lay some thin planks on top.*

2 *Use a workbench to screw the boards in place on the batons, then saw off the overlap. Repeat this process for the opposite side of the compost bin.*

3 *Attach a base and top board to the two prepared sides so that the open sides have the same proportions as the other two sides of the bin.*

4 *Fix more boards to the open sides so that the box is fully formed, but leave the bottom two from one of the sides to form a hatch to empty the bin.*

5 *Saw off any overlap from the boards to give a good even edge, and ensure all the screws are tight. Sand off any rough splinters from the sawn edges.*

6 *Make the roof using two "A"-shaped pieces (as shown), ensuring that the bottom edge is just narrower than the sides. Fix more boards to this.*

7 *Fix two hinges to the board above the open side and attach a door that will allow access to empty the bin. This is made of two more wooden boards.*

8 *The finished compost bin can now be placed in the garden and used to make compost. It can be painted to ensure it lasts longer and looks good.*

equal amounts of browns and greens set in layers to keep the compost moist but not too wet, and supply the decomposing organisms with essential nitrogen and carbon.

EQUIPMENT

There are many different composting methods and containers, and the type you choose will vary depending on the amount and type of organic waste you will be composting. For most people, the choice is a relatively simple one between a composting container – such as a cone – or an open heap.

At its simplest, a compost heap is made by piling up your organic waste in the garden. The urge for tidiness means that most build a container for the material or purchase a commercially made container, the cone shape being a popular choice because it's compact and ideal for small gardens. It's usually made of plastic and has a long life; the manufacturers often claim that the contents don't need to be turned although the tumbler bin, like a barrel, is supported by a metal frame, making it vermin-proof, and can be easily swung over. The only drawback is that such kinds only deal with small amounts of waste and almost never heat up. What is more they are less accessible or even completely inaccessible to some wild creatures.

Compost heaps, on the other hand, can deal with large volumes of waste. They can also be made large enough to generate heat, although not all will, and this helps the composting process and attracts some wildlife that will shelter here in the cooler months. The bottom of the pile must have contact with the soil so that creatures can gain access. Note that heaps work best when turned. If you bag your compost after about a year, it will continue to decompose in the bag and become finer and drier. When you do bag it up, put anything too coarse back in the heap for further decomposition, as the in-bag maturation tends to be rather slow and will not easily deal with larger items. Once mature, it can be used as a wonderful soil conditioner.

WON'T A COMPOST HEAP SMELL?

If you are adding the right things in roughly the right proportions, there shouldn't be any problem. Most compost heaps that smell are either lacking air or are too wet. In either case, the answer is to aerate the heap by turning and loosening it with a fork and, preferably, by adding some dry material at the same time.

Above: *Sieving compost is the best way to remove larger pieces that have not fully decomposed. These can be returned to the heap to break down further.*

WEEDING AND WEED CONTROL

The term weed may seem peculiar in the context of a wildlife garden, where so many plants might be native wildflowers. It is important to remember, though, that the term does not automatically refer to a native plant and, indeed, many of the most notorious weeds in towns and the countryside are imports. Removing these plants is as essential in a wildlife garden as in any other, and may even improve the habitat as a result.

Above: *Buttercups are regarded as weeds by many gardeners, but their cheerful yellow flowers are much loved by many insects.*

WHAT IS A WEED?

Answer: A plant (often unsightly) that establishes itself in a garden, with no help from us, and which proceeds to compete with those that we have planted. Weeds are highly competitive species that rob cultivated specimens of nutrients, light and, most important, water. In fact uncontrolled weed growth may ultimately kill ornamental plants, which are often much less vigorous, and will often seriously inhibit their development. For most of us, a weed's "unwantedness" is its major crime.

Weeds are able to take control because they are species that have evolved to colonize, compete and become dominant. Most of them specialize in getting established on disturbed ground – often found in a garden – and usually have rapid growth rates when compared to cultivated plants. In natural habitats their competitive capabilities are held in check by the equal demands of neighbouring plants, but such equilibrium is very rare in the average garden.

While many common weeds are native plants and owe their competitive edge to this fact alone, many others are introduced plants that become weeds because they do not have the constraints of their natural habitat. They are often the most serious weeds in a garden, and can sometimes become so troublesome that they become a national problem. Don't make the mistake of thinking that a pretty plant can't become a weed. It can. Choose your plants carefully to avoid introducing problems.

Finally, note that a few plants, such as Japanese knotweed, no matter how tolerant you may be, are simply weeds that must be removed for the well-being of your garden. They will resist all efforts to eradicate them and, as any gardener knows, the only really successful strategy for weed control is persistent weeding.

COMMON TYPES OF WEEDS

There are many plants that can become weeds if they get out of control or grow where you don't want them to. Often they are native plant species that are able to take advantage of the conditions within your garden, and can be quite persistent.

Annual meadow grass A very common annual weed thriving in just about every situation in a garden. Very variable and adaptable, and able to grow and set seed all year round if the winter is mild.

Bittercress This diminutive plant is very common in container-grown plants, and often grows in mild periods in winter. Sheds abundant seed and can become invasive.

Chickweed Commonly found on soil that is well-cultivated and rich in organic matter. Spreads to make a large mat and produces seed prolifically. Seed lies dormant for years.

Couch grass This perennial grass spreads via underground rhizomes that often form thick masses in the soil over time. Very difficult to eradicate from borders, but can be tamed and weakened by constant cutting.

Dandelion The dandelion is quite a showy plant, often appearing in lawns, with a strong tap root. Readily regenerates by seed and by root unless the whole plant is removed.

Dock A persistent perennial that is difficult to dig out, with very tough roots that can regenerate from even a small section left in the ground. Seeds prolifically if not controlled.

Ground elder A spreading and smothering weed that is happiest in a loamy soil, which it can rapidly colonize. The white, spreading roots often go down deep, and it resists efforts to dig it up.

Horsetail Non-flowering plants that mainly spread via the thin, black roots. Often covers large areas, and is very difficult to dig out as the brittle stems and roots break easily when pulled, and regenerate.

Nettle Extremely common weed in gardens, primarily because it needs high fertility and disturbed ground.

Bittercress

Chickweed

Couch grass

Ground elder

Horsetail

Nettle

CHEMICALS

As a rule of thumb, don't use them. The majority of herbicides (or weedkillers) are toxic compounds that can affect the flora and fauna in your garden. The exception is where highly persistent weeds cannot be effectively controlled by hand weeding or mulches. While this situation is mercifully rare, plants such as Japanese knotweed have become a real problem in recent years, and threaten both garden and natural habitats in parts of Western Europe.

HAND WEEDING

Simply pulling out weeds, digging them up or using a cultivator, such as a hoe, is usually the least detrimental method of weed control. There is little skill in using most hand-weeding implements and, provided that you are careful, little and often is all that is required. The real trick is to be able to recognize weeds when they are very young, even when they are just seedlings, and remove them then.

MULCHING

A mulch is a layer of material that is laid over the soil, or other growing medium. It should be laid on a bare soil surface that is warm and moist, with autumn being the ideal time, although it can also be applied in the spring after the soil has warmed up. Many types of mulch will suppress the germination of weed seeds, and some will also benefit wildlife by introducing organic matter.

Below: *Dandelions can become troublesome as they spread quickly by means of the plumed seeds that follow the bright yellow flowers in late spring.*

Mulching an established border will help keep the plants' roots warm in winter and cool in summer. It also reduces soil water loss through evaporation, partly by shading the soil surface. The weed control benefits are mostly due to the mulch preventing the germinating weed seedlings from reaching the sunlight, or by "drawing" the weed up so that it is spindly and can be easily removed. It will not, however, inhibit established weeds, especially vigorous perennial ones, which must be removed by hand the moment they appear.

If a mulch is laid to a sufficient, even depth – 5cm (2in) or more – it will develop a dry, dusty surface that will deter the germination of weed seeds that land on it. While this is only a temporary measure, it can help reduce the need for weeding at the busiest times of year. Synthetic materials are unattractive, but can be useful if you choose the permeable types, which allow the passage of air and water. Indeed, some organic materials, such as grass clippings, can pack down on the surface and form a water-resistant layer. Finally, note that mulches encourage surface rooting, and that the mulching must be continued if the plants are not to suffer in the future.

Mulching also aids plant development by gradually raising soil fertility and encouraging nutrient cycling. Furthermore, natural, organic mulches will actually harbour many beneficial insects, such as carnivorous beetles, which will help keep the plants healthy by eating pests, including slugs and caterpillars.

MULCH TYPES AND THEIR BENEFITS TO WILDLIFE

The materials that can be used for mulching are varied in their composition and effects. They are generally classified into organic and inorganic types. Organic mulches are mainly bulky materials of living origin. Inorganic mulches, on the other hand, include some naturally occurring but non-living materials such as pebbles and gravel, as well as synthetic materials of artificial origin. In the inorganic category, the materials may be further subdivided into loose fill and sheet materials. The six main kinds are:

Bark and composted woodchip Makes an excellent material because it is recycled, and will gradually break down and yield organic matter to the soil below. It also lowers the chance of weeds germinating, and is possibly the best material for encouraging beetles due to its open nature.

Garden compost Often makes a first-rate mulch, increasing soil fertility and encouraging beneficial insects, but it can also be an excellent place for germinating weeds to become established, and large quantities can be difficult to produce.

Straw A moderately good material to use around the base of plants in the summer, particularly under fruiting strawberries. While surprisingly durable, it eventually rots down. It should be chopped into short lengths prior to use.

Black polythene Quick and easy to lay, and a common material that can be readily obtained from many suppliers. It does not allow for water penetration into the soil though, and is generally best restricted to use under paths or for temporary coverage.

Woven plastic sheet An improvement on black polythene, although it also has the disadvantage of denuding the organic content from the soil below by preventing it reaching there. Use in similar places to polythene as a water-permeable substitute.

Grit, pebbles, gravel or sand These inorganic materials are very durable, although they often become incorporated into the topsoil layer because of the actions of worms and other organisms. They are ideal in dry gardens, around alpine plants, and as a topping around potted plants.

Bark

Straw

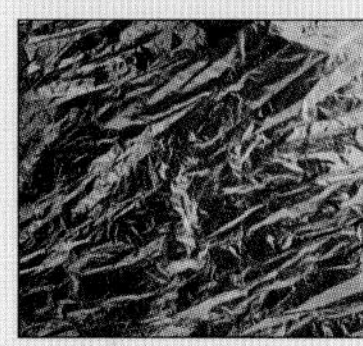

Black polythene

Gravel

Above: *Snails and slugs are a problem in any garden if their number gets too high. Beer traps can help to control them.*

PESTS, DISEASES AND DISORDERS

While the vast majority of the creatures and other organisms in the garden don't cause any harm, a small number can sometimes become your worst enemies, seemingly intent on devouring crops and damaging the appearance and overall vigour of other plants, possibly shortening their lifespan. Controlling them might be easier than you think, though, and wildlife gardens have a whole "army" of helpers to help you do this.

DEFINING A PEST

In the simplest terms, a pest is a creature that eats a plant. Many culprits are visible – although a few are very small and may even be microscopic – and they are usually present in large numbers. That is not always the case, however, and a single large pest, such as a deer, may affect many plants in quite a short time, often in a single visit. Pests may be host specific or more general in their feeding habits.

WHAT IS A DISEASE?

A disease describes the symptoms caused by a small (usually microscopic) parasite that attacks the plant's cells, possibly causing extensive harm before any obvious symptoms appear. Plant diseases are usually caused by fungi, bacteria or viruses.

A fungus is a small unicellular or colonial mass of cells, often with complex life cycles. Most are beneficial or benign to plants. The vast majority are only evident at the reproductive phase, and they may go unnoticed unless serious harm occurs.

Bacteria, on the other hand, are very simple (unicellular) organisms, only some of which are capable of life outside their host (victim) species. They too usually parasitize individual cells, and often reproduce and spread rapidly once an infection occurs. The most common source of harm occurs when they release poisons into the cell. Bacteria can be very hard to treat because they live inside the plant cells.

A virus is quite unlike the other two disease-causing agents. All viruses are incapable of functioning outside the host cell, and they consist of a shell that contains a small amount of very basic genetic material. This is used (once inside the cell) to cause the host cell to produce copies of the virus. The host cell then usually dies, and damage often spreads through the copies.

DISORDERS

A disorder is a condition whereby the growth or internal functioning of the plant physically deviates from the norm. The most common cause is an environmental stress – such as nutrient imbalance or lack of light. Disorders differ from temporary stresses (e.g. wilting) because they cannot be readily reversed, even if the cause is promptly removed. Plants suffering a disorder often resemble diseased or pest-stricken plants, and may become sicker than if they had been attacked by a pest or disease-causing organism.

Left: *A scarecrow was a traditional way of discouraging birds, although in truth, they are often more ornamental than useful.*

RECOGNIZING THE SYMPTOMS

Knowing what is likely to harm the plants you intend growing is the best starting point. Only a few insects are actually harmful, and learning which are pests and which are not is vital. In addition you will be well advised to find out which plants are susceptible to particular pests, and learn what are the signs. In many cases, the pest or disease will be visibly present, allowing an easy diagnosis. Get into the habit of looking closely at all your plants and checking for early symptoms of attack. Disease symptoms can be tricky to diagnose, but a few of the commoner ones are outlined here.

Blight is usually noticed as a softening and death of tissue in patches, whereas damping off is a localized blight of the stem near the soil. Wilt is sudden wilting, usually of the stem tip, whereas foot rot (affecting the lower stem) and root rot are often less visible without close examination.

Anthracnose usually refers to any skin tissue where black lesions appear, with leaf spots specifically affecting that area. Scab also affects the skin, being a hard, corky layer on the stems, leaves and fruit. Canker is an area of flaking or bleeding bark tissue, whereas yellowing and mosaics are often disease-related.

A few other disease-like conditions can be less threatening, and are actually an interesting addition to the diversity in your garden. Galls – and there are many of them – are a hyperplasic deformation of the plant tissue, and are often caused by tiny mites, midges or wasps. They are mostly harmless and can occasionally be extremely curious shapes. Other deformations also occur, such as "Witch's Broom", and they can have a variety of causes including bacteria, fungi, mites, aphids, and even mistletoe. On the other hand, a plant may simply be showing a genetic abnormality, such as fasciation, where a normally round stem is flattened, looking as if many stems have fused together.

PREVENTION IS BETTER THAN CURE

The best way to control problems is to ensure that your plants are healthy by giving them the right conditions. Healthy plants are often more resistant to diseases and stresses, and a healthy, balanced garden, full of the appropriate plants, is also the ideal environment for beneficial organisms. Traps, barriers, scaring devices and repellents can all be effective methods of dissuading pests, provided they do not prove too tempting or disruptive to the more desirable creatures.

BENEFICIAL ORGANISMS

By attracting beneficial organisms, you'll be well on the way to balancing the ecology of the garden and removing the majority of threats posed by pests.

All pests tend to become numerous and, as such, they are almost always a food source for a whole array of predators (species that eat them), parasitoids (creatures that lay eggs that hatch and eat them), and parasites (diseases of the pest). You can actually buy all three for use in the greenhouse, but they are often less effective outdoors. In the latter case, it is often better to enlist the help of a local volunteer force. Your garden can easily become a haven for many beneficial insects that are attracted by the plants or the habitat, and they'll reward you by eating as many of the offending insects as possible. With an army of natural pest killers on your side, matters will improve as their tireless efforts to devour the pests will keep their number in check.

Below: *The larvae of ladybirds are particularly voracious predators of a range of insects, and are especially fond of aphids.*

BENEFICIAL PREDATORS

Many familiar creatures that visit or inhabit gardens are voracious predators, and help control the numbers of pests. Some are very common and, by encouraging them, you can help restore a natural balance in the garden.

Frog, toad and newt All amphibians are carnivores and eat an array of garden pests. Toads tend to be particularly good in this respect, and all amphibians can be attracted by a pond to breed in and cover such as rock piles and long vegetation.

Ground beetle A fierce-looking beetle living among the litter layer, just above the soil, where it hunts its favourite prey – the slug. The beetle is common everywhere, and can be encouraged by mulching and leaving areas untouched.

Hedgehog It eats a variety of garden pests. Encourage it by providing brush piles or a nesting box, and dense growth next to hedge bottoms.

Hoverfly Though the adults are vegetarian, feeding on pollen and nectar, the larvae are voracious predators of aphids. Encourage the adults into the garden by planting flat umbelled plants, and those with daisy flowers.

Lacewing A strange, graceful, night-flying insect; the larvae are among the best of all garden predators. They attack and eat a whole range of insects, favouring aphids.

Ladybird Though inconspicuous, the larva is the most voracious predator of aphids.

Robin Carnivorous bird that normally catches its prey on the ground after seeing movement from a perch above. Often follows gardeners digging the soil to catch unearthed grubs.

Slow worm Not a worm but a legless lizard, feeding on slugs and earthworms, but will also eat insects. Prefers damp and warm habitats, and hibernates under piles of leaves in winter.

Spider Probably the most important predator in the garden. Catches mostly flying insects in webs, although some species are specialists at ambushing prey. Spiders vary considerably in size and can be found in every type of habitat.

Wasp Renowned for its sting and reviled for this reason. An incredible hunter, particularly of caterpillars in early summer. Can be a problem if they nest in or near houses and other buildings.

Frog

Ground beetle

Hedgehog

Hoverfly

Lacewing

Ladybird

Robin

Slow worm

Spider

Wasp

PRUNING

Pruning is a necessary activity in the garden, especially when plants become too big and unmanageable, or perhaps to try to encourage better flowering or rejuvenate older specimens. While sometimes a little confusing to the beginner, there is no great mystery surrounding pruning and, like most jobs in the garden, it merely involves the application of simple and straightforward principles. Follow these guidelines and in no time at all you'll be pruning with confidence.

Above: *A garden shredder is an ideal way of recycling prunings, as the shredded material can be used in making mulch for the garden.*

WHY PRUNE?

The main reason to prune is to control a plant's growth. It may outgrow its space or need to be shaped for aesthetic reasons. But pruning can also improve the flower size of some shrubs and climbers, and maintain a regular supply of new growth valued for its attractive colours (e.g. dogwoods).

CHOOSING THE RIGHT TOOLS

Secateurs are used to snip through thinner growth, up to about 15mm (½in) in diameter. For thicker growth you will need a pair of loppers that are used on branches up to 2.5cm (1in) thick. Use them when you can't reach in with secateurs, for instance in dense, tangled shrubs. Normally, loppers should not be used for very thick branches because they may easily be damaged, although several models of ratchet-operated loppers can cut through growth of up to 5cm (2in).

Above these thicknesses you will need a pruning saw. Again many designs exist, but the most useful is the curved or Grecian type, and a bow saw for really thick wood. Always make sure you have the right tools for the job. If you don't, it will make the job harder, and you may actually end up causing more harm than good by either breaking the tool itself or by making untidy or ragged cuts that increase the chances of disease.

DECIDING WHAT TO DO

The first and simplest thing that you can do is to remove all dead, dying, damaged or diseased wood. Remember, though, that deadwood is very important to some wildlife, especially what is called "standing deadwood" in a tree. This is often removed to ensure that dead branches do not fall suddenly, and should be left on the ground for wildlife and not removed and burned as is often recommended. Diseased material, on

GOOD AND BAD PRUNING

Above: *Cuts should be made like this one, just above a bud or pair of buds. Make sure the cut does not get too close so that you don't damage the delicate buds.*

Above: *Leaving too long a stub above the buds will result in a piece of deadwood that can act as an entry point for fungal diseases. This can affect the rest of the branch.*

DOS AND DON'TS OF PRUNING FOR WILDLIFE

Whilst pruning always employs the same basic methods, the choice of how and when to prune can have serious implications for wildlife.

- **Do** identify the shrub or tree, and check its pruning requirements.
- **Do** leave piles of thicker branches on the ground for wildlife. Log and brush piles can provide escape cover, nesting and den sites for many species and, if placed along the edge of water, can be an important habitat for amphibians and reptiles.
- **Do** thin shrubs over a two- to three-year period in preference to one hard pruning session to allow them to make new growth while still producing fruit and flowers.
- **Do** leave "standing deadwood" where possible, especially stumps and boles of dead trees for wildlife.
- **Don't** prune and deadhead shrubs until late winter to allow the birds to feed on berries and seed heads.
- **Don't** prune in spring because this will disturb nesting birds.
- **Don't** compost diseased material as this will infect other plants. Remove and burn it to avoid re-infection.
- **Don't** worry if you see fungus growing on deadwood because it cannot infect live material.

USING PRUNINGS TO CREATE A HABITAT

1 *Collect prunings from a variety of healthy plants, and drive some short stakes into the ground, ensuring they are firmly in place.*

2 *Lay down bundles of long, straight branches horizontally behind the stakes. Pack them together tightly to make narrow spaces, which will provide excellent cover for insects in all seasons.*

3 *Cover the packed pile with loose material and add a layer of leaves. Place larger logs in front to help secure the prunings and to create an even more diverse habitat, attracting more species.*

the other hand, should be removed and burned, especially if there is a chance that it will spread and affect other plants.

Criss-crossing branches and crowded growth should also be cleared, with their removal prompting the appearance of new growth in many species. This is normally then followed by the removal of any unwanted growth that is obstructing paths or crowding out adjacent specimens. Always take care when doing such pruning because removing large amounts of plant material may cause the plant to assume an unbalanced form that is difficult (if not impossible) to counter with further pruning.

Once you have cleared this material, it is possible to see what further work needs to be done. Creating balance, form and a pleasing shape requires a keen eye, and it is worth taking your time, intermittently viewing your work from a distance.

Finally, note that the real results of pruning may not always be apparent for months and, in the case of trees, years.

PRUNING CUTS

The two basic pruning cuts are heading (the removal of a part of a shoot or limb) and thinning (the removal of the entire shoot or limb). Heading stimulates re-growth near the cut and is the most invigorating type of pruning cut, resulting in thick, compact growth and a loss of natural form, as found in a formally pruned hedge. Thinning, on the other hand, generally provides a more natural look, with only around one-third of the growth being thinned at any one time, leaving the natural flowering and fruiting cycle to continue. Thinning is often the best type of pruning to favour wildlife, although the dense growth promoted by heading does provide good dense cover for some species, such as nesting birds.

Pruning cuts should always be cleanly done using sharp cutters or a saw, and always avoid tearing. When removing a whole limb, try to leave as short a stub as possible. If you are heading (i.e. shortening) a branch, make your cut 3mm (⅛in), or just less, above a bud and always ensure that the bud is not damaged while cutting. And remember, if you cut the wrong stem or branch, that's it. Always check that you know what effect its removal will have before cutting.

TIMING OF PRUNING

Many woody ornamentals are pruned according to their date of flowering. Spring-flowering plants, such as forsythia, are normally pruned only after they bloom because pruning them during the dormant season will remove the flower buds formed the previous autumn. Summer-flowering plants, on the other hand, are generally pruned during the dormant winter season. As a rule of thumb, avoid heavy pruning during late summer and autumn because this can remove berries and seed needed by wildlife, and in spring to avoid disturbing nesting birds.

CUTTING A HERBACEOUS BORDER

1 *Herbaceous borders will always look better after a tidy-up, and this will also allow light to get to the crowns and encourage strong, healthy new growth in spring.*

2 *Try to leave cutting back herbaceous stems until the early spring, if possible, as old stems often act as a vital refuge for insects, including many beneficials in winter.*

Above: *A field of cowslips is a good feeding place for early emerging bees and long-tongued flies that will in turn pollinate them.*

RAISING NATIVE PLANTS FROM SEED

Seed is the principal way in which flowering plants produce a new generation. It is also the way that they ensure genetic diversity in a population and so collecting and sowing seed of trees, shrubs, grasses and flowers is extremely worthwhile. Native plants are often best for wildlife, and those that are native to your particular locality will be the best of all for attracting the local wildlife.

WHY DO IT?

The two advantages of collecting seed and raising your own plants are, first, saving money and, second, helping the local environment.

Native plants may be quite variable across their range, and the slight difference between local populations is called their provenance. If these plants occur naturally without being planted, they are called indigenous plants. Commercial supplies of seed usually come from seed or plant material from a different area or, in some cases, from another country. Therefore, though the plants are often genetically very similar, they may not always be best suited to the conditions in your area. By gathering and propagating local seed, then, you are helping to maintain the natural variety of native plants across a wide range.

WHAT TYPE OF SEED TO COLLECT

This depends on what kind of garden you want. Diversifying your lawn, for instance, will need different plants to those for creating a woodland edge. Once you have a clear plan, you can decide where to collect the seed.

Above: *The seed of a cowslip is very easy to harvest. Simply gather the ripe seed heads and gently rub them to release the seed. It is best sown fresh, or store in a paper bag.*

THE BEST PLACE TO GATHER IT

Your own garden is obviously the easiest place to collect seed. The best policy before you collect any seed from land that is not your own is to first ask for permission from the landowner. Remember to check whether the plants you intend collecting from are rare or endangered because some species might be protected, making it illegal even for the landowner to take seed, and collecting seed of any wild plants should be limited to small amounts.

When you visit the site, you must be able to make a clear distinction between plants that have become naturalized and those that have always grown there. A good place to look may be land earmarked for building because new developments are often built on land with native plants.

HOW TO HARVEST SEED

There are three main kinds of seed. The commonest and easiest type is that which can be collected, dried and stored prior to sowing. Berries and softer fruit are slightly more difficult, and often need the soft flesh removed before they can be sown. The seed is usually short-lived and must be sown at once to retain its viability. Nuts, and many larger kinds of seed, are also difficult to store because they will only germinate when fresh. Berries and nuts should only be collected after they have fully ripened, usually once they begin to fall off the branch.

Whichever type you are collecting, you must remove only a small or modest amount from the plant. Unless you need a very large number of plants, you will need only a small amount of seed. Remember to

MACERATING AND FLOATING BERRIES

1 *Lay the ripe berries on a firm surface and cover with a large plastic sheet. Squash the berries by pressing them underfoot.*

2 *Pour the squashed berries into a bucket full of water and leave for several days. The soft parts of the fruit will separate from the seed.*

3 *The seed will sink to the bottom and the fruit and skins will float. These can be poured off. Wash the seed and it is then ready to sow.*

collect from more than one plant to get as much diversity as possible. If the seed pods are not quite ripe, you can always put them in paper bags and allow them to dry and burst open.

THE FIRST STAGE

Germination is the growth of the embryonic plant inside the seed. This embryo lies in a dormant state, only barely alive until this time; some seed, such as poppy, can survive successfully in this dormant state for 50 years or more. Most seed, however, is capable of lasting for only a few years before the embryo dies and the seed becomes unviable. The term "viable seed" is used to describe seed that is alive and in a healthy state, thereby allowing germination. As time passes, the amount of viable seed usually decreases under normal storage conditions, and seed is best sown fresh.

To germinate, seed requires moisture, warmth and oxygen. Most seed germinates best at 18–24°C (65–75°F) and, although most seed will happily germinate in light, some – such as periwinkle (*Vinca*), pansy (*Viola*) and verbena – germinates best in the dark.

While most seed is easy to grow, a few species have specific germination requirements. Bought seed has specific instructions on the packaging, but collected seed might require a bit of guesswork. As a general rule, small dust-like seed such as thyme (*Thymus*), basil (*Ocimum basilicum*) and begonia needs light to germinate. Make sure that the seed is well pressed into the moist compost, but do not cover it. Larger seed, on the other hand, is most commonly covered to twice its thickness, preferably with finely sieved compost.

Some seed can be a little tricky to germinate, and the commonest problem is caused by a lack of cold-temperature dormancy. Cold dormancy is mostly required by plant species that originate from cooler climates. The solution is stratification. This simply involves covering the seed in damp material, such as compost, leafmould or sand, depending on the seed size. Large seed can be kept in organic matter, but smaller seed is best mixed with sand to make sowing easier later on. Keep it in a refrigerator at about 4°C (40°F) for up to three months, when it can be removed, being ready to germinate. Oak (*Quercus*) and hellebore (*Helleborus*) seed needs such treatment to break dormancy.

SOWING SEED

1 *Fill a seed tray with seed compost. Don't use general purpose compost as this is too rich in nutrients. Water well using a watering can with a fine rose, and allow to drain for around an hour.*

2 *Sow the seed carefully. With larger seed you can place a couple of seeds in each of the cells in a modular tray; smaller seed can be mixed with fine sand to make it easier to spread evenly.*

3 *Unless the seed is of a plant that needs light to stimulate germination, the seed must now be covered. Do this with sieved compost or vermiculite so that all the seed is just covered.*

NATIVES V EXOTICS

While gardens are usually full of imported plant species, native species are often considered to be the best option for the wildlife in your area and the surrounding habitats.

PROBLEMS WITH INTRODUCED PLANTS	ADVANTAGES WITH NATIVE PLANTS
• Many introduced species have short flowering seasons, many of which occur at the same time in high summer to benefit the retail garden trade.	• They tend to be the best for nurturing and supporting wildlife all year, and their flowering times often coincide with the life cycles of native animals.
• Cultivated plants often have flowers unsuited to native pollinators. This is usually because they have large, colourful or double flowers, or because they are native to other countries.	• Most native flowering plants are able to survive only in an area with the appropriate pollinating insects. Their flowers will therefore nearly always be suited to the local species.
• Introduced plants are often the result of intensive breeding programmes, and do not always offer the same advantages for native wildlife when they are used in landscape settings.	• Many native plants are becoming rare due to habitat loss and competition from introduced weeds. Incorporating native plants in landscaping is a small step towards reversing this trend.
• Garden plants can escape and become invasive because they have few species that eat them and control their numbers. This often reduces the biological diversity of surrounding natural areas, as they compete with native species.	• If they escape your garden they cannot become invasive weeds because they are usually kept in check by animals eating them, or through competition from other plant species.
• Cultivated plants often perform poorly away from their native environment, and must have intensive cultivation and care to ensure their survival.	• They are invariably well adapted to the local climatic conditions, having had many generations to shape them into the fittest possible race for the area, and once established, need less intensive care.

DIVISION, CUTTINGS AND LAYERS

Above: *Bulbs, such as these tulips, naturally form offsets that can easily be divided to produce many more plants at no extra cost.*

Most new plants are reproduced from seed or spores. In certain circumstances, however, plants produce offspring in other ways, enabling you to grow new plants quickly and easily from existing stock, and often involving very little specialist equipment. Plants propagated in this way are said to have been propagated "vegetatively" or "asexually", and this is one of the most interesting and rewarding areas of gardening.

VEGETATIVE PROPAGATION

The vegetative parts of the plant are the stems, roots and leaves. In certain circumstances all these parts can be used to produce a new plant, although the ease varies considerably between species. Most fruit trees, for instance, are propagated asexually, using a bud or a twig from a tree that produces exceptionally good fruit. When this bud or twig becomes an adult tree, it has the same qualities as the parent tree and is essentially an identical clone.

BEST PARTS FOR PROPAGATION

Plants may be propagated from many different parts and, in certain species, specialized roots, stems and leaves have a tendency to form new plants, and can be used for propagation.

Rhizomes usually grow underground and, although they appear root-like, are actually horizontal stems that often send out roots and shoots. Stolons are similar to rhizomes, but usually exist above ground level and sprout from an existing stem. Irises and bamboos are common examples of plants propagated from rhizomes and stolons. Runners are similar to stolons but arise from a crown bud and creep over the ground. Good examples include strawberries and spider plants (*Chlorophytum comosum*).

Bulbs, such as tulips (*Tulipa*), onions and lilies (*Lilium*), consist of swollen leaves on a short stem. They are easily propagated from natural offsets that form next to the parent bulb, or from sections of the bulb itself. In some species, such as lilies, individual scales can be separated and propagated. Lilies also produce small bulbils in their leaf axils that will become bulbs if grown for 2–4 years in a rich, light soil. This procedure also applies to plants that form offsets from corms, such as gladioli (*Gladiolus*).

Corms are similar to bulbs and are often confused with them. Structurally, however, a corm is different, consisting of a stem that is swollen as a food store. It is shorter and broader than a bulb. The leaves of the stem are modified as dry, thin membranes that enclose the corm and protect it against injury and drying. Good examples include the crocus and gladioli. True corms are usually propagated from offsets produced by the "parent" plant or from seed.

Tubers are underground swollen stems or roots that store food, such as the potato, used individually to produce new offspring, and generally sold as seed potatoes. Root tubers of the dahlia, cyclamen and anemone can be divided while dormant, provided that each new segment has a bud attached that will form new shoots.

ROOT CUTTINGS

Some plants can be propagated from roots. To produce a new plant from a root cutting, there must be a shoot bud present or it must be possible for the cutting to form one. The ability of root cuttings to form these buds depends on the time of year. The dormant season is usually best with phlox and euphorbia, two examples of plants that can readily be propagated from root cuttings.

The cuttings should be taken from newer root growth, making cuttings 3.5–10cm (1¼–4in) long from roots that are 1–1.5cm

MAKING DIVISIONS

1 *Lift the herbaceous plant as a whole clump and insert two forks into the clump. Prise the clump apart to divide it.*

2 *Work the ground using a fork, and incorporate organic matter at the same time to produce an ideal planting medium.*

3 *Place the divided sections in their final positions before planting them with a spade. Use your heel to firm them in.*

4 *The divided sections quickly establish and fill the space in between. Dividing rejuvenates the plant and encourages growth.*

TAKING CUTTINGS

1 *Fill a seed tray with seed and cutting compost and level this using a flat wooden board. This will ensure that the compost is filled all the way to the brim.*

2 *Prepare your cuttings by taking short sections of the tips and carefully removing the lower leaves as close to the stem as possible, using a sharp knife.*

3 *Insert the prepared cuttings into the compost, making a hole with a narrow stick. Make sure that the leaves do not touch the compost, or they may rot.*

4 *Water with a fine rose on a watering can to firm the cuttings in. Place them in a propagator or on a warm windowsill and cover with a plastic sheet.*

(⅜–½in) in diameter. Cut straight through the end of the root closest to the stem, but cut the other end at a slant. This helps you to remember which end is the top (the straight cut) and which is the bottom. Cuttings taken from dormant roots are placed in a moist rooting medium at 5°C (41°F) for around three weeks before they are planted in small pots. Thereafter, they are kept moist and warm in a bright location to encourage growth until ready to plant out.

STEM PROPAGATION

Many trees, shrubs and herbaceous plants are propagated from stem parts. The two commonest methods are layering and stem cuttings.

The main difficulty involved in producing new plants from stem cuttings is keeping the stems alive while they form new roots. Some stems root better when the wood is soft and growing, others root best from mature wood. Cuttings taken from plants that are actively growing are called softwood cuttings. They are taken from first-year growth that has not yet become woody. Many flowering shrubs are propagated by softwood cuttings, with late spring and early summer being the best times for the majority of species.

Take cuttings 5–10cm (2–4in) long. Larger cuttings produce larger plants sooner, but they are prone to more rapid water loss. Make cuts slightly below a leaf node (the point where the leaf meets the stem) and remove any leaves on the lower section. Insert the cuttings into the compost, making sure that no leaves are touching each other or the compost. Remove any cuttings immediately if they die, and transfer individual, healthy cuttings to small pots once they start growing, following rooting.

Cuttings taken from mature growth are hardwood cuttings, and are taken when the plant is dormant. Cuttings can be taken two weeks after leaf fall but before new buds open next spring. Select healthy wood that was produced the previous summer, about pencil thick, and cut into sections of approximately 15–20cm (6–8in). Several cuttings can often be made from the same branch. The bottom cuts are made just below a node, and the upper cuts slightly above a bud (again, the upper cut should be slanted so that a cutting can't be inserted into the compost upside down).

Bury cuttings vertically in moist, sandy topsoil or sand, leaving 2.5–5cm (1–2in) showing, and put them in a cool, shady place, taking care not to let them freeze. In spring, remove the cuttings from storage and plant at the same depth in pots or open ground, in a sheltered position in dappled shade. Keep them moist until a root system forms, and transplant them the following spring while they are dormant.

LAYERING

Plants that are difficult to root from cuttings can often be propagated by layering. Bend a young, flexible branch down to the soil, peg it down and bend the tip back up, supporting it clear of the ground, and cover the bend with soil. At the point of the bend, roots will form as the bend interferes with the flow of sap. Sap flow can be further reduced by twisting the stem, or cutting a tongue in the lower side of the bark with a sharp knife. The bend will need extra covering through the summer to encourage stem rooting. Plants suited to this method include magnolia and hazel (*Corylus*).

DIVISION

Usually practised only on herbaceous plants, division involves cutting or breaking up a crown or clump of suckers into segments, creating new, vigorous plants. Each segment must have a bud and some roots. The clump is carefully dug up and split with two spades or forks, or is chopped up with a spade or large knife if the clump is firmly massed. Autumn-flowering perennials are commonly divided in spring, while those flowering in spring and summer are best done in autumn. Pot-grown plants can also be divided, with one pot giving rise to many offspring.

Below: *Choosing the right plants from a nursery can help increase your stock. To get value for money, choose crowded pots that are in need of dividing.*

GETTING A CLOSE-UP VIEW

Most gardeners will have at one time lifted a stone to reveal many tiny creatures darting here and there to escape the light. Such sightings are a real thrill and, with a bit of patience, you can get a close look at this whole new world. A good way to start is just to sit quietly and watch birds eat on a feeder, or see the butterflies flit from flower to flower. Many species are very shy, though, and you'll need to hide to get a good view.

Above: *By fitting a wall box with a small solar-powered light, you can see night-flying species as they visit, attracted by the glow.*

WHY CREATURES ARE SHY

Many animals are understandably shy of people because their survival depends on their alertness to danger and potential predators. When you observe a creature you're actually like a predator. You stop, turn your eyes directly on the creature and then slowly move towards it – essentially stalking it. Its first reaction is to assume that it's being hunted and to flee. This sort of flight response is instinctive in many creatures as a result of aeons of evolution, and can be difficult to overcome unless you mask your intentions.

THE FLIGHT RESPONSE

There are many ways that creatures detect the presence of a potential predator. Some will pick up scents, so the wind direction will make a difference, while others have very acute hearing.

Movement is an obvious trigger, especially when it's sudden. Even if you have managed to get close without disturbing a creature, it may well be aware of your presence. A sudden movement may be mistaken for the start of an ambush attack and it'll flee. Even if you stay at a respectful distance and keep still, the effect of binoculars or cameras can prove alarming to many creatures. This is simply because they look like large eyes, and seem closer than they actually are.

TEMPORARY CAPTURE

This is a good way of seeing some creatures, provided you are careful not to cause them harm or distress in the process. Remember that their behaviour can be aggressive if they feel threatened. Wild creatures will become as alarmed when encountering you as they do when meeting a predator.

The most obvious candidates for capture are pond creatures that can be caught and briefly placed in a jar where they can be studied. Small mammals, such as mice and voles, can be captured in a humane trap, but don't keep them in it for long because this will distress them unnecessarily (the traps are "humane" only in the sense that they do not kill the creatures). Never attempt to trap larger animals – even squirrels or rabbits – because they can become quite aggressive when threatened, and they have sharp teeth that can do a lot of damage. Whatever you do catch, the golden rule is to put it back where you found it as soon as possible, and never handle it.

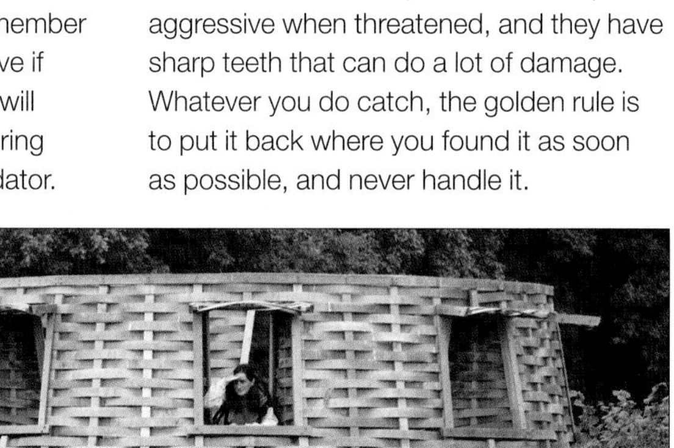

Right: *If you have a very big garden, you could set up a large permanent hide to observe visiting wildlife species without disturbing them.*

POND DIPPING

1 *Move a small-gauge net slowly through the water in a gentle, side-to-side swishing motion for about half a minute.*

2 *For identification, carefully empty the contents of the net into a shallow white bowl containing a little pond water.*

3 *The white background makes a good contrast with the creatures so they can be easily identified using a simple "spotter" guide.*

4 *Don't keep the animals in the tray for too long. Always return them to the water as quickly as possible to minimize stress.*

LURES

To get a close look without capturing a creature, use a lure. Moth traps are an obvious example where a light is placed under a white sheet to attract them. Some bird feeders can be secured to a window by suction cups so that you can observe the birds close up. Indeed, feeding is an excellent way of luring even larger animals close to the house, but never overestimate this trust, and avoid trying to interact with them because they can still be aggressive. And never try to make them tame in case they trust all humans, some of whom might be out to kill them.

SPYING

A hide is really just a tent, albeit one made specially for the purpose, with a small opening for you to watch through. If they cannot see you and you remain quiet, animals will often come amazingly close.

Binoculars or a telescope are an excellent aid, and a night scope can yield amazing results. Smaller aquatic creatures in a drop of pond water can be looked at under a microscope. You will be amazed what else is lurking there.

It's now even possible to look into the homes of some creatures. It's relatively easy to put a small surveillance camera in a nesting box, and these micro cameras send a video link direct to a television monitor. If you get one with infrared lighting it is even possible to see what is happening at night.

The simple rules for watching wildlife are to be quiet, avoid sudden, quick movements, give yourself plenty of time and, most of all, be patient. Binoculars, telescopes and a telephoto lens on your camera will enable you to get a close-up view, and see undisturbed wildlife. Never rush or pursue wildlife, be considerate, and always avoid causing unnecessary stress.

Above: *A nest box can become a wonderful opportunity to observe nature by using "spy-camera" technology inside the structure.*

Limit time spent observing wildlife because encounters with people can alter their normal behaviour. Stay clear of mothers with young, nests or rookeries, and never herd, chase or separate a mother from its young or try to handle the young, even if they appear to be orphans – the mother may well be watching from a safe distance.

MAKING A TEMPORARY HIDE

1 *Making a hide doesn't need specialized equipment – just a large cardboard box, paints, stakes and a little creativity.*

2 *Open out the cardboard box and paint it. The pattern or colour is not important; your body shape will be hidden behind it.*

3 *Preparing the hide can be great fun and is something that the whole family or friends and neighbours can join in with.*

4 *To support the cardboard, drive a few thin stakes into the ground until they are firm enough to support the weight of the hide.*

5 *Hides are traditionally made of dull-coloured material, some with military-style camouflage. In the case of a garden hide, the colour is rarely important. Gardens are often full of extreme contrast, and so why not make a colourful hide that children will love?*

RECORDING WILDLIFE IN YOUR GARDEN

Once you have designed and established your wildlife garden, you'll probably want to know how successful it has been. Making a record of which animals choose to either visit or take up residence is an important way to judge the success of your garden and can be tremendous fun too. The essential thing to remember is that you should be discreet in your activities. Try not to disturb the animals too much.

Above: *Sketching wildlife can be a relaxing hobby and has the added advantage of teaching you to look closely at the creatures.*

TAKING PHOTOGRAPHS

Photographing wildlife can be a frustrating affair because the creatures in question are so elusive and easily frightened. If they aren't startled by your presence, the camera lens often looks like a big eye and timing that perfect shot can be almost impossible. Even easily seen creatures, such as a familiar garden bird, may fail to pose at the right moment. It is simply a matter of patience.

IDENTIFYING SPECIES

Always try to identify the species of wildlife accurately, and in the case of many creatures that's easily done using illustrated books. Some creatures, though, tend to have a large number of species, many of which look quite similar, birds being a good example. If you get a rare visitor it is often difficult to identify it straight away. Always look closely because most creatures have distinctive characteristics, making later identification possible in books or on the Internet. Assume that it is something common until you have any evidence to the contrary.

Above: *Photographs are an ideal way to accurately record the wildlife in your garden, but getting a really good shot can take a lot of practice and patience.*

MAKING NOTES

The easiest and most obvious way to collate any notes is to keep a diary of what you have seen through the year. This has the advantage of helping you to build a picture of what is happening, and you can compare years to see if your garden is gradually attracting more species and to predict what species will turn up at a particular time.

In addition, you could draw up a plan of the garden and mark where you see most species, perhaps extending those areas that are most successful. You could also record which flowers the bees and butterflies prefer, and when particular flowers start to bloom. Adding notes on the weather will flesh out the picture.

DRAWINGS

Even non-artists can gain a lot from trying to draw a creature. The most important technique is to look carefully and take in the detail. You can use simple sketches for basic shapes, and record something of a creature's movement by using sequences of line drawings, as well as studying typical poses, such as a squirrel sitting upright. Details and notes of the eyes, wings, legs and coloration should all be made.

CALLS AND SOUNDS

If a creature is very difficult to see, there might be a good chance that it gives its presence away by a call or sound. Many creatures – birds being a prime example –

Left: *Make notes about the animals you see, paying special attention to the plants they are visiting and the time of day.*

Right: *A large textbook can be cumbersome; a short field guide showing common species is often much more valuable when you are out and about.*

SETTING UP A GARDEN TRANSECT

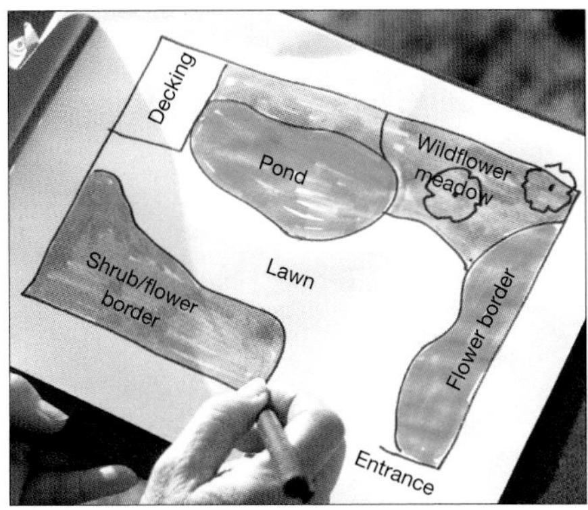

1 *Draw a rough sketch of the area that you intend to keep records on. This needn't be particularly detailed but should show the positions of major habitats in your garden.*

2 *The transect should have several locations where you make observations. Stand still for a few minutes at each and avoid any sudden movements, as this may alarm animals.*

3 *You can always take a portable chair along with you and sit for a set duration of time to record the resident wildlife. Try not to hurry as you might miss some of the shyer creatures.*

communicate using an extensive vocabulary of sounds. These often allow you to identify them without even getting a sighting.

Things are not always as they seem though, and often different sexes have different calls. For example, most people think that the tawny owl goes "twit-twoo". In fact the "twit" (or more accurately "ke-wick") is the female's contact call, and the "twoo" (or more accurately "hoo-hoo-oooo") is the male's territorial call. People assume the "twit-twoo" is one bird when it's actually a conversation between two owls. Learning to recognize the sounds that animals make can take time, but it is a fascinating way to appreciate what is out there without needing to stalk and cause unnecessary stress.

KEEPING RECORDS

Scientists call regular recording sessions that are carried out on a weekly basis using books, binoculars, camera and notebook a "transect". If you want to do the same in your garden, you could simply pick a few different areas around the garden, such as flower borders, shrubs or a woodland edge, and spend five minutes at each place, taking notes about the species seen.

Try to collect similar information each time, including notes on the weather, species seen and which plants they were on, if relevant. Don't forget to add notes about any unusual behaviour or other interesting snippets, sticking in drawings, photographs, feathers, fur, fallen leaves or empty seed cases. All can be kept with information about where and when you found them.

RECORDING A GARDEN TRANSECT

Use a sheet like this to record wildlife in the garden. It is better to choose one species at a time to record. Split the garden into sections and record the different types that visit each section. Record the information on a weekly basis usually from spring through to autumn (and winter if the animals chosen are active in this period). If the records are kept year-on-year you can soon establish if your wildlife numbers are increasing or decreasing, and this will determine if any changes need to be undertaken in your garden to improve the habitat.

Butterfly recording
Temperature: 27°C — Date: 18th July
Wind speed: Slight — Sun/cloud cover: Sunny, no clouds

	Garden sections				
Type of butterfly	**Flower border**	**Wildflower meadow**	**Pond**	**Shrub/ wildflower border**	**Total number**
Small tortoiseshell	III			~~IIII~~	8
Painted lady	I	II			3
Peacock	II			III	5
Comma		I	I		2
Red admiral	III			II	5
Meadow brown		~~IIII~~ IIII	~~IIII~~ ~~IIII~~ I		20
Orange tip		I			1
Small white					0
Large white	II	III	I	II	8
Small copper		~~IIII~~ II	~~IIII~~	I	13
Number of butterflies visiting each section	11	23	18	13	**Total for week** 65

CARING FOR WILDLIFE

While natural habitats can be very rich in wildlife and natural diversity, gardens often lack the space that some of the larger species require. Fortunately, though, our gardens can provide their own set of rich pickings, often in the leaner seasons of winter and early spring, when natural food sources are scarce. By planning your garden carefully, you can provide hibernation and nesting sites and a year-round supply of food. You'll give many species a real boost and, in turn, your garden will also flourish, with natural predators promptly getting rid of any pests.

Left: *A habitat stack is the ultimate in purpose-built accommodation for a range of garden creatures, and is great fun to make.*

Above: *While most butterflies are happy to visit garden flowers for food, a butterfly feeder is a great way to see them close up.*

Above: *Birds naturally suffer food shortages in the winter months. They can be boosted by providing food supplements at this time.*

Above: *Standing deadwood is an extremely important home for many species, while for others it provides shelter or hunting grounds.*

Above: *The bright yellow flowers of this* Tagetes *attract many insects, especially bees, which find pollen and nectar there.*

PLANTS AS FOOD

Food is the single most important element that a wildlife garden must provide. Even the smallest window box on an upstairs balcony can act as a feeding station for passing visitors. If creatures find food, one of their most vital necessities is satisfied and they rarely stray too far from it. The real trick is to ensure there is a supply all year round, and the natural seasonality of plants throws up some interesting challenges and ultimately solutions where feeding wildlife is concerned.

SEASONALITY

When feeding garden wildlife, you need to make sure that you provide food over as long a period as possible, which is why you should try to have some flowering and fruiting plants every month of the year, if possible. Remember, too, that flowers attracting insects will in turn attract predators, such as birds, which may also need to feed.

Winter flowers are useful because they help those few hardy, winter-emerging insects. Late winter is especially important because some species, woken by a mild spell, will not be able to survive until spring without food. You can also stretch the season with annuals – sown in several batches over a few weeks – to add continuity of flower.

FLOWER SHAPE

In general, creatures are attracted to a flower by some reward. Nectar provides an instant source of sugary energy, and pollen is rich in protein. Visiting creatures may eat one or both of them, and the flower is often shaped according to the way in which these visitors feed. As a general rule, flowers that are large and showy, fragrant and nectar-rich, have usually adapted to attract animal pollinators.

These plants, of course, exclude those that have been bred by humans to be large and showy. Double-flowered cultivars often have little in the way of nectar or pollen, and some large-flowered kinds, such as the garden pansy (*Viola* x *wittrockiana*) and its cultivars, have flowers that are so large and slippery that bees cannot easily land on them. In the case of wild pansies, however, they can grip the smaller, more rigid flower and these less showy species are the greatest asset to wildlife.

While there are a number of plant species that attract a whole plethora of creatures, many pollinators have specific preferences as to the types of flower they like to visit. Bees, for example, tend to visit flowers whose petals form a wide surface providing a landing site, whereas butterflies and hummingbirds tend to visit flowers whose petals form a protective cup or tube. Flowers that open at night often target night-flying insects, particularly moths, although certain water lilies (*Nymphaea*) attract night-flying beetles. Some orchids even attract male moths by mimicking the sexual parts of a female moth, while also producing a pheromone-like scent. It follows that you should choose as wide a variety of flower shapes as you can, and always choose those that most resemble the wild form.

Left: *Fruit is an ideal food for a whole range of garden wildlife, including insects, some mammals and especially birds that rely on this seasonal bounty to supplement their diets. This often brings conflicts because fruit, such as this raspberry, is as enticing to them as it is to us. Always ensure that there is enough fruit for birds, and protect "your own".*

FLOWER SCENT

Bees are usually attracted to flowers that are sweetly fragrant and produce nectar. Moths are also attracted to flowers that have a strong, sweet scent, whereas butterflies generally seem to be guided by the colour of the bloom although they, too, are often attracted to sweet scents, especially that of fallen fruit. Flies are a large and complex group with some, such as hoverflies, preferring open, flat composite blooms or umbels. Some specialized flowers, such as those in the arum family, attract carrion-feeding flies or beetles using a foul odour, although the majority of pollinating beetles are attracted to flowers with a spicy smell.

FLOWER COLOUR

While there is no single best colour for a wildlife plant, certain colours do tend to attract better than others. Remember, though, that the colours that you see may not be the same as those seen by a pollinator. Many pollinators see in ultraviolet, as well as the visible spectrum accessible to us, and the best colours for them may be invisible to us. Bees, for example, often favour flowers that are yellow or blue, but most of them have ultraviolet markings that act like landing lines, guiding the bee in to the nectar.

Hummingbirds almost always favour yellow, orange or red blooms with long necks that bear large amounts of nectar. Butterfly-pollinated flowers are also usually brightly coloured, with many species being especially fond of purple or red flowers, whereas those used by moths tend to be yellow or white because colour is not important for night visitors. Beetles also seem less enticed by colour, often favouring white, yellow or dull blooms.

FRUIT AND SEED

Once a plant has flowered, gardeners often remove the dead heads before the seed is set. This prolongs flowering and helps them build up food reserves for next season. It also has the unfortunate consequence of removing a valuable food source for wildlife, particularly during the winter. You can help by not deadheading flowers, and if you choose plants that don't eject or drop the seed as soon as it ripens, when it may germinate or rot in the soil, you can ensure a longer-lasting supply of food. Sunflowers (*Helianthus annuus*), many grasses, cardoons (*Cynara cardunculus*) and globe artichokes are good examples of seed heads which persist into winter.

Since berries are a well-known source of nourishment for garden wildlife, berrying trees and shrubs should be grown wherever possible to help birds and mammals. Try to choose a range of species that have berries over a long period. Spring is the time when there are often fewest available; one shrub that does have berries ripening then is the spotted laurel (*Aucuba japonica*).

SACRIFICIAL OFFERINGS

Any serious wildlife gardener will want to make compromises, either by growing plants that are intended to be eaten by visiting creatures, or by encouraging those we normally regard as weeds. Nettles are a prime example of a plant that can support a wide range of wildlife. The stinging nettle (*Urtica dioica*) has a reputation for providing for many species: 100 species have been recorded on it, though it more usually supports up to 40 species. The best results need a patch around 3m² (32sq ft), but if you have a smaller garden you may want to consider growing the related hop (*Humulus lupulus*). Although it supports fewer species, it's an excellent food plant for many butterflies and moths, takes up much less space and doesn't sting. Ultimately, the real message is not to be too upset if a few of your plants are eaten. It is all part of garden ecology, and you should take comfort in the sight of the vast numbers growing healthily.

TOP ORNAMENTAL PLANTS FOR WILDLIFE

The wealth of wildlife found in a garden is determined by the type of plants selected for it. This panel lists some of the best plants to entice wildlife into an area.

	PLANT NAME	WILDLIFE ATTRACTED
	TREES AND SHRUBS	
	Butterfly bush (*Buddleja davidii*)	An excellent plant for butterflies and other nectar-feeders, including bees and moths. Can self-seed and become invasive.
	Crab apple (*Malus*, especially *M. sylvestris*)	All apples are excellent for wildlife, especially older specimens with deeply creviced bark. Bees visit the flowers in spring; many species feed on the fruit in autumn.
	Lavender (*Lavandula angustifolia*)	The scented blooms attract many different species of bee and bumblebee, as well as several species of butterflies.
	Rosemary (*Rosmarinus officinalis*)	Almost unrivalled in its ability to attract honeybees, butterflies and hoverflies, all attracted by the copious nectar.
	Rowan (*Sorbus aucuparia*)	The flowers are great for feeding bees and other insects in spring; the berries are consumed by many bird species.
	CLIMBERS	
	Golden hop (*Humulus lupulus* 'Aurea')	Caterpillars of several butterflies and moths feed on the foliage, which also attracts other leaf-feeding insects and their predators.
	Honeysuckle (*Lonicera periclymenum*)	Bumblebees, and especially moths, are attracted to the flowers in the evening. Fruit-eating birds take the berries.
	HERBACEOUS PLANTS AND ANNUALS	
	Borage (*Borago officinalis*)	Attracts bees when in full bloom due to the abundant nectar. Readily self-seeds and is at home on dry or stony soil, in full sun.
	California poppy (*Eschscholzia californica*)	Attracts hoverflies, bees and bumblebees. Once sown, will self-seed freely around the garden.
	Fern-leaved yarrow (*Achillea filipendula*)	An abundance of hoverflies can be found "nectaring" on the flowers in summer. Also attracts bees and bumblebees.
	Honeywort (*Cerinthe major* 'Purpurascens')	Bees love the blue flowers and congregate in vast numbers. Readily self-seeds, eventually creating large colonies. Loves hot, sunny borders.
	Ice plant (*Sedum spectabile*)	Sedums are loved by butterflies, bees and hoverflies because they're a valuable, late summer source of nectar.
	Michaelmas daisy (*Aster novi-belgii*)	In late summer and autumn, butterflies and bees visit the flowers. Birds also eat the seed after ripening.
	Miss Willmott's ghost (*Eryngium giganteum*)	Extremely attractive to many species of bee and bumblebee during its long flowering period from early to late summer.
	Red valerian (*Centranthus ruber*)	One of the best flowers for butterflies. Rapidly spreads via seed, and can become invasive if not kept in check.
	Summer phlox (*Phlox paniculata*)	Attracts large numbers of various nectar-feeding adult butterflies and moths from late summer to early autumn.
	Sunflower (*Helianthus annuus*)	Birds, such as greenfinches and bullfinches, eat the seeds. Also visited by honeybees and bumblebees when in flower.
	Tall verbena (*Verbena bonariensis*)	Attracts a whole host of butterflies, moths and hummingbirds. It self-seeds easily, with seedlings flowering the same year.
	BOG GARDEN AND WATER PLANTS	
	Hemp agrimony (*Eupatorium cannabinum*)	Attracts butterflies and bees. As well as looking fantastic, this plant is one of the best at providing adult butterflies with nectar.
	Water lily (*Nymphaea alba*; one of many superb nymphaeas)	Adult frogs and dragonflies like to bask on the floating oval leaves, which also provide cover for tadpoles that swarm below the surface of the water.

PROVIDING EXTRA FOOD

Cold winters and hot summers can be harsh times for garden creatures for a variety of reasons, and the extremes of temperature often cause intense physical strain to all the creatures within the habitat. Food shortages can occur at such times because insects, fruit or flowers might become scarce during extreme weather. You can help wildlife by providing some extra food, enabling them to endure these lean times.

Above: *A live-food feeder can help a variety of birds that rely on live prey to feed their young. Use them in spring and early summer.*

LIMITED NATURAL FOOD SOURCES

During harsh times of the year, many garden creatures either hibernate or migrate to a better climate and, in so doing, avoid seasonal food shortages. This particularly helps creatures that have specific dietary needs. Hibernating species often emerge in times of relative plenty, but for those species that remain active for the whole year, there are times of extreme hunger, as well as times of surplus. As one group of migratory species leaves the garden to seek food elsewhere, others often migrate into the garden and take their place, so there is no reason why your garden should not be full of life all year round.

The hardest time for most year-round garden residents is during the autumn and winter. Natural foods are still available in the form of berries, seed heads and a few late surviving insects but, as winter really begins to bite, food demands become more pressing as non-hibernating creatures compete for the dwindling natural resources. Their plight is not helped by the fact that many creatures enlarge their foraging areas, and conflicts may arise when new individuals enter the garden in search of food.

Below: *Natural food, such as these rowan berries (*Sorbus aucuparia*), is always the best option, but seasonal shortages may necessitate additional feeding.*

Above: *Millet bunches hung in the branches of trees and shrubs can help overwintering birds, which will be attracted to the seeds.*

For all the creatures in a garden, additional food can be a lifeline. Not only are you helping the ones that have been present all summer but a wider community, including migratory birds, which may have travelled thousands of miles to be there.

THE BEST FOOD

When deciding which animals to feed, remember that by habituating any wild animal to food in your garden, you are making that place an important part of its territory. Also that all the animals in your garden (save domestic pets) are still wild and, as such, may behave aggressively if they feel threatened. Even small creatures, such as squirrels, have been known to be highly aggressive once the fear of humans is lost, and you must weigh up the chances of any conflicts before you commence feeding.

As a rule, most mammals are perfectly capable of finding the food they need although some, especially those living in urban areas, will benefit greatly from any additional nourishment that you can provide. If you do decide to supplement their diet, the amount should be limited and targeted for times when their natural food sources are scarce.

Badgers, for example, benefit from additional feeding in the drier months or when the ground is frozen. They are naturally omnivorous and will often eat worms and insects as well as plant material and fruit. They do not hibernate, and the winter can be harsh as food is often scarce. They can be fed small amounts of canned, cereal-based dog food with lightly cooked meat, cheese, peanuts and fruit. Such supplements can help badger cubs survive harsh summer conditions, and it is a good way to entice them to an area where you can watch them. But remember that encouraging badgers into your garden can be a mixed blessing because their natural digging and foraging can be very destructive. And if they extend their territory into your garden, they may come into conflict with domestic pets, and, being large, strong and potentially ferocious, can cause serious injuries.

Some gardeners love to feed squirrels, whereas others resent their habit of stealing bird food and their occasional habit of damaging trees. They do not hibernate, and although they will hide snugly in their drey in really cold spells, they remain active for the whole year. In fact, giving them their own food may actually reduce the incidences of damaging behaviour – since this is usually associated with food shortage – and dissuade them from bothering the bird feeders.

Place food away from windowsills or doorways so as to discourage them from coming into the house, or becoming too familiar with people. No matter how tempting it may be, you should not feed them from the hand or they'll start to associate people with food. And despite their innocent and cuddly look, they can become quite aggressive and inflict a very painful bite. Place their feeding stations away from those for the birds, and consider using a purpose-made squirrel feeder that will not attract birds.

Hedgehogs are one garden visitor that few of us have any qualms about feeding, being non-aggressive, beneficial and the perfect guest. They have a varied diet, and you can encourage them to visit by providing them with dog food mixed with biscuits, or even by providing a specialist dried hedgehog food (any food should always be accompanied by fresh drinking water). While they do hibernate in winter, they are active when the conditions are mild enough to favour their prey – insects, slugs and other invertebrates – and you should only stop feeding them when it is really cold.

WHEN TO FEED WILDLIFE

Winter is the best time to feed because that's when food is scarce. Many mammals that live in gardens all year round are omnivores, and extra food is a good way of ensuring that they are healthy for the following spring. Remember that many birds and some smaller mammals principally visit gardens in the winter to exploit the diversity of food available in this varied habitat.

Above: *A simple butterfly feeder made from a wooden frame contains a sponge soaked with sugar water to tempt insects to feed.*

MAKING A BUTTERFLY FEEDER

1 *Butterflies normally find enough food in flowers, but they will readily feast on ripe fruit and fruit juices.*

2 *Suspend a shallow dish on thin chains and place a range of chopped fruit pieces in the dish.*

3 *To prevent drying out in warm weather, soak the fruit in some fruit juice to keep it moist and release the sugars.*

Gardens are often quieter in the colder months, also making them an ideal retreat. Take stock of what is visiting and feed accordingly.

Spring is a time of seeming plenty but, for many creatures, it can be a hungry gap. While everything is stirring into life, many creatures start their annual cycle of breeding and raising young, adding to the demands of collecting food. Remember that if you have been feeding creatures through winter, more of them survive and demands on natural sources may be temporarily excessive. Keep feeding through spring, judging the demand and reducing the amounts as conditions improve.

Summer is the time when you should provide very little food, except to try to attract more interesting species. Butterflies are best provided with flower nectar, but can be encouraged to visit a purpose-made feeder.

Autumn sees the whole cycle recommence. Gradually reintroduce feeding for your active winter residents, but don't forget about the hibernating species as they need to build up their strength for the coming winter too.

PROVIDING EXTRA FOOD

Whilst wild animals are instinctively very adept at finding food from natural sources, they might well appreciate a bit of help, especially in the winter months.

Pet food Providing a small amount of pet food mixed with water is often an ideal supplement for hedgehogs, foxes and badgers, etc. Only leave a small amount, removing and replacing it daily so that it doesn't go off.

Live food Some species only ever take live food and, while this is difficult to provide in the case of larger animals, small garden visitors, such as songbirds, relish this valuable supplement. Mealworms are ideal and are easily purchased.

Leftovers Kitchen leftovers, such as cake, cooked rice or other natural food items, are generally fine for most wildlife species. Fat drawn from roasted or grilled (broiled) meat is excellent. Avoid any spicy, salty foods, or items that have gone off.

Bought items These include peanuts, raisins and purpose-made foodstuffs formulated for particular species. The latter are usually excellent but can be quite costly. However, they are designed for specific dietary needs and do save a lot of time.

Hedgehog food

Mealworms

Cooked rice

Peanuts and raisins

BIRD FEEDERS

Even a well-stocked garden can be a harsh and unforgiving place for wildlife as the winter draws in. Late autumn marks the time when many birds will visit your garden, seeking extra supplies of food. These birds are welcome visitors, since they add much-needed life and colour as the days grow darker. But feeding can be beneficial throughout the year, especially in spring when the young are born and adults must find even more food to feed their growing families.

Above: *Small perching birds are able to take advantage of hanging bird feeders, safe from competition from larger birds.*

WHY BIRDS NEED EXTRA FOOD

By supplementing bird diets with extra food, you are arguably maintaining a falsely high population of birds in your garden but this, in turn, helps some species to survive when their natural habitats have disappeared. It is therefore important that you keep feeding once you have started because the birds will soon come to depend on it. By choosing the right foods, and offering them in different bird feeders around the garden, you can attract a wide range of species.

POSITIONING BIRD FEEDERS

Different species of birds have different feeding habits. Hanging food is ideal for members of the tit family, placed high enough up so that cats can't get at it. If the food is too exposed, however, the birds may be in danger from sparrowhawks, unless there is nearby cover, such as trees and hedges. Avoid placing feeders near bird boxes because the numbers of attracted birds can put off nesting parents.

The bird tables sold in many garden centres are frequently more ornamental than functional, but have the benefit of being off the ground, thereby reducing the chances of other foraging animals, such as mice and rats, getting at the food. A bird table with a roof can help to keep rain off, but is not essential. The simplest design is usually the best, and often proves to be the easiest to clean and maintain.

DIFFERENT FEEDERS

By using a wide range of bird feeders, you can provide a greater variety of food items. In doing this, you will increase the chances of more species visiting your garden.

Bird feeder table – spring Bird tables are excellent for a range of larger birds that perch or stand in order to eat their food.

Buzzard table Not really an option for most gardens, although congregating birds often attract predatory birds that may feed on them.

Glass/plastic feeder – spring Glass or plastic feeders are usually filled with mixed seed, made accessible through a series of small hoppers in the side.

Half a coconut – spring (or any time) A coconut sliced in two is an excellent way of providing food for small, clinging birds. Can be filled with suet or seeds.

Squirrel-proof feeder To discourage squirrels, make bird food inaccessible. This feeder has a cage to protect the seed.

Wire feeder – spring Wire feeders are mostly for peanuts, and are useful because they prevent birds from choking on whole nuts.

Buzzard table

Glass feeder

Half a coconut

Squirrel-proof feeder

Some birds readily forage on the ground, and a few actually prefer this. Putting food on the lawn – away from shrubs that can be hiding places for predators – will favour these species. Don't put too much out at once because this encourages rats and mice, and avoid using the same patch repeatedly so as to reduce the risk of disease.

DRINKING SUPPLY

Maintain a reasonably clean water supply at all times, ideally in shallow containers for the birds to use for bathing as well as drinking. Never add salt or any chemicals to the water, even if there is a tendency for it to turn green. If it does, change the water regularly, cleaning the container and placing it out of direct sunlight wherever possible. A garden pond with shallow areas can also be useful, but a bird bath has the advantage that you can change the water regularly to ensure that the risk of disease is minimized. Water is especially welcome on a cold, frosty morning when natural supplies may be frozen. If a bird bath is on the ground, other animals, such as hedgehogs, can also drink from it.

GIVE BIRDS VARIETY

Birds, like many wild creatures, enjoy a range of food, much of which is easy to obtain. In certain cases this can be leftovers, although this can be a variable commodity so don't solely rely on it. Seed, such as black sunflower seed, peanuts or the wild seed mixes sold for the purpose, is useful and can easily be supplemented with such items as pinhead oatmeal or porridge oats, sultanas, shredded suet and toasted breadcrumbs. Other popular items for the bird table include canned sweetcorn and fresh fruit, broken (not cut) into pieces.

The more different food types can be left in different positions and types of feeder, the better. Whole peanuts are best avoided

MAKING A BIRD FEEDING STATION

1 *Start by choosing a range of glass/plastic, wire, cage and open feeders that will support a wide variety of bird species.*

2 *Either use an existing dead tree or insert a couple of large branches firmly into the ground to act as supports for your feeders.*

3 *Securely attach the feeders to the branches using thin, pliable wire, twisted around the branches or old branch stumps.*

4 *Once you have hung the feeders, check to see which get used. If some remain unused, replace them with more popular types.*

during the nesting season because they can choke young nestlings. They should be chopped, if left on a table, or placed in a mesh peanut feeder from which adult birds can take only small fragments. Always avoid using any form of dried food, such as uncooked rice or dried bread, because this will swell in a bird's stomach and can even be fatal.

Some birds, robins in particular, can benefit from supplements of live food, such as mealworms, particularly during the late winter period when food is scarce and their breeding cycle commences. The worms can easily be purchased from pet shops or by mail order, and can be placed on tables or in specialist feeders. Whatever you decide to place out for the birds, make sure that you stick to natural foods, rather than chemically altered or processed items, such as margarine.

KEEP IT FRESH AND CLEAN

Only leave out as much food as can be consumed in a day or two, and never allow food or feeding debris to accumulate because it can rapidly spread disease.

DIFFERENT TYPES OF FOOD/SEED

The variety of seed and other food supplements available for birds has increased vastly in the last few years and all of these have their own merits and will be preferred by different species, according to their dietary and feeding preferences.

Black sunflower seed More commonly known as the "oil sunflower", this seed – as its name suggests – is rich in oil and ideal for winter-feeding a range of garden birds.

Coconut fat Half coconuts are ideal for filling with a mixture of suet – rendered animal fat – seed and other dried foodstuffs that suit clinging feeders such as tits.

Dried mealworms These freeze-dried grubs are an excellent source of protein for carnivorous birds.

Fat ball A ball of suet into which other dried foodstuffs have been incorporated. It is usually hung in nets or special feeders.

Fruit suet treats Mainly for bird tables or hanging feeders, this suet-based cake is best made with moist, dried fruit and peanut granules, and is popular with larger birds.

Grain Consists of any commercially grown crops in the grass family, including wheat, millet, maize and oats.

Mixed seed Consists of various seed types for a wide range of birds, and is often of variable quality.

Niger Sometimes called thistle seed, this tiny black birdseed, cultivated in Asia and Africa, is high in calories and oil content, and is quickly devoured, especially by finches.

Scraps A variable commodity, and best included only as extra titbits. Avoid dried foodstuffs that can swell in the stomach; also spicy or over-processed items.

Striped sunflower seed Has a lower oil content than the black variety, and is useful in the spring when natural foods become more abundant.

Suet cake This block type of suet food is used on a table, and contains a seed mix that provides a balanced diet for many species. It is ideal for feeding birds when you are away, although the fat content can sometimes attract scavenging mammals, such as rats, to a table.

Black sunflower seed

Fat ball

Fruit suet treats

Mixed seed

Niger

Suet cake

Above: *Flowers such as this aubretia are useful for attracting early aphids that in turn allow predator numbers to increase.*

FEEDING BENEFICIAL CREATURES

In any garden, pests will proliferate if we don't maintain the balance of nature. But for every pest, a natural predator exists. By encouraging these predators, unwanted species can be controlled, but be prepared to give the predators a helping hand to get them started. If pest numbers get too high, the predators might not easily control them. By giving predators an early boost, you can improve their chances of reducing the pests.

WHY FEED BENEFICIAL CREATURES?

The balance of nature is a cycle whereby different populations rise and fall in direct relationship to the abundance of food. Creatures that hunt widely for dispersed food will need a large territory to satisfy their needs, and creatures that feed on more abundant species will, of course, become more abundant themselves. In the garden, we want to ensure that certain creatures are present to control predators, and if we can feed them, they are more likely to flourish and stay where we want them.

Many beneficial species can be given a boost by providing some form of supplementary feeding to increase their numbers early in the year, or quite simply to attract them to the garden. Once there, they are able to begin eating pests, and feeding them means that seasonal fluctuations in their numbers can be avoided. In a small, enclosed garden, for example, it would be quite easy for a hedgehog to be trapped and run out of food. By feeding it, you help it through hungry periods and maintain its useful presence. Equally, some insects, such as ladybirds, can be helped with an artificial food supplement hung in the garden in a special feeder. It attracts and nourishes these useful beetles, and enables them to maintain a high population early in the season. By feeding them, you are maintaining an artificially high number of these useful creatures, and consequently will reduce numbers of their prey.

Below: *Hedgehogs are excellent pest-controlling animals, and can benefit from a supplement of dried mixed seed and wax-worms in the spring.*

Many beneficial insects have different needs depending upon their life stage, and a surprising number eat pests when they are larvae but are partly or wholly vegetarian as adults. Plants can be chosen to feed the adults and even to attract their (or their offspring's) prey. To maintain a variety of beneficial insects, then, you will need to make provisions for all these stages. The simplest approach is to maintain a diverse habitat. The more varied your garden is, the more species you will maintain and ultimately, the more beneficial creatures there will be.

Finally, note that the term "beneficial creature" is really only of particular relevance to gardeners. All garden creatures have some benefit, and it is up to us to recognize what these are, and to seek a balance, according to the needs of our own garden.

FOOD SOURCES

Each species of beneficial insect has its own particular diet, and that may change according to availability or which life stage it is passing through. Some, such as lacewings or hedgehogs, are generalists, feeding on several different species, while others, like hoverfly maggots, exclusively eat aphids and therefore have a specialized diet.

In the case of more general feeders, the garden often contains several alternative kinds of prey. This, of course, increases the chance that the hunters will stay in the garden and perhaps breed there. Specialists, on the other hand, such as ladybirds, will fly away if there are not enough small, soft-bodied insects – such as aphids and scale insects – to support them and, especially, their voracious larvae.

It is a simple fact of life. If you want to encourage predators to take up residence then you first have to encourage their prey – the very pests you want to get rid of.

TOLERATING SOME DAMAGE

While pests sometimes eat more of our garden plants than we would like, a healthy garden has a balanced ecosystem, with severe outbreaks of problem creatures being mercifully rare. As a wildlife gardener, you must learn to accept some level of damage to many of your plants. A few holes in some of the leaves or flowers won't make

MAKING A LADYBIRD FEEDER

1 *Ladybird feeders are relatively simple constructions, consisting of a length of bamboo cut at angles so there is a "long side", some ordinary garden twine and a feeding compound.*

2 *Slightly moisten the food block (bought from a specialist supplier) and break it up so that it forms a spreadable paste, by lightly working it between your fingers until soft.*

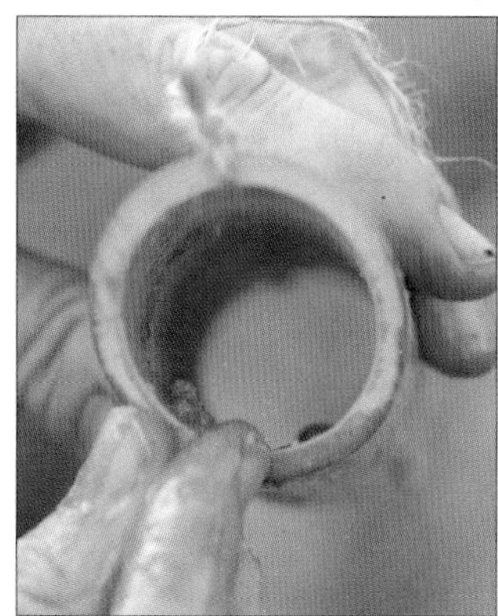

3 *Smear the mixture on to the inside of the feeder, putting it on the shorter side that will hang lowermost on the feeder. Spread it evenly on the bottom and sides of the inside surface.*

4 *Hang the feeder on a piece of twine with the long side uppermost to keep out the rain and preserve the food paste. Hang it in light shade in an out-of-the-way corner.*

them less attractive or useful. Don't be blinded by advertisements and their promise of blemish-free plants. Nature isn't like that.

PLANTING TO ATTRACT "BENEFICIALS"

Many flowering plants will attract the vegetarian adults of beneficial insects whose larvae are predators of pests. The adults need to feed upon the nectar or pollen, and attracting them is a vital first step in encouraging them to mate and lay eggs so that the larvae can start eating the pests. The poached egg plant (*Limnanthes douglasii*) attracts large numbers of hoverflies, and various parasitoid wasps will be attracted if you plant white alyssum (*Lobularia maritima*). Both hoverflies and wasps are dependent on proteins from pollen and carbohydrates from nectar because of their active lifestyle, and to form their eggs.

Korean licorice mint (*Agastache*), feverfew (*Tanacetum parthenium*), pot marigold (*Calendula officinalis*) and yarrow (*Achillea millefolium*) are also excellent at attracting a wide range of creatures, including the "beneficials". The best results are gained when you plant them on the edges of a border or bed in a sunny spot.

Ladybirds and some other beneficial insects will even lay their eggs on some plant species in the absence of aphids. The best plants for such egg-laying are stinging nettles (*Urtica dioica*), ivy (*Hedera*), gorse (*Ulex*) and hawthorn (*Crataegus*), as well as umbelliferous herbs such as angelica, chervil (*Anthriscus cerefolium*), parsley (*Petroselinum*) or coriander (*Coriandrum*).

Other plants are valuable because they harbour pests, and act as a larder for predators. Nasturtium (*Tropaeolum majus*) is one such example that is practically guaranteed to attract aphids before the surrounding plants. Aubretia (*Aubrieta*) and nettles are especially useful because they attract some of the earliest aphids, and enable the army of "beneficials" to get an early season feed. Remember also that many bird species eat aphids or larger pests, such as caterpillars, and by planting seed-bearing annuals, native trees and hedges you can enjoy the benefit of their efforts in spring and summer.

Finally, don't be in too much of a rush to tidy the garden in early winter. Excessive trimming of hedges and cutting back of herbaceous plants means that there will be nowhere for the beneficial insects to shelter. Even when you do clear up, don't burn any garden waste unless it is diseased because it may carry the eggs and pupae of overwintering beneficial insects.

Below: *The white alyssum,* Lobularia maritima, *is a superb plant for attracting highly beneficial parasitic wasp species that flock to feed on the flowers.*

PROVIDING NATURAL SHELTER

Shelter is essential if wildlife is to hide from the elements and predators, and many creatures also need cover for nesting. There are many different types of natural shelter, and some can easily be recreated in the garden. The best kinds are those made of natural materials, especially if they are the by-products of other garden tasks, since they will blend in with the surroundings and will not cost you anything.

Above: *A pile of logs is a great hiding or sheltering place for many creatures, especially if it is situated near a food source.*

THE BEST KINDS OF SHELTER

Top of the list come natural forms of shelter. Every part of most natural habitats supports a range of creatures, many of which have specific adaptations enabling them to live there. Fortunately, many of the natural shelters found in the wild can be recreated in the garden.

The first thing to remember is that decay is an essential natural process by which nutrients are cycled and recycled thanks to a whole host of species. If your garden contains a lot of plants, then you will be familiar with the amounts of green waste produced over the year, with one of the most useful habitat-forming materials being deadwood. It provides food and shelter for hundreds of species, including many that eat it or live within its confines. In addition, thicker branches may be used to create specific habitats such as log piles or log pyramids. Building a log pile is quick and easy, and you can make a real five-star habitat by carefully constructing your pile.

LOG PILES

If you have a limited amount of space, just pile up a few old logs or stumps, and partially cover them with leaves and smaller brushwood in an out-of-the-way corner. If you have enough space, though, you could consider making a log-pile hotel. Start by making the base out of six or eight large, untreated logs, ideally with the bark still on, 1.8–3m (6–10ft) long and 10–15cm (4–6in) in diameter. Stack them so that they are stable, with a variety of runways and spaces between to allow access for larger creatures. Once you have finished the base, add large branches criss-crossed to cover the logs. Continue adding more branches of a gradually smaller diameter so that you end up with a domed structure about 1.2–1.5m (4–5ft) high. If you want a smaller pile, just reduce the dimensions accordingly, but try to keep the thickness of the base logs the same. Ideally you should place your log pile between two habitats, and make sure that at least half of it receives direct sunlight.

You can enhance the pile by adding piles of flat stones along the edges to serve as basking sites and tight crevices, and planting some native plants around it to soften its appearance. Remember not to destroy fruiting bodies of toadstools that spring up around the pile as they often harbour dozens of rare insects.

OTHER HABITATS

Standing deadwood is another important habitat that, if it cannot be left on the tree, can be recreated. You can recreate some of its benefits by making a log pyramid. Stand a series of logs of varying thickness in a hole, dug some 30–45cm (12–18in) deep. Leave from one-third to one-half their lengths out of the ground. Fill in around them with the excavated soil, and pile this higher on one side. Plant some native plants around it to soften its appearance, and give additional shelter for other wildlife. Try drilling holes in some of the logs to provide homes for solitary bees.

Left: *Tree bark naturally becomes fissured and gnarled, creating many tiny nooks and crannies for small creatures to hide in.*

Above: *Vegetation is always an excellent source of shelter. A dense planting of grasses and flowers will protect many creatures.*

TIPS ON PROVIDING SHELTER

Providing shelter is an essential part of any wildlife garden and can be done quite simply using a range of naturally occurring materials that are readily available.

Plant a variety of shrubs, trees and herbaceous plants Some bird species may find them attractive as nesting sites, but even if they nest elsewhere, these plants will attract birds, albeit for only a few minutes.

Large evergreen shrubs They provide winter shelter for many species. Low-growing evergreen plants are ideal for small animals, such as shrews, which stay active all year round.

Grass cuttings Left in heaps in a sunny spot, these attract reptiles, such as grass snakes, which use them for egg-laying or as a warm hideout on cool nights.

Mounds Use unwanted rubble to build a stone and earth mound – great for hibernating newts and lizards. Smear yogurt on the rocks to encourage lichens.

Old logs Drill holes in these for solitary bees or place by a pond for an egg-laying site for some dragonflies. Many creatures will hide inside the decaying wood.

Rocks and twigs These provide shelter for ground-dwelling species, including toads and voles, which enjoy hiding in small crevices or under decaying logs or stumps. A length of drain or tubular material provides protection from predators and the weather.

Cotoneaster

Old logs

Rocks

Twigs

Herbaceous plants are ideal for close planting and provide plenty of cover. This type of planting is helpful to a variety of species, including many insects as well as the creatures that prey upon them, such as shrews and hedgehogs. If the ground is thickly covered with plants, the insect numbers increase, and the plant debris makes useful hibernation sites.

Lawns can also be an excellent habitat, particularly when left to grow long. Many animals, including insects, spiders, toads, frogs, slow worms and small mammals, find cover in areas of long grass throughout the summer months. The grass gives them places to feed, hide from predators and nest. Wait until midwinter before you cut the grass, raking off cuttings and composting them. To add interest, you can try planting late flowering grassland plants in these areas.

Water and poolside planting provides good habitats for aquatic creatures, and also cover for any creatures that are approaching and leaving the pool. If you don't have space for a pond, provide a birdbath or shallow pool, and keep it filled all year round, letting birds drink there and restore their plumage.

Mulch and litter layers covering soil serve as a protected habitat for ground-dwelling creatures, including larger insects, amphibians and some reptiles, which can sometimes be seen basking on mulched surfaces. These are unable to thrive if the soil is regularly cultivated. While cultivating the soil has obvious advantages in terms of growing certain plants, leaving some areas undisturbed has tremendous benefits for these creatures, many of which are useful predators. Not cultivating all your ground at once, and leaving undisturbed areas as wildlife refuges is the best solution, although a hedge bottom or well-mulched shrub border is very useful.

All trees and shrubs are also very beneficial, and support a rich population of invertebrates and larger animals. Evergreen plants are especially good for providing cover all year, and provide all-round structure in the garden. Climbers are a favourite nesting site because the supporting wall on one side and camouflage of leaves on the other provides safe protection. Remember to include some thorny shrubs, such as barberry, pyracantha, mahonia and roses, which offer hide-aways and nesting sites.

MAKING A LOG PILE

1 *Begin by digging out a shallow pit to a depth of around 30cm (1ft) in a shady spot where creatures will not be disturbed, preferably in a shrub bed or under a tree.*

2 *It is best to use a range of logs that are different ages. Arrange some of them in the pit, putting the thickest ones at the base and building up with smaller ones.*

3 *Fill the spaces between the logs with the excavated soil and pile some up around the edges. Wood chips could also be used.*

4 *Cover the finished pile in leaves, twigs and old litter. You could plant ferns or ivies to soften the appearance of the log pile.*

CONSTRUCTING EXTRA SHELTERS

We cannot pick and choose which creatures enter our gardens – they choose us – but we can definitely maximize the possibilities and opportunities for them. The best policy is to provide shelter for those creatures that you know are nearby. Find out what is in your area by talking to neighbours or asking local wildlife groups; provide the appropriate accommodation and wait to see if those creatures take up residence.

Above: *A bat box in a sheltered, shady spot in the garden can act as a temporary resting place for these night-flying predators.*

NESTING AND BIRD BOXES

It is never the wrong time to create nesting places, and even if it's not immediately used by the intended creature, it will almost certainly be used by some form of wildlife. Remember that nest boxes may be used by one species at a certain time of year, and by another in a different season. Many summer roosting or nest boxes, for example, are used as winter hibernacula (hibernating sites), being vacated in early spring before the summer residents return.

As many gardens lack natural types of shelter for wildlife, the best way to help creatures is to provide them with an artificial substitute. There are many types to choose from that can either be bought ready made or created at home. Over time, and as your garden habitat improves and diversifies, you may need to increase their numbers according to the needs of the wildlife.

The majority of shelters are essentially boxes mimicking natural crevices in trees that have often disappeared due to human management of forests and woodlands. The relative importance of cavities and crevices varies according to which country you are in. The total number of Australian animals that use tree hollows, for example, is around three times greater than in North America, and twice as great as in South Africa. In situations where hollows are important but in short supply, expect many species to try and take up residence in the boxes provided. The greater the range of sizes and shapes of these artificial crevices, the greater the number of species that might reside in your garden.

Above: *A toad house placed near water can be an ideal sheltering spot for these useful garden amphibians in daylight hours. Hide it among vegetation to keep it cool.*

Below: *A butterfly roosting house provides safe, dry shelter for these beautiful insects. Put verbena or buddleja inside to attract them.*

CUSTOM-MADE SHELTERS

Until recently, if someone talked about providing boxes in the garden, they'd almost certainly have been thinking of birds. The last few years, however, has seen a surge in interest in the provision of homes for other creatures, and gardeners are now providing breeding and shelter sites for a wide range of animals, including insects, amphibians and mammals. Examples include nest boxes for mason bees, bumblebees, bats and hedgehogs, as well as shelters for ladybirds, lacewings and other insects. Some gardeners prefer the designed look of commercially produced shelters and nest boxes but, if your budget is tight, or you prefer the more rustic look, you can easily make your own.

DIY

While an ever-expanding array of nest boxes is now available, most are very easy to make and require only the simplest tools and equipment. All the facilities found in the more expensive shelters and nest boxes can be provided in other ways. For example, a good hibernating or breeding shelter for hedgehogs can be made by piling up dry leaves in a quiet corner, and leaning a sheet of plywood over it to keep off the worst of the rain.

Shelter for insects and other invertebrates can be made in dozens of simple ways, for example by drilling holes of different sizes into a piece of hardwood and leaving it undisturbed in a sunny corner of the garden, or try a bundle of hollow stems or canes, placed in a pipe, and left in a quiet hot spot. Minimum disturbance is essential.

LACEWING HOTELS

One of the easiest shelters to make is a lacewing "hotel", helping these creatures – whose larvae are voracious predators of aphids – hibernate in large numbers, ensuring that there are always plenty of them. From late summer on they are looking for shelter for the coming cooler months.

Simply cut the base off a large plastic drinks bottle using a pair of scissors, and keep the lid on. Roll up a length of about 1m (3½ft) of corrugated cardboard so it fits loosely inside the bottle, and trim so that it doesn't poke out. Then push a piece of wire through the bottle sides and across the bottom to stop the cardboard falling out, and bend the ends round to keep it in place. Now hang it up using a piece of strong string tied around the neck of the bottle, and place it in a tree, shrub, hedge, or against a fence covered by climbing plants. A particularly good site is near an outside light or lit window. To help attract visitors, spray the cardboard with a widely available pheromone liquid. You can put the "hotel" in a shed from mid-autumn to late winter in frosty areas, otherwise leave it alone.

Above: *This lacewing hotel is a hibernation site for these useful garden predators. It can be taken down and stored in a shed over winter and put out again in spring.*

Above: *Bat boxes fixed to trees should be placed in threes on all but the sunniest side, because bats change their roosting preferences through the year.*

BEE BOXES

Solitary bee boxes are also easy to make and can be very simply made, involving nothing more than a few canes or hollow stems. If you are using bamboo canes, you will need six or seven approximately 6–10mm (¼–⅜in) wide; cut them into pieces about 15cm (6in) long, avoiding any knots in the cane. Then gather them into a circular bundle, and tie them firmly together in two places with wire, garden string or twine, twisting it tight. Alternatively, put them inside an old can. Hang the bundle at about eye-level at a slight angle so that the entrance holes are slightly lower than the opposite end, in a sheltered, sunny spot, for example under the eaves of a garden shed.

Lastly, remember that this construct may well become home for other unexpected residents. Nature is no respecter of your intentions. If another creature wants to live there, it will. Some bumblebees, for example, will nest in bird boxes and, although they are very docile, may sting if threatened, so never evict any residents.

MAKING A SOLITARY BEE NESTING BOX

1 *Using an old can (making sure there are no sharp edges) or similar food container, paint the outside to help prevent rusting in wet weather as it ages.*

2 *Cut some old bamboo canes to the approximate length of the can using a fine-toothed saw or a pair of very sharp secateurs. Discard any split ones.*

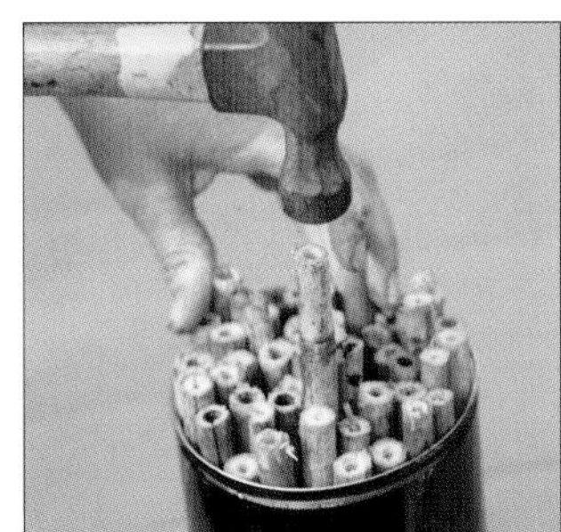

3 *Place the cut canes into the can and pack them in. Use a hammer to bang the last few in tightly, thereby avoiding glue, which would produce fumes.*

4 *Place the finished can in a sheltered, sunny spot, at around eye level and at a slight angle, so that the open end is just lower than the closed end.*

BIRD BOXES

In recent years, bird boxes have become a familiar sight in many gardens, chiefly because people like to see birds raising their young. Boxes have been extremely valuable for many birds because they provide alternative, artificial nesting sites for many species, but before you erect one, decide what kind of bird you are trying to help. Different birds have different needs. Choosing the wrong type of box or putting it up in an inappropriate place may mean that it is not used.

Above: *A bird feeding a brood of chicks, such as these common redstarts, is a wonderfully rewarding sight in a garden.*

WHICH BOXES TO CHOOSE

If bird boxes are to be used immediately, they need to be in place by the start of the breeding season, and that usually means late winter. However, there is never a wrong time of year to put one up, and they often provide winter shelter. A box so used is more likely to be used again next season.

Recent years have seen an explosion in the range of commercially produced bird boxes, and numerous designs are now available to suit a range of garden birds from martins and swifts, tawny owls and wrens, to starlings, sparrows and tits. Small-scale specialist producers of bird boxes can be found on the Internet.

Only trust solid, simple designs and beware fussy, ornate ones because they're often useless. If you are buying a box it needs to be waterproof, but it must have a drainage hole in the bottom to allow any water that blows or seeps in to escape. If there's any standing water, it will make the box cold, might lead to disease, and will

DIFFERENT TYPES OF BIRD BOXES

There is no standard, accurate design for a bird box. What birds really need is a secure and weatherproof home, safe from predators. Do remember, though, that different bird species have different preferences regarding the type and location of a box.

With a front hole The size and shape of the hole varies with the species you intend attracting. Small birds such as tits need round holes around 2.8cm (1⅛) wide whereas larger birds like woodpeckers need rectangular holes that are 6cm (2¼in) or more.

With an open face Many birds, including European robins, wrens, wagtails and thrushes, prefer this design, and the opening width varies accordingly, from 4cm (1½in) for wrens to 12cm (4¾in) for flycatchers and thrushes.

Duck box Usually large and square for attaching to poles sunk in water, keeping predators away. The rectangular entrance is reached via a ramp-like ladder.

Communal box Birds such as house sparrows form communal nests, commonly in the eaves of houses. Modern energy efficiency means that many former nest sites have been sealed off, however, and the house sparrows often have difficulty in breeding. A communal nest box can help these species and is best attached as high as possible on the shady side of a building.

Martin box Swallows and house martins can have difficulty finding nest sites, and the smooth walls of modern buildings often cause nests to fall, sometimes with the young inside. Near roads, vibration caused by heavy vehicles may also shake nests loose. Artificial nests, made of a wood and cement mix, are attached to an artificial overhang and ready for immediate use.

Owl box These vary considerably in their design and are often more of a tube than a box. Smaller owl boxes are used by other large birds as they are often at least three times the size of a standard bird box. While there are many designs, all need a well-drained floor and easy access for cleaning at the end of the season, and are best placed in a large tree in the lower to mid canopy.

Tree creeper box Tree creepers build nests that have contact with the trunks of thick-barked trees such as oak (*Quercus*), alder (*Alnus*), poplar (*Populus*) or pine (*Pinus*), and so the boxes must be open at the back. They are fixed to the tree with wire attached to each side or with wooden blocks and the entrance holes face downward and are located at the side of the box.

Open face box

Duck box

Communal box

Martin box

Owl box

Tree creeper box

MAKING A BIRD BOX

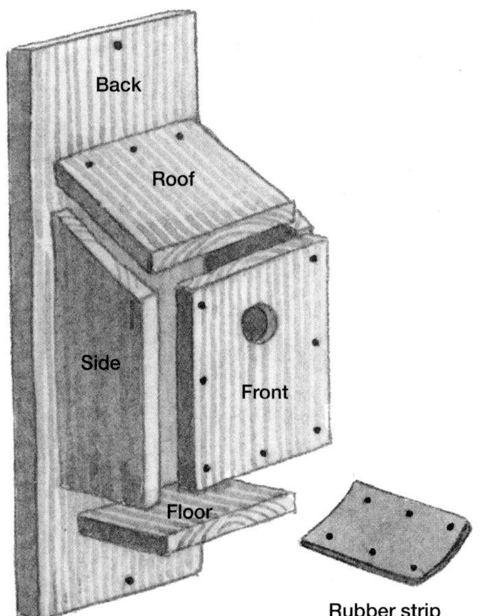

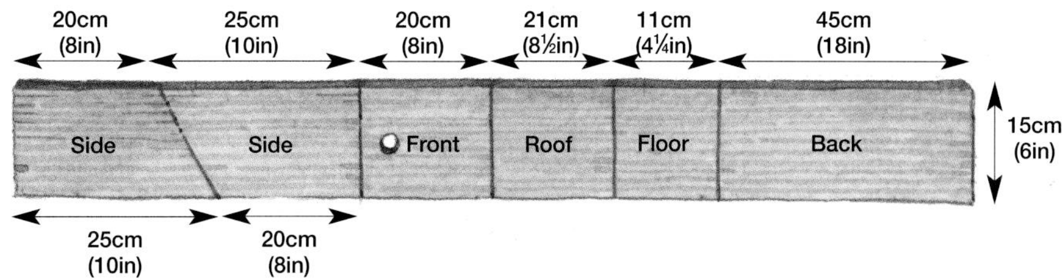

1 *Measure the dimensions and mark them clearly with a soft pencil and a "T" square. Mark the names of each section.*

2 *Cut the pieces using a sharp carpentry saw and put them to one side. Sand off any splintered edges to the wood.*

3 *Carefully screw the sections together. Don't use nails as these can cause the wood to split, allowing water into the box.*

4 *On the front face of the box, make a hole with a large drill bit. Attach the roof, using the rubber strip as a hinge.*

5 *Fix the bird box in the garden, choosing a suitable spot out of direct sun and high enough to be out of reach of predators.*

increase the chances of rotting the box. For the same reason, make sure that the base of the box is inside the sides and not fixed to the bottom or water will seep straight into the bottom. The lid must fit tightly, preferably with a hooked catch to prevent predators, such as squirrels or cats, from getting in and eating the chicks. If a box has a perch under the entrance hole don't buy it because birds will not use it, and it is perfect for hungry (predatory) squirrels to stand on. Lastly, avoid using any boxes that have been heavily treated with preservative. They could prove poisonous to the adults or chicks and, what is more, the fumes will be off-putting to birds.

When you buy bird boxes, make sure that they are accompanied with instructions and other useful information regarding their positioning to maximize the chances of birds taking up residence. The best brands may also offer advice on how you can improve your garden to suit particular species. Buying a bird box from a reputable supplier is probably the simplest (if most expensive) way to achieve success.

FIXING A BIRD BOX

It is not difficult to fix a bird box, but choosing the right position is important, and it must be fixed securely so that it doesn't fall when occupied. Although boxes can be fixed at 1.8m (6ft) above ground, they can be placed higher than this, and a height of 3.7m (12ft) or more will defeat many predators, as well as preventing overly curious children from investigating.

When positioning a bird box, make sure that it is protected from prevailing cold winds and hot sun, preferably giving it a shady aspect or wall that faces away from the strong midday or afternoon sun. Try to ensure that the birds have a fairly clear flight path to and from the nest, and try to angle the box slightly downward to help exclude rain. Remember that birds are often territorial and, in most cases, don't like being crowded together. Leave some space between the boxes unless providing for communal species such as sparrows.

MAINTENANCE

Inspect the box in late summer or early autumn, and remove any nesting material or other debris. This helps to remove parasites that otherwise build up and, if you want to make the box attractive for small birds over winter, add some loosely packed clean straw. In late winter, clear the box out again ready for the nesting season. Finally, give the next batch of nesting birds building materials such as string, cloth, wool, dried grass and excess hair from your cat or dog.

HIBERNATION SITES

During winter, many creatures go into a state of suspended animation known as hibernation, usually for several months. They do this to avoid harsh conditions and shortages of food. Many overwintering species (those that do not migrate to avoid the winter) adopt this strategy. Overwintering species choose a wide range of hibernating sites. Many have very specific requirements, and if you provide what's required, you may well see them again next year.

Above: *A rock garden situated next to a pond provides lots of crevices for hibernating animals, including amphibians such as frogs.*

WHAT IS HIBERNATION?

The state of inactivity experienced by many overwintering species is triggered by short day lengths, cold temperatures and scarcity of food. Some larger garden animals hibernate, and most insects do so in response to the shorter days which tell of the approaching winter. Most insects hibernate as eggs or larvae, although a few overwinter as adults. The hibernating animals are quite defenceless at this time and need a secure place to protect them. It is essential, then, that we help these smaller garden occupants, as well as the larger more charismatic creatures.

HOW ANIMALS HIBERNATE

Most insects hibernate as eggs or larvae, emerging as adults in spring or summer. Some species overwinter as adults, and a few, including honeybees and the occasional butterfly, can still be seen flying in mild spells during winter as they forage on winter-flowering plants.

Reptiles, amphibians and insects are all cold-blooded, and must anticipate the onset of cold conditions so as not to be caught out when the temperature drops. They need to find a sheltered, frost-free place to hide and become completely torpid, where they remain until temperatures rise again in spring.

Mammals are different because they generate their own heat to keep themselves warm, getting the energy to do so, and the energy to grow and move about, from their food. They tend to hibernate because food becomes scarce in winter, and they may use up more energy looking for food than is gained from eating what they find. Different mammals have different ways of overcoming the problem, however, and while some react by hibernating, others are active all year round.

MAKING A HABITAT STACK

1 *Place a layer of bricks on to bare ground. Arrange them to provide crevices for animals that like cool, dark places – especially newts.*

2 *Put old pallets on top and stuff them with straw. This offers burrow opportunities for mammals and hibernation sites for invertebrates.*

3 *Place layers of logs and bricks to provide a range of dark, dry recesses for creatures, such as spiders and woodlice, to hide in.*

4 *In the next layer of pallets, roll up sheets of corrugated cardboard, cutting them to the right length. These will encourage lacewings.*

5 *Drill the ends of some of the cut logs to create nest holes for solitary bees and hiding places for other small insects and invertebrates.*

6 *Keep making successive layers, packing old roof tiles with stones to create a drystone wall-type habitat for insects and reptiles.*

7 *There are no real rules about what you can include in your stack. As with all artificial habitats, you should cater primarily for creatures in your own neighbourhood. You can use any materials that you have available to hand, and the finished habitat stack will become a unique and beautiful feature in its own right.*

HELPING HIBERNATING ANIMALS

There are several ways in which you can help hibernating animals. Firstly, don't tidy up any sites too soon, and avoid the urge to dispose of all the organic matter that lies around throughout the year. Many insects hibernate in grass tussocks and hollow, dead plant stems; a late autumn clearance will often devastate their populations. Leave piles of autumn leaves in corners to create hibernation sites for a variety of insects, and avoid raking leaves from borders any later than mid-autumn, so that you avoid disturbing any hibernating creatures.

Nest boxes can be cleared and part-filled with straw in early autumn to help overwintering animals. Nooks and crannies, such as those found in walls, rock piles and elsewhere in the garden, are ideal places for hibernation – don't tidy them.

Artificial homes can also be bought for many species. These will help creatures to survive in greater numbers through the winter. A lacewing box, for example, can increase survival rates for these useful insects – that devour aphids the following spring – from around 5 per cent to as high as 95 per cent.

An alternative to buying artificial lodgings is to make them yourself, using odds and ends from around the house and garden. The ultimate example is a habitat stack, which is a bit like a hibernation city for your garden wildlife, and can incorporate a whole range of hibernation sites in one "multi-storey complex". Many creatures can benefit from such a diverse place, and the whole construction can become a decorative – if eccentric – and interesting feature in your wildlife garden.

Above: *A drystone wall is a wonderful habitat for creatures that make their homes in narrow crevices or use them for shelter. It is also a very attractive ornamental feature.*

DIFFERENT TYPES OF HIBERNATION SITE

The garden can be a great place for wildlife to overwinter in, safely tucked up in their hibernation sites. It is important to know what and where these hibernating creatures are if you want to avoid disturbing them, and vital if you want to provide extra sites for them.

Burrows Some creatures, such as bumblebees, simply burrow down into the soil to avoid the winter weather. Leave some patches of ground uncultivated until spring.

Compost heaps An attractive hiding place for some amphibians and rodents, attracted to the cool, moist conditions. Wait until late winter before moving a heap and disturbing the inhabitants.

Drystone walls Contain a multitude of nooks and crevices, offering safe, secluded shelter for an amazingly diverse array of creatures, including amphibians, reptiles, insects and spiders.

Herbaceous plant stems Leave old plant stems until the following spring to provide many insects with a safe hiding place. Start to clear them away as the weather warms up, but leave on the ground for a few days to let the inhabitants escape.

Insect boxes There is an increasing array available on the market, designed to help garden insects nest and overwinter. You can make your own using common household items such as cans and bamboo stakes.

Leaf piles The perfect place for many species to shelter in. Often rich in overwintering insects and may also contain amphibians, rodents and hedgehogs. Ideally, leave undisturbed through the winter.

Log piles Replicating piles of fallen branches and offering overwintering sites for many amphibians and insects as well as wood-boring beetles, these are excellent and easy features to include in a wildlife garden. Hide them among shrubs for extra cover.

Mulch Often rich in species, such as ground beetles and centipedes, that devour garden pests. They too often hibernate there and, by cultivating the ground in the winter, you can expose and kill them.

Ponds Water is an ideal place to spend winter because the temperature is relatively stable. Most aquatic life does not really hibernate but merely slows down, although male frogs often hibernate in muddy pond bottoms.

Sheds and outbuildings An ideal place for some species, such as butterflies, to spend winter. Any creatures found there are best left until spring.

Standing deadwood Attracts many creatures, especially wood-boring beetles, and will be colonized by numerous fungus species. In searching for grubs, woodpeckers often make holes that may later be occupied by other creatures.

Tree cavities Contain a number of overwintering creatures, such as insects, mammals and even amphibians seeking wind-free shelter. There are few times of the year when such cavities would be empty.

Burrow

Mason bee box

Leaf pile

Log pile

Pond

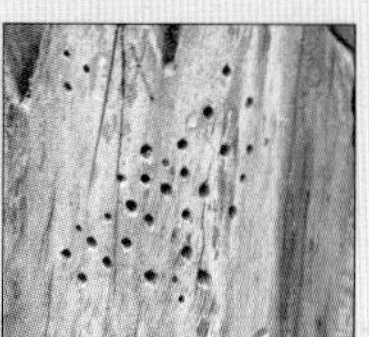

Standing deadwood

CALENDAR OF TASKS

WINTER

EARLY WINTER

- Make bird boxes when work in the garden is quiet, and erect them in suitable places. The birds will get used to them before nesting in spring.
- Place a little bedding, such as dry straw or moss, in new nest boxes to encourage birds to use them.
- Reposition any boxes that have not been used for two years or more.
- Continue feeding resident birds, and introduce high-energy foods, such as fat balls, to help birds through the forthcoming cold weather.
- Provide food from now onwards, until warmer weather arrives for non-hibernating mammals.
- Dig over the soil in the vegetable patch if it is not too wet, and leave for the frost to break it down. Resident birds will search the overturned ground for grubs and insects.
- The compost heap can be emptied and the contents incorporated into the vegetable patch with single or double digging.
- Start to plant out deciduous shrubs and bare-root trees.

MIDWINTER

- If water in the birdbath freezes, thaw it out with boiling water because birds still have to drink and bathe in cold weather.
- Float a rubber ball on a pond or birdbath to prevent the water freezing over.
- Purchase seeds of annuals and herbs for growing next spring.
- Continue to plant out deciduous shrubs and bare-root trees.
- Winter, as well as autumn, is an ideal time to plant out containerized plants because they will grow new roots deeper into the soil before the winter rains cease. If you plant in a dry spring, containerized stock will struggle to find adequate moisture, and the growth will be checked.
- Prune fruit bushes and trees, such as blackcurrants and apples, because the plants are now dormant. This can be continued into late winter.
- Take hardwood cuttings and layers of deciduous shrubs.
- Be sure to feed resident birds at this time, as the coldest weather and dwindling natural foods make life hard for them.

LATE WINTER

- Clean and remove old nesting material from bird boxes because lice and fleas will overwinter and infect new chicks next spring.
- Do not clean out ponds because newts, toads and other creatures will start to migrate here from their winter sites to breed.
- Mulch around shrub borders on a warm day when the soil is still damp.
- Trim one side of the hedge before birds begin to nest, and leave the other side to be pruned next year. This will ensure flowers and fruits every year.
- Plant climbers, such as honeysuckle (*Lonicera*) and clematis, in an established hedgerow to provide a rich nectar source in summer.
- An ideal time for planting a deciduous mixed hedge if the soil is dry enough to work on. This task can be carried out any time during winter.
- Remove any fish from a pond to stop them eating tiny young frogs, toads and newts in spring.
- Under glass, start to sow annuals, such as trailing lobelia and petunias, for summer bedding. Vegetables can also be started off indoors.

SPRING

EARLY SPRING

- Continue sowing annuals and vegetables under glass.
- Cut back herbaceous plants towards the end of this period to provide the maximum shelter for overwintering insects.
- Compost old herbaceous stems. Cut them into small pieces so that they decompose quickly.
- After pruning, mulch herbaceous borders with light material, such as old compost or bark. Mulching with manure can often rot a plant's crown.
- Lift and divide established herbaceous plants every 5–6 years. Compost any dead material, often found in the centre of old clumps.
- Do not put out whole peanuts on the bird table because they may choke chicks. Feeding whole peanuts can recommence after the nesting season is over.
- Put out protein-rich live food, such as mealworms, for birds to feed their chicks.
- Hedgehogs emerging from hibernation will benefit from a bowl of cat food or specialist hedgehog food, which is sold at many garden centres.
- Commence mowing.

MID-SPRING

- Scarify a lawn, and then make a moss ball out of all the debris collected. Hang the ball up in a tree for birds to collect for nesting material.
- Top dress lawns after scarification to encourage beneficial soil organisms, such as worms, into an area of short grass.
- Construct a new pond for planting up next month. Make a list of all the plants needed, and order from a supplier.
- Sow a wildflower meadow mix after preparing the soil. This will entail removing the topsoil to reduce fertility. This can also be carried out in autumn.
- Sow seeds of hardy vegetables outdoors. Cloches may be needed to warm up the soil and provide protection.
- Seedlings of summer-flowering annuals and vegetables grown indoors can be moved to cold frames for hardening off, before planting out.
- Make solitary bee boxes and hang them in a sheltered, sunny position.
- Start weeding, and don't let up.

LATE SPRING

- Plant up hanging baskets and containers to encourage wildlife, and put outside at the end of spring.
- Plant out summer bedding plants, such as nicotiana and verbena, after hardening them off.
- Plant up a new pond when the water starts to warm up and the plants are ready to burst into new growth.
- Sow seeds of hardy annuals, for example sunflowers (*Helianthus annuus*), directly into annual or mixed borders.
- Sow seeds of hardy vegetables outdoors; no protection is needed.
- Remove tree stakes that have been supporting trees for over 1 year.
- Feed containers and hanging baskets with a weak, organic liquid feed to encourage flowers and attract pollinators.
- Record all wildlife present, to help you plan your future projects.
- Carry on weeding throughout the growing season, especially around seedlings. Where possible, mulch borders with old compost.

Feed the birds with high-energy fat balls

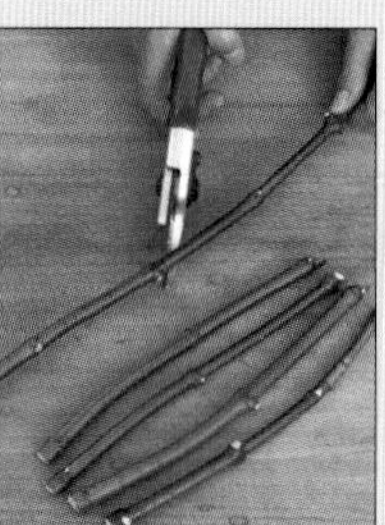

Take hardwood cuttings of deciduous shrubs

Plant a deciduous mixed hedge

Lift and divide herbaceous plants

Hang up butterfly boxes in a sunny position

Remove year-old tree stakes

SUMMER

EARLY SUMMER

- Prune out the old growth from spring-flowering shrubs, such as forsythia and flowering currants (*Ribes*).
- Sow seeds of spring-flowering bedding, e.g. wallflowers (*Erysimum*) and forget-me-nots (*Myosotis*).
- Deadhead early spring-flowering herbaceous plants to encourage a second flush of flowers.
- Protect fruit crops from birds. After harvesting, remove nets and allow the birds to forage on the excess fruits.
- Start to water hanging baskets and containers if they dry out, and continue to feed on a weekly or fortnightly basis.
- Make a bird hide for you and the children. Use binoculars to watch the activity in and around garden nest boxes and feeders.
- Butterfly spotting becomes easy as the new broods emerge. Buy an identification guide to name the different species.
- This is also a good time to go pond dipping with children.

MIDSUMMER

- Continue weeding. Remember to compost each time, separating perennial weeds into a separate bag.
- Continue grass cutting. When composting, mix it with brown material, such as dead leaves, to prevent the compost heap from turning slimy.
- Lightly trim hedges after flowering to encourage dense growth for winter.
- Turn the compost heap every two weeks, and water it during dry weather. Take care not to disturb snakes and bumblebee nests.
- Keep birdbaths and ponds topped up with stored rainwater because tap water can be very alkaline, and to avoid wasting mains water.
- Do not use pesticides during summer when infestations of aphids can be troublesome. Let beneficial insects tackle the problem. Use organic plant oils and soft soap to reduce pest numbers until this happens.
- Note how beneficial insect numbers are quickly increasing, provided no chemicals have been used.

LATE SUMMER

- Clear out overgrown ponds.
- Leave the hauled-out vegetation and soil from the pond at the side for a few days to allow inhabitants to return to the water. After this duration of time, recycle the plant material on the compost heap.
- Only clear out up to one-third of a pond at any one time.
- Trim the nectar-rich, summer-flowering herbaceous plants to encourage a second flush of flowers.
- Site a hedgehog box under a hedge or log pile to enable wildlife to get used to it before it is used in autumn. Add some bedding.
- Fill bird boxes that are no longer in use with straw to provide hibernation sites for bumblebee queens and other insects.
- Take semi-ripe cuttings of many species of shrubs.
- Cut down about a third of a nettle patch to promote new growth. Late-flying butterflies will prefer laying their eggs on new leaves.
- Put out hibernation boxes for beneficial insects, such as ladybirds.

AUTUMN

EARLY AUTUMN

- Put netting over a pond to stop leaves falling in. The leaves can be used to make leaf mould.
- Collect seeds from garden plants to sow next year. They should be stored in a paper bag to allow the seeds to breathe and prevent mould.
- Build a "habitat stack", log pile or drystone wall to provide overwintering and hibernation sites for a variety of animals.
- Leave any annual herbs, such as dill, or vegetables (carrots and lettuce) to flower to boost the nectar supplies for autumn insects.
- Start to plant out bulbs that will flower the following spring.
- Sow a wildflower meadow mix while the ground is warm – the seeds will germinate quickly. In the preparation, remove the soil for best results.
- Now or in mid-autumn, remove the summer-flowering plants in a hanging basket and replace with spring-flowering plants.
- Create piles of leaves and small twigs under vegetation, as these make ideal hibernation spots for small mammals.

MID-AUTUMN

- Do not cut down old herbaceous stems in autumn because insects will overwinter in the crevices and hollow stems.
- Leave seed heads of oil-rich species, such as lavender and evening primrose, for seed-eating birds.
- Assess all the garden plants for their wildlife value.
- If redesigning part of the garden, make sure that any new plants are wildlife-friendly, providing berries, nectar, pollen and nesting material.
- Plant out spring bedding plants for flowering next year. Use plants such as single-flowering wallflowers (*Erysimum*) and forget-me-nots (*Myosotis*).
- If the soil is not dry, plant new containerized shrubs, climbers and trees.
- Plant out potted wildflowers, such as cowslips (*Primula*), in areas of grass.
- Pick ripe berries off bushes, e.g. hawthorn (*Crataegus*), and remove the fleshy covering before sowing.
- Lift and divide herbaceous perennials before the ground becomes too wet.

LATE AUTUMN

- Clean out the greenhouse from top to bottom to eradicate any pests and diseases, and to allow maximum light penetration over the winter months, especially if plants are being grown in it.
- Find out which bird species are resident in your area, and buy the appropriate feeders and food.
- Build a bird-feeding station close to shrub or tree cover.
- Start to feed the birds over the cold winter period. Feed with a variety of foods to encourage different species into the garden.
- If you intend using live food feeders, be prepared to continue this through the whole winter to ensure the wellbeing of carnivorous birds.
- Continue to plant out containerized shrubs, trees and herbaceous plants.
- Begin winter pruning of deciduous shrubs and trees. Save larger prunings to create log piles around the garden.
- Shred smaller twigs and make hibernation piles using branches and fallen leaves. Create a leaf-mould compost heap.

Make a bird hide for you and the children

Turn the compost every two weeks

Site hedgehog boxes under shelter

Build a habitat stack for various wildlife

Pick ripe berries off bushes to sow

Shred twigs to make wood chips

INDEX

A
Acer negundo 73
Achillea filipendula 77, 109
Achillea millefolium 43, 115
Agastache 115
A. foeniculum 39
Alcea rosea 39
alder buckthorn 41, 69
Allium giganteum 39
Allium schoenoprasum 76, 80, 83
alyssum, white 115
Amaranthus caudatus 43
amphibians 33, 36, 37, 57, 117
Anchusa azurea 41
anemones 100
Angelica 115
A. sylvestris 43
anise hyssop 39
Anthriscus cerefolium 115
aphids 114, 115
Aponogeton distachyos 67
apple 42, 43, 73
crab 35, 71, 109
aquatic life 117
Aquilegia vulgaris 39
Aralia elata 39
Argyranthemum 85
Artemisia vulgaris 43
Aster novi-belgii 109
Aster x *frikartii* 41
Aubrieta deltoidea 114, 115
Aucuba japonica 109

B
badgers 110
balm, bee 39, 80
balm, lemon 43
barbed wire bush 41
barberry, Japanese 42–3
basil 80, 83, 99
bats 15, 118, 119

bean, scarlet runner 39
beech 42
beech, southern 71
beehive compost bin 86, 91
bees 6, 9, 108, 116, 117
bee borders 38–9
bee boxes 33, 35, 118, 119
beetles 93, 95, 108
Begonia 99
bellflower 39
beneficial organisms 95, 114–15
Berberis 50, 51, 117
B. thunbergii 42–3
bergamot 39, 80
berries 109, 110
bird's foot trefoil 41
birds 6, 7, 9, 10, 55, 115
attracting 24, 30, 32
bird border 42–3
bird boxes 37, 118, 120–1
feeding 107, 112–13
positioning feeders 31, 35, 37, 112
wildlife corridors 19
bistort 41, 43
bittercress 92
blackberry 73
blackcurrant 43, 82
blackthorn 69
bladderwort 67
bog gardens 31, 33, 37, 49, 67
borage 39, 76, 109
Borago officinalis 39, 76, 109
borders 30, 31, 32, 33, 35
bee border 38–9
bird border 42–3
butterfly border 40–1
cutting back 97
flower borders 76–7
box elder 73
bramble 73
breeding sites 11, 18
Buddleja 77
B. alternifolia 41
B. davidii 109
B. 'Lochinch' 41
Butomus umbellatus 67
butterflies 7, 9, 10, 108
butterfly border 40–1
egg-laying sites 31, 36, 47
feeding 41, 107, 111
butterfly bush 109
fountain 41

C
cabbages 82, 83
Calendula officinalis 85, 115
Callitriche stagnalis 67
Caltha palustris 67
Campanula latifolia 39
Campanula rotundifolia 63
candytuft 41
Capsicum 83
Cardamine pratensis 76
Carpinus betulus 42
carrot 63, 79, 82
caterpillars 7, 40, 41
catmint 39
Ceanothus impressus 39
centipedes 54
Centranthus ruber 41, 109
Ceratophyllum demersum 67
Cercis siliquastrum 39
Cerinthe major 'Purpurascens' 39, 77, 109
chard 83
chervil 115
chickweed 92
chives 76, 80, 83
Chlorophytum comosum 100
chrysanthemum 85
Cirsium rivulare 39, 79
Clematis tangutica 39, 75
climate 13, 20, 26, 58
climbers 33, 35, 74–5, 117
clover, red 39, 63
Colletia hystrix 41
columbine 39
compost heaps 37, 90, 123
composting 12–13, 90–1
coneflower (*Echinacea*) 77, 79
containers 81, 83, 85, 88
coriander 115
Coriandrum sativum 115
Corylus 83, 100
C. avellana 51, 69
Cotoneaster 51
C. horizontalis 39, 43
cowslip 63, 98
Crataegus 115
C. monogyna 33, 50, 51, 69
Crocus chrysanthus 100
crucifixion thorn 41
currant, flowering 39
cyclamen 100
Cynara scolymus 82

D
Dahlia 100
D. Collerette Group 41
dandelion 92
Daucus carota 63, 79, 82
daylily 83
deadwood 37, 52, 56, 107, 116, 123
deer 53
Dianthus barbatus 41
Digitalis purpurea 39
Dipsacus fullonum 43
diseases 50, 94, 95
dock 92
dragonflies 11, 15
ducks 120
duckweed, lesser 67

E
earthworms 54, 55
Echinacea purpurea 77, 79
Echinops nitro 39
elderberry 43, 51
Elodea (pondweed) 49, 67
Eryngium planum 77
Escallonia 'Langleyensis' 41
Eschscholzia californica 39, 109
Eupatorium cannabinum 41, 109
evening primrose 43

F
Fagus sylvatica 42
fennel 79
feverfew 115
firethorn 43, 51, 117
Foeniculum vulgare 79
forget-me-not, field 43
foxglove 39
Fragaria vesca 43
frogs 15, 64, 65, 95, 117
fruit 31, 41, 109
fungi 50, 55, 116, 117

G
Gladiolus (gladioli) 100
globe artichokes 82, 109
golden club 67

golden rod 43, 76
gooseberry 43
gorse 39, 115
grasses 92
grasshoppers 46
ground beetle 95
ground elder 92
guelder rose 43

H
hanging baskets 11, 35, 83, 85, 88
harebell 63
hawthorn 33, 50, 51, 69, 115
hazel 51, 69
Hebe 'Great Orme' 41
Hebe salicifolia 39
Hedera helix 41, 75
hedgehogs 9, 95, 111, 114, 117, 118, 119
hedges 11, 19, 31, 32, 33, 37
  dead hedges 56, 57
  hedgerows 50–1
  planting 68–9
Helianthus 76
  H. annuus 43, 109
Heliotropium arborescens (heliotrope) 41, 77
Helleborus (hellebore) 99
Hemerocallis 83
hemp agrimony 41, 109
herbs 11, 31, 115
  herb garden 80–1
hibernation 7, 110, 118, 119, 122–3
hides 102, 103
holly 40, 42, 43, 51
hollyhock 39
honesty 43
honeysuckle 51, 75, 109
honeywort 39, 77, 109
hop 41, 109
hornbeam 42
hornwort 67
horsetail 92
hoverflies 15, 95, 108, 114, 115
Humulus lupulus 41, 109
Hyssopus officinalis (hyssop) 80

I
Iberis amara 41
ice plant 39, 41, 109
Ilex aquifolium 40, 42, 43, 51
Indian cress 85
insects 33, 36, 37, 55, 114, 115, 119, 123
invertebrates 117, 119
Iris pseudacorus (flag iris) 67
ivy 41, 75, 115

J
Japanese angelica tree 39
Japanese pond lily 67
Jasminum officinale 75
jays 43
Judas tree 39

K
Knautia arvensis 63, 79

L
lacewings 95, 114
  lacewing hotels 35, 37, 118, 119
lady's smock 76
ladybirds 7, 15, 95, 114, 118
  feeders 115
Lathyrus latifolius 39
laurel, spotted 109
Lavandula angustifolia (lavender) 43, 80, 109
lawns 32, 33, 46, 62, 117
leaf piles 123
Lemna minor 67
lettuce 83
Leucanthemum vulgare 63
licorice mint, Korean 115
lilac, Santa Barbara 39
Lilium (lily) 100
Limnanthes douglasii 39, 115
Lobelia erinus 85
Lobularia maritima 115
log piles 35, 37, 56, 116, 117, 123
Lonicera 51, 75
  L. periclymenum 109
Lotus corniculatus 41
love-lies-bleeding 43
Lunaria annua 43
Lycopersicon esculentum 82

M
magnolia 100
Mahonia 117
  M. aquifolium 43
Malus 73
  M. 'Red Sentinel' 42, 43
  M. sylvestris 35, 71, 109
mammals 110, 111, 117
marigold 115
  English 85
  marsh 67
marjoram 41
martins 19, 120
Melissa officinalis 43
Mentha 80
  M. aquatica 67
mice 7, 52, 102
Michaelmas daisy 109
millet (*Panicum*) 110
millet (*Pennisetum*) 76
Miss Willmott's ghost 109
Monarda didyma 39, 80
Morus rubra 71
moths 103, 108, 109
mountain ash 35, 42, 43, 71, 73, 109
mugwort 43
mulberry 71
Mycorrhizae 55
Myosotis
  M. arvensis 43
  M. palustris 67
Myriophyllum spicatum 67

N
nasturtium 115
Nasturtium majus 85
Nepeta x *faassenii* 39
nests 11, 118, 120
nettle, stinging 92, 109, 115
newts 95
Nicotiana 76
  N. sylvestris 85
Nothofagus alpina 71
Nuphar japonica 67
nutrients 13, 88, 89
Nymphaea 49, 66, 67, 108
  N. alba 67, 109
Nymphoides peltata 67

O
oak, English 71, 99
Ocimum basilicum 80, 83, 99
Oenothera biennis 43
Oregon grape 43
Origanum majorana 41
Origanum vulgare (oregano) 41, 80
Orontium aquaticum 67
owls 120
ox-eye daisy 63

P
Panicum miliaceum 110
pansy 99, 108
parsley 115
pea, perennial 39 
Pennisetum glaucum 76
periwinkle 99
Perovskia atriplicifolia 39
pests 94–5, 114–15
Petroselinum (parsley) 115
Petunia x *hybrida* 85
Phaseolus coccineus 39
Phlox paniculata 41, 109
Pinus sylvestris 71
poached egg plant 39, 115
Polygonum bistorta 41, 43
ponds 28, 30, 31, 32, 33, 36, 37, 117
  planting 66–7
  pond dipping 102
  wetlands 48–9
  wildlife ponds 64–5
pondweed (*Elodea*) 49, 67
pondweed (*Potamogeton*) 67
poppy, California 39, 109
potagers 82
Potamogeton crispus 67
predators 11, 14–15, 102
  beneficial 95, 114, 115
Primula veris 63, 98
propagation 100–1
pruning 96–7
Prunus spinosa 69
Puccinia graminis 50
Pyracantha coccinea 43, 51, 117

Q
Quercus robur 71, 99

R
reptiles 37, 57, 117
Rhamnus frangula 41, 69
Rhizobia 55
Ribes 83
  R. nigrum 43, 82
  R. sanguineum 39
  R. uva-crispa 43
robins 24, 95, 113
rock piles 57, 117
Rosa (roses) 33, 51, 73, 75, 117

R. canina (dog rose) 39
R. 'Mermaid' 39
R. rubiginosa (briar rose) 69
rosemary 80, 109
Rosmarinus officinalis 80, 109
rowan 35, 42, 43, 71, 73, 109, 110
Rubus fruticosus 73
rush, flowering 67

S
sage
bog 79
Russian 39
wood 39
Salvia nemorosa 39
Salvia uliginosa 79
Sambucus niger 43, 51
Scabiosa atropurpurea 41
scabious 41
field 63, 79
sea holly 77
Sedum spectabile 39, 41, 109
seeds 109, 98–9
shrews 15, 117
shrubs 33, 37, 117
planting 70–1
wall shrubs 74–5
slow worms 95
slugs and snails 55, 94
snakes 117
snakeweed 41
soil 17, 22–3, 27, 54–5
Solidago virgaurea 43, 76
solidaster 79
song thrushes 14, 42
Sorbus aucuparia 35, 42, 43, 71, 73, 109, 110
sparrows 24, 120
spider plant 100
spiders 11, 18, 55, 95, 117, 123
squirrels 72, 102, 110–11
Stratiotes aloides 67
sunflower 43, 109
swallows 13, 120
sweet William 41

T
Tanacetum parthenium 115
Tanacetum vulgare 43
tansy 43
Taraxacum officinale 92
Taxus baccata 42, 43
teasel 43
thistle, globe 39
thistle, plume 39, 79
Thymus vulgaris 80, 84, 85, 99
tits, blue 15, 42
toads 15, 48, 95, 117, 118
tobacco plant 85
tree creepers 120
trees 11, 19, 31, 33, 35, 37, 55, 117, 123
planting 70–1
removing stakes 72
woodland 52–3
Trifolium pratense 39, 63
Tropaeolum majus 115
Tulipa biflora (tulip) 100

U
Ulex europaeus 39, 115
Urtica dioica 92, 109, 115
Utricularia vulgaris 67

V
valerian, red 41, 109
vegetables 11, 24, 31, 33
vegetable gardens 82–3
Verbena bonariensis 41, 77, 79, 99, 109
verges 19
vervain, purpletop 41, 77, 79, 99
Viburnum 73
V. lanata 69
V. opulus 43, 73
Vinca 99
Viola 99
V. x *wittrockiana* 108
voles 102, 117

W
walls 11, 33, 57
drystone 56, 64–5, 123
wasps 95, 115
water 11, 18, 32, 34
drinking 64, 112
water features 35, 64, 66
water use 59
water hawthorn 67
water lily 49, 66, 67, 108
white 67, 109
water milfoil, Eurasian 67
water mint 67
water soldier 67
water starwort 67
watering 88, 89
wayfaring tree 69
weeds 92–3
wetlands 48–9
wildflower meadows 31, 33, 36
establishing 62–3
grasslands 46–7
willow tunnels 30, 31
window boxes 11, 35
woodland 52–3, 72–3
woodpecker, greater spotted 43
worms 54, 55

Y
yarrow 43, 77, 109, 115
yellow floating heart 67
yew 42, 43

Z
Zinnia elegans 41

ACKNOWLEDGEMENTS

AUTHORS' ACKNOWLEDGEMENTS

Thank you to Writtle College and their staff for allowing the use of their grounds and glasshouses to take many of the photographs.

Thank you also to the following people who worked as models for the photography: Edward Anderson; Peter Anderson; Lin Blunt; Dave Campbell; Benjamin Crosby; Jane Dobson; Felicity Forster; Simon Grundy; Lucy and Florence Kedman-Watts; Denis Lloyd; Gemma, Oliver and Oscar Mackman; Christine and Luca Mailbaum; Rachel and George Nutton; Charlotte, Olivia and James Power; Donna Sheringham; Chris Steward; Graham Thompstone; Mary Venables; Jackie Wright.

We would also like to thank Ben Wincott for his garden design advice and drawings.

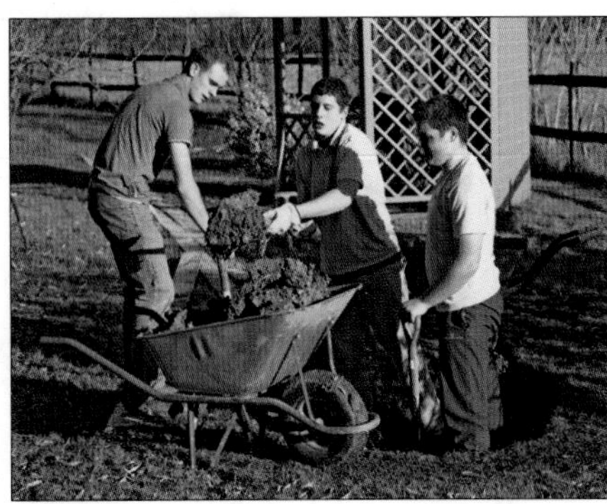

PUBLISHER'S ACKNOWLEDGEMENTS

The publisher would like to thank the following for kindly allowing photography to take place in their gardens: Jane Dobson, Chelmsford; Debbie Hart, Bocking; Stuart and Maj Jackson-Carter; Kew Gardens; Christine and Michael Lavelle; Pam Lewis, Sticky Wicket; RHS Hyde Hall; RHS Rosemoor, Devon; RHS Wisley, Surrey; Writtle College, Chelmsford.

The publisher would also like to thank the following for allowing their photographs to be reproduced in the book (t=top, b=bottom, l=left, r=right, c=centre, f=far):

Dave Bevan: 14t, 31bl, 55cr, 82 panel fl, 109 panel 8th from b.
Frank Blackburn/Ecoscene: 68t, 70t.
Corbis: 85 panel fl.
Lucy Doncaster: 87c.
Felicity Forster: 116.
iStockphoto: 6 panel tr.
Michael Lavelle: 115b.
Charles Lightfoot: 11bl.
papiliophotos.com: 19br, 36br, 42t, 43tl, 43tr, 50t, 52t, 95 panel 3rd from bl, 98t, 120t.